Lectures on Logic

Studies in Continental Thought

John Sallis, EDITOR

Georg Wilhelm Friedrich Hegel

Lectures on Logic
Berlin, 1831

Transcribed by
Karl Hegel

Translated by
Clark Butler

Indiana University Press
Bloomington and Indianapolis

Publication of this book is made possible in part with the assistance of a Challenge Grant from the National Endowment for the Humanities, a federal agency that supports research, education, and public programming in the humanities.

This book is a publication of

Indiana University Press
601 North Morton Street
Bloomington, IN 47404-3797 USA

http://iupress.indiana.edu

Telephone orders 800-842-6796
Fax orders   812-855-7931
Orders by e-mail iuporder@indiana.edu

Published in German as Georg Wilhelm Friedrich Hegel's *Vorlesungen über die Logik (1831)*. Transcript by Karl Hegel. Edited by Udo Rameil with Hans-Christian Lucas. © 2001 by Felix Meiner Verlag, Hamburg.
English edition © 2008 by Indiana University Press.

The paper used in this publication meets the minimum requirements of American National Standard for Information Sciences—Permanence of Paper for Printed Library Materials, ANSI Z39.48-1984.

Manufactured in the United States of America

Library of Congress Cataloging-in-Publication Data

Hegel, Georg Wilhelm Friedrich, 1770–1831.
  [Vorlesungen über die Logik. English]
  Lectures on logic: Berlin, 1831 / Georg Wilhelm Friedrich Hegel;
transcribed by Karl Hegel; translated by Clark Butler.
     p. cm. — (Studies in Continental thought)
  Includes bibliographical references and index.
  ISBN 978-0-253-35167-8 (cloth: alk. paper) 1. Logic I. Butler, Clark, date II. Title.

B2944.V652E5 2008
160—dc22
                                                           2007048893

          1 2 3 4 5 13 12 11 10 09 08

Contents

Contents

Translator's Introduction

This introductory discussion concerns the context and state of the text along with a small number of general rules adopted in its translation. The first three sections, which address the text and its context in relation to Hegel's other works and to the history of philosophy, are intended even for beginning students of the logic.[1] The last three sections address more especially Hegel scholars, since they seek to justify my decisions regarding certain translation issues on which such scholars have not always agreed. Throughout all six sections a recurrent theme will be the complex relationship between Hegel and his near contemporary Friedrich Heinrich Jacobi (1743–1819).

1. The Text

This book has its source in lectures by Georg Wilhelm Friedrich Hegel (1770–1831). His name appears as the author on the title page of the German edition. But, like many posthumous works, this is not a book expressly intended by the author. He delivered lectures, but did not intend their publication as a book. But the lectures did constitute a potential book by Hegel, which his son Karl Hegel (1813–1901) penned as a manuscript, and which has become actual due to the German editors— chiefly Udo Rameil, with the collaboration of Hans-Christian Lucas— and the support of the Hegel Archiv in Germany.[2]

The first thing beginning readers must keep in mind is that Hegel's works on the science of logic are not in any sense treatises on formal logic. This is true despite the fact that Hegel first turned to write his *Science of Logic*[3] after the publication of his *Phenomenology of Spirit*,[4] upon receiving a request from the Royal Bavarian Ministry of Education to write a formal logic text for use in the kingdom's secondary schools.[5] To be sure, his science of logic treats the concepts of judgments, syllogisms, definition, and proof in its third and last part on the self-concept, but this does not make the *Science* or *Lectures* a logic textbook. The *Lectures* are far more a treatise in rational theology in which the author abandons himself to the life and internal self-development of the divine *logos* at work since the true Parmenidean onset of the history of philosophy.[6] And this is so even though Hegel understood that the science of logic could be used non-theologically as a study of the universal and necessary thought determinations or categories of thinking.[7]

At first glance the Lectures on Logic seem to be Hegel's commentary on the first book of the third edition of his *Encyclopaedia of the Philosophical Sciences*.[8] They thus suggest self-interpretation, self-explication, but this impression is not the whole truth. The *Lectures* should not be taken merely as a kind of commentary since they are a self-contained exposition that can be understood even without reading the *Encyclopaedia*. Nonetheless, they contain periodic explicit references to selected paragraphs of that work.

Often the German manuscript of the *Lectures* begins a paragraph with a number in parentheses from the 1830 *Encyclopaedia* (e.g., §19), but many of the German paragraphs do not begin this way. If the German edition of the lectures omits a paragraph number at the beginning of a new paragraph, the present edition sometimes identifies a slightly later *Encyclopaedia* paragraph—in which Hegel typically introduces a new technical term or transition—in brackets *within* the paragraph of the lectures in which the term or transition is introduced, not at the start of the paragraph.

2. Interpolation in the Text

A further general comment on the translation has to do with interpolations in this text which was never intended for publication, and which indeed was first published only very recently. The editors of the first collected works of Hegel did not draw on Karl Hegel's transcript of these lectures in constituting the published additions (*Zusätze*) in the *Encyclopaedia*'s logic.[9] Thus not even brief excerpts of it appeared in print in the nineteenth century. The manuscript was in private hands until a few decades ago when its owners transferred it to the Hegel Archiv for expert review.[10] The German editors took nearly two decades to decipher the script and edit the text, which was published late in 2001. The manuscript contained a fairly large number of brief omissions which could only be filled in by interpolation, though Udo Rameil notes that most of his interpolations were quite obvious and resolved no ambiguity controversially.

The present translation contains interpolations beyond those in the Rameil edition. Rameil puts his interpolations in brackets, and they may be consulted in the German edition. Bracketed interpolations in this edition are my own. Interpolations in the text were needed to produce a text that could serve as more than Karl Hegel's personal manuscript, and Rameil largely provided these basic interpolations. Further interpolations, which I have sought to provide, were needed to produce a readable text for those who are not Hegel scholars. I have sought to limit these interpolations to those that are necessitated by the text and needed for a smooth reading. I have sought to exclude from my interpolations and footnotes any interpretive comment that would seek to resolve in a controversial manner any real ambiguity left in Karl Hegel's transcript.

In producing a book such as this, editors and translators face a choice between letting the ambiguity and incompleteness of Karl's words stand, or filling in what is missing through their contextual awareness of the Hegelian opus as a whole. Hegel scholars typically prefer the first solution, which allows them to complete the text with their own contextual knowledge. But beginners who hope to use this volume as an initiation to Hegel's logic will tend to prefer the second solution. By bracketing interpolations beyond those of the German edition, this translation seeks to address both audiences. Hegel scholars remain free to judge these additions.

However, in some cases I have added words without placing them in brackets as explicit interpolations. For instance, I have rendered the text gender-inclusive in this way. I have also done so when a few extra words help the reader keep in mind what Hegel has referred to and is still referring to in the text. Thus, when Hegel introduces "essence" in the logic of essence, he makes it clear that he means "the abstract inner essence of immediate being." Afterward, Karl Hegel's abbreviated transcript may simply mention "the essence," but I have sometimes reminded the reader of Hegel's meaning by making it repeatedly explicit that he is still talking about the abstract essence of being.

Footnotes to this translation occasionally cite classical texts in the history of philosophy to which Hegel refers, or provide possible alternative wordings of the translation. Suggestions as to how to resolve possible basic philosophical ambiguities of the text in different ways—as implied, for example, by the fact that some reputable Hegel scholars read the science of logic as theistic while others do not—may be reserved for commentary elsewhere.

One hope behind this translation has been that for some it may, for the first time, make the science of logic not only readable but teachable, whereas it has often proven inscrutable even to many professional philosophers. Since the science of logic for Hegel is an ideal reconstruction of the real history of philosophy, its understandability for philosophers who are not specialized Hegel scholars will be assisted by recalling clas-

sical philosophers and their particular ways of identifying reality that
come to be reconstructed on the level of pure thought in Hegel's logic:
e.g., Parmenides, Heraclitus,[11] Plato, Aristotle, Plotinus, Anselm, Descartes, Spinoza, Leibniz, Locke, Hume, Kant, Fichte, Schelling, and Jacobi. Some idea of these different historical philosophers, if held in
mind, makes the development of pure imageless thought in the logic
easier to follow. Students who have not yet studied the whole prior history of philosophy will need to form a general representation of each of
these historical philosophical positions in order to enjoy a similarly fa-
cilitated comprehension of Hegel's science of logic.

These lectures, with the help of rudimentary knowledge of key classical philosophers, are the most readable introduction Hegel himself
provides to his logic. But they do not replace his *Science of Logic*, which
has some sections (e.g., on reflection) that do not even appear in the
Lectures.[12] The *Encyclopaedia* outline of the logic may be viewed as a guide
to the subsequent lectures and, as we have noted, the lectures were
keyed to that outline. The Karl Hegel transcript does not key them to the
Science of Logic, and this translation does not attempt to do so either. The
Encyclopaedia previews in outline the lectures, which then illuminate
the *Encyclopaedia*. As often happens when a thinker is present with his
listeners, Hegel expresses himself more clearly in his lectures than in
either the *Science of Logic* or the *Encyclopaedia*. The *Science of Logic* was
largely written at night during the first years of Hegel's marriage, as he
was a gymnasium rector during the day, with a view to earning an
eventual university professorship.

The Hegelian authenticity of the lectures does not seem to have
been disturbed by Karl Hegel's transmission. This is due to the intelligence of the young man, and to his desire to assimilate his father's
logic accurately. His transcript was surely not verbatim. Karl could
only recreate what he had heard and taken down in notes according
to the spirit, not always the exact letter. But of two known transcripts
of the 1831 logic lectures, Karl's is recognized as far superior in quality.[13] Still, it would be false to claim that his transcript records only
Hegel's words or all his words. The claim that this is a new, previously
unpublished book by Hegel is implied by the appearance of his name
on the title page of the German edition—a convention we have maintained in the present edition. Yet ambiguity remains. Scholarly correctness obliged the German editors to add a disclaimer that quite
technically the volume, as a reconstruction of the lectures after the
fact, is "the product of another author, namely, the transcriber."[14] Karl
Hegel was not a tape recorder. The *Science of Logic* will always have
greater authority. But these lectures may very likely be read as the best
available preparation for and help in reading the larger *Logic*.

3. The Science of Logic and the History of Philosophy

Research into parallels between passages in the *Lectures*, the *Encyclopaedia*, and other works and lectures by Hegel will be rewarding even though the *Lectures* can be read on their own. The editor of the German edition has, in his notes, done most of the work of tracing such parallels. Yet readers of the English edition can fruitfully, and without great difficulty, do much of this work for themselves. It largely suffices to keep within arm's reach copies of Part One of the 1830 *Encyclopaedia of the Philosophical Sciences*, the *Science of Logic*, and the *Lectures on the History of Philosophy*.[15] Consultation of the *Lectures on the History of Philosophy* is as important as consultation of the first two volumes, which are expositions of the science of logic itself. The reason is that Hegel believes the history of philosophy to be the unfolding of the logic empirically, amid the contingent events and personalities of empirical history.[16]

Despite Hegel's warnings that prefaces to a science are what is least in importance,[17] the paradoxical length and, at times, brilliance of his own prefaces and introductions have led most anthologizers to privilege them, especially given the difficulty of excerpting Hegelian systematic science. In the *Lectures on Logic*, the systematic exposition is of course what is most important. The introductory essay on Kant and the following one on Jacobi have importance as intellectual history, and as a commentary on the philosophical landscape of Hegel's time. However, they are also an internal self-introduction to Hegel's science of logic itself. If, according to Hegel as he is commonly interpreted, there are no thought determinations outside the complete circle of such terms in the science of logic,[18] any introduction to this science must be internal to it. It must be the science of logic itself awakening to self-consciousness.

The introduction to the *Lectures* records the self-discovery of the science of logic in the history of philosophy in four stages. First there is classical metaphysics from Parmenides (born 515 BC) to Christian Wolff (1659–1754). This position starts by taking what is immediately given, in abstraction of the larger context to which it is relative, to be an absolute or non-relative whole. Parmenides started it by identifying what Hegel calls "the absolute" as mere indeterminate being. Its last great representative for Hegel is the seventeenth-century philosopher Leibniz.

Second there is the skeptical critique of classical metaphysics, highlighting the fact that what is immediately given is what it is only through its relation to what is other than it. This critique of classical metaphysics was most systematically developed by Immanuel Kant (1724–1804). Clearly in Hegel's view the progress of the history of philosophy was accelerating in the modern world, since Kant and the last two stages of this history which follow it date from the eighteenth century.

The third stage is an attempt to reject the skeptical critique of classical metaphysics and to retreat back into the position of classical metaphysics before Kant. This results in a dogmatic reassertion that what is immediately present is absolute or not relative to what is other than itself. This position was represented in Hegel's own time by Jacobi. Parmenides and Kant are of course in the front rank of world-renowned philosophers. But it is remarkable that Hegel elevates his contemporary, Jacobi, to such a position in his overall concept of the history of philosophy.

Forsaking any attempt to think and know God, Jacobi in a broadly romantic sense took the immediate feeling (*Ahnung*) of God, what Friedrich Ernst Daniel Schleiermacher (1768–1834) would call a feeling of absolute dependence on the Infinite, to be a universal fact of consciousness regardless of the cultural context.[19] Clearly this was not a return to Parmenides' identification of "the absolute" with an objective abstract Being, an object of thought in which consciousness loses itself. Indeed, Jacobi makes something subjective, a fact of subjective consciousness, out to be absolute. The feeling of dependence on God is not itself the absolute, but it is immediately given to all human consciousness.

Jacobi must deny the validity of the entire history of classical metaphysics, of its attempt to know God by hard thinking, in order to acknowledge the alleged absolute immediate fact of contact with God by feeling. So his return to the position of taking what is immediate to be absolute is not a return to classical metaphysics—the attempt to know God by logical argument. In trying to go back before Kant, Jacobi in the end cannot entirely evade Kant. He concurs with Kant's skeptical denial of our ability to know God.

The last of the four stages followed by this history of philosophy is Hegel's own stage of embracing the Kantian critique of classical metaphysics and then advancing beyond it rather than seeking to fall back to a prior standpoint. Hegel reconstructs the metaphysics of what is immediate by including what is other than it, its mediation. He holds neither God nor consciousness to be merely immediate or directly given. Whatever is immediate is abstract in relation to a larger whole. Only a larger whole to which it is relative can be truly absolute. Thus to take what is immediately given merely by itself to be absolute is to falsely make it out to be absolute. In Hegel's typical way of expressing himself, we say that what is immediate is self-mediated by its other which is ultimately none other than an expansion of itself.

Both the introduction and systematic exposition of *Lectures on Logic* will be more understandable to those with some prior knowledge of the history of philosophy. Hegel held that his logic reconstructed the history of philosophy on the level of pure thought. Students approaching these lectures will, as I have said, have an advantage if they have some familiarity with the history of philosophy from ancient times to Hegel's own time. Yet understanding the lectures does not require the reader to be an Aristotle or Kant scholar. Hegel assumes that modern readers carry around within themselves a distilled but tacit common understanding of each great philosopher. Aristotle's perspective as a cultural deposit or residue inhabits some corner of the mind of each contemporary reader with a solid education in general culture.

In editing the German edition of the *Lectures on Logic*, Udo Rameil has acted on behalf of Hegel, heeding Hegel's presumed intention of reaching a wider audience. Hegel published only four books in his lifetime,[20] making a strategic decision to disseminate his philosophy orally through lecture courses to both followers and a wider public.[21] This decision was made with the realization that certain students would take notes and reconstruct the lectures as fully as possible while their recollection was still fresh.[22] The practice was and to some degree still is common in European universities. These reconstructions would be intended for the personal use of the student, but the transcripts would also sometimes be shared with others. Hegel accommodated himself to the circulation of these transcripts, without personally endorsing any of them. He did not personally endorse the transcript contained in this volume, even though it was made by his own son.

Yet this transcript is unusual in a number of respects that suggest it may have more authority than others. The transcriber, Hegel's son Karl, would have a fairly distinguished academic career himself as a university historian.[23] He was a philosophy student in 1830–1831 at Berlin University where his father taught. He still lived at home with his father when he took this course on logic in the summer of 1831, the last course Hegel was to teach before his death. Karl had by then already embraced his father's philosophy. Though he would never specialize in the science of logic, he understood that it was the basis of the entire Hegelian system. He took class notes, and afterward reconstructed the lectures for himself, with the aim of appropriating their content for himself as the foundation for his further study of Hegel's philosophy of history. We may surmise that he did not wait for his father's death in November of that year to begin his reconstruction. His version of the lectures was not undertaken in memory of his father, but in an attempt to internalize his father's thought. It is likely that Karl worked out his prose version of the lectures at least in occasional direct communication with his father in the months before the latter's unanticipated death. It would be surprising if Hegel was unaware of Karl's project. He may have looked over his son's transcript and even have occasionally discussed it with him. Indeed, the transcript seems a bit too good to come from an unassisted eighteen-year-old. But we have no evidence that the philosopher ever saw the transcript as leading to the publication of a book.

Hegel's terse outline version of his logic in the *Encyclopaedia* contrasts with the expansive but often difficult exposition in his earlier *Science of Logic* (1812–1816). His decision to communicate his philosophy orally by lectures implied an understanding that its propagation would occur within an oral tradition among his students, but also allowed that some of these students could and would publish books. He did not request that any transcripts of his lectures *not* be published. He only said that he could not vouchsafe for the evenness of their quality.

In the present translation, "the science of logic" is often abbreviated as simply "the logic." I often reinstate the word "science" because Hegel viewed his logic as science in the strictest sense. The growing prestige of the positive sciences later in the nineteenth century caused Hegelians some embarrassment over the word. Some Hegel scholars today still hope to escape that embarrassment by downplaying the "science" in the science of logic. But as a translator faithful to Hegel's intentions, I have concluded that the scientific purpose of these lectures cannot be honestly downplayed. The reader will have to judge whether Hegel, as some have suspected,[24] was a scientific charlatan. To the extent that these lectures prove readable, they will tend to show that Hegel has not resorted to obscurantism to hide the alleged fact that he had no science. To the extent that they still fail to be reader-friendly, readers will have some reason to suppose the contrary. We cannot treat the matter here in a translator's introduction, but this volume may help to reopen the question as to whether there is a Hegelian science of logic.

4. Jacobi and Hegel's Prepositional Mode of Discourse

Having characterized the text as a whole and its context in both Hegel's life and the history of philosophy, we now go inside the text to take up particular translation issues. First a general comment. The translation of *canonical* philosophers cannot entirely escape the method of rational interpretation. We must translate Hegel's words (1) so that they are intelligible in English and (2) so that they express, consistent with the German text lexically and syntactically, a maximum of surprising insight *discovered* in the text as worthy of a canonical philosopher, without importing extraneous thought into the text. Even if these lectures represent an easier point of access to Hegel's science of logic, their sense is not always obvious. In completing the translation I have had to weigh various interpretive hypotheses which remain open to discussion. I have sought to abandon myself to the life of the text and to rethink it accurately, and I have been most encouraged by the efforts of well-trained and careful readers of the manuscript who have helped me correct numerous passages where I originally fell short.

Passing on to a few technical issues in the translation of particular
terms, I first want to recall an important terminological connection between Hegel and Jacobi. Hegel was greatly influenced by Jacobi's "prepositional" mode of discourse, which serves to highlight relations. Prepositions such as "in," "within," "outside," "beside," "upon," "before,"
"after," "for," and "by" all express relations. The classical subject-predicate discourse of Aristotle did not similarly stress relational thinking,
since for him relational predicates were accidental. For Hegel the absolute articulates itself in essential dynamic relations between its moments, i.e., prepositionally.

The translator must wonder whether prepositional discourse can
replace subject-predicate discourse as easily in English as it does in
German. Jacobi's prepositional discourse reflects the German language, in which separable prepositional prefixes to verbs are both ac-
cented in pronunciation and highlighted by being thrown all by themselves to the end of the clause. If we say that lordship and bondage *hebt
sich im Stoicismus auf*—which literally translated is to say that it raises
itself beyond itself into Stoicism *up there*—the upward direction of the
movement clearly becomes essential. In translating the lectures on
logic I have opted to preserve in the English, as much as possible,
Hegel's prepositional idioms: upon itself (*an sich*), for another (*für An-
deres*), upon itself (*an ihm*), outside itself (*ausser sich*), within itself (*in
sich*), for itself (*für sich*), upon and for itself (*an und für sich*), at home
with oneself (*bei sich*). Thus where "*für sich sein*" could be translated as
"being on its own account," I have preferred "being for itself."

The decision to retain the prepositional mode in the translation keeps
the English closer to the German original, and helps express Hegel's
stand against non-relational subject-predicate thinking. Prepositions
are integral to the grammatical essence of German, but not to that of
English. That is part of what Hegel considered the speculative genius of
the German language.[25] Yet the German influence brought to bear on
this translation will not, I believe, be destructive of its readability. The
assumption is that English, with a little help, can be taught to speak
speculative philosophy.

A recurrent preposition for Hegel, "*an*," is already found in Kant's "*Ding
an sich*," commonly translated as "thing in itself." My preferred translation
of "*an*" in the Hegelian context is not traditional. "*An und für sich*" translated as "in and for itself" is well established in French—Sartre's "*en soi et
pour soi*"—as well as in English. "In and for itself" is so well established that
a translator may be inclined to prefer the translation tradition even if it is
not faithful to Hegel's original meaning. But when a choice seems necessary between an author's intentions and the meaning assigned to an author by the consecrated history of the text's reception in translation, I have
preferred fidelity to authorial intentions. So I owe the reader an explana-

tion as to why I view "being in and for itself" as a familiar, even reassuring, but ultimately inaccurate way of glossing over the meaning of *"Anundfürsichsein,"* which is better translated as "being upon and in itself."

In Hegel's distinct usage, the preposition *"an"* connotes the potentiality for receiving some further actual form. Putting the translation tradition aside, I translate *"Das Kind ist an sich aufgewachsen"* as "The child is already *upon itself* an adult." This means that it is already essentially an adult for those who place it in a class with other children whom they have seen actually grow up. The reflective thinking of persons who have seen this can place or posit upon a newborn child an adulthood which is not yet directly observable in it.

The science of logic aims, we have mentioned, at pure imageless thinking.[26] It may seem odd, given this opposition in the science of logic to pictorial representation (*Vorstellung*), that *"an"* can have a spatial connotation. That Frankfurt is upon the river Main, for example, can be intuited in perceptual space and then represented in imagination. Frankfurt-am-Main is Frankfurt *at* or *upon* the Main. It is not Frankfurt *in* the river! What is *upon* something lies upon its surface.

As for adulthood, it is no more *in* the child than Frankfurt is *in* the Main. The difference between the two relations is that Frankfurt and the Main coexist spatially at the same time, while the adulthood temporally *succeeds* the child at a later time. Associated with this is the fact that *"an"* in *"Frankfurt am Main"* is the *"an"* of location which takes the dative case in German, while *"an"* in *"Das Kind an sich"* is the *"an"* of directionality which takes the accusative case. When we say that the child is upon itself an adult, we mean that the child is directed to the actualization of its essential potentiality in being succeeded by the adult it becomes. Hegel does not uphold preformism, the view that there is an actual little adult hiding in every child, awaiting its chance to come out in the open.

Actual adulthood and childishness are incompatible and cannot coexist in the same subject, whether in perception or in imagination. Being Frankfurt and being the Main are also incompatible in the same subject. A city is a city and not a river. But the Main is simultaneously found in something adjacent, while an adult is found as a successor subject to the child. Being the Main does not eventually displace Frankfurt in the way in which adulthood displaces childhood. We imagine an adult when we perceive a child, but eventually we perceive an adult in place of the child.

A further advantage to translating *"an sich"* by "upon itself" rather than "in itself" stems from Hegel's separate use of *"in sich."* The German *"in sich"* could well be translated as "in itself," though I have used "within itself." A second point is that *"in,"* as well as *"an,"* has a spatial connotation. Yet Hegel intends no literal physical space connotation of either German preposition. His use of the prepositions projects only thought space. (Such thought space is also projected by contemporary symbolic logic when we say that a conjunction *contains* two conjuncts.)

Yet Kant's *"Ding an sich"* may still be translated as "thing in itself" to capture his distinct intent. The thing in itself for Kant is walled off from any relation to other things, from anything in the way of what Hegel calls the thing's being for the other. Hegel passed from Kant's understanding of *"Ansichsein"* in *"Ding an sich"* to his own understanding of *"Ansichsein"* issuing in *"Anundfürsichsein,"* and in the transition *"Ansichsein"* shifted in meaning. Moreover, the shift brought the meaning of *"an"* closer to its meaning in ordinary German.

5. Hegel's Logic, Jacobi, and the Specter of Panlogicism

A second comment on a particular translation issue remains to be made. I often prefer to translate *"Bestimmtheit"* ("determinateness") as "determination," *"Existenz"* as "the existent," and *"Körperlichkeit"* ("corporeality") as "the body."[27] Hegel himself admitted the year before these lectures, in his review of Karl Friedrich Göschel (1784–1861), that his style of writing tended to mislead readers into supposing that he was in effect the panlogicist who many since have supposed him to be.[28] He conveyed the idea that the absolute is nothing but a bloodless ballet of unearthly logical categories. This gave the impression that only *corporeality* had true existence, not individual bodies, or that only *existence* was a true entity, but not individual existents.

Hegel confessed to Göschel that this practice was polemically motivated by his stand against the romanticism of Jacobi and of Jacobi's despised followers—e.g., Schleiermacher, or even worse Fries—who denied the possibility of any true conceptual grasp of reality. The absolute, for these romantics, could only be intimated by feeling. Hegel wanted to reinstate a conceptual grasp of reality, and overcompensated stylistically by suggesting that reality was nothing but concepts, essences, or universals. His actual position is that the system of conceptual categories indeed grasps, but never exhausts, the absolute. The potential for ever-new, longer editions of his *Encyclopaedia of the Philosophical Sciences* is proof that his systematic philosophy, while true in general, remains a living system by continually expanding to embrace more of the absolute in its self-particularization.

In this translation I have heeded Hegel's professed true intent, and have thus corrected his panlogicist writing style that has left so many readers puzzled, and that has put so many off Hegel. These lectures on logic give us good reason for supposing that Hegel, far from being a panlogicist, was in fact a nominalist[29] who held that universals existed only for us as concepts abstracted from singular individual entities:

> [I]f I say "red," the predicate expresses a universal characteristic that at once belongs to blood and various other objects. Yet what I have before me is only a singular red, this determinate red thing. Yet this same red also assumes the character of universality which at once belongs to me [insofar as I have abstracted it from what is singularly red]. But one is no more able to single out color in general in contrast to any singular color than to refer to the animal in general as opposed to referring to this dog or this elephant. The elephant in general, the dog in general, the species does not objectively exist. The genus is something still more general, which once again falls to me as subject.[30]

My correction of a traditional interpretation of Hegel's philosophy, which is well grounded in Hegel's own statement, has led me, in an attempt to communicate his meaning in a less off-putting way, to correct a mode of expression which he himself criticized in 1830, but which still remained an ingrained habit of his in the 1831 lectures.

---

6. Three More Translation Decisions

To briefly mention another practice adopted in this translation, I translate *"der Begriff"* as "the self-concept," not simply as "the concept" which is the more usual English translation. This is to make more explicit Hegel's thought that the concept grasps itself in its object. Your concept of the other is your own self-concept in and through the other. We are translating a text, but more fundamentally we are translating intelligible thought expressed in German into the same intelligible thought expressed as well as possible in English. I take *"der Begriff"* as elliptical.

A second translation issue concerns the term *"Materien"* in relation to *"Eigenshaften."*[31] The noun *"Eigenschaften"* is translated as "properties" understood as exemplified universal determinations, while a *"Bestimmung"* is a determination that may or may not be exemplified. To refer to the universal determination of being watery as a property is thus also to implicitly refer to a *matter* which has that property. This is to draw on the established sense of "a matter" where it means "a material substance of a particular kind or for a particular purpose, e.g., 'a vegetable matter.'"[32] A living organism has the property of being watery, but another way of saying this is to say that, since being H_2O is exemplified by 97 percent of the organism, the organism possesses "a chemical matter" whose property is to be watery. A rose as perceived has the sensory quality of being red as one of its properties, but another way of saying this is to say that it contains as one of its matters a visual surface that has the sensory color property of being red. Hegel says that a thing's property is a matter,[33] meaning, I take it, that its property is what it is only in and through some matter (*Materie*) that exhibits the property. I have followed an established translation tradition by rendering "*Materie*" as "matter," but I do not think we need be puzzled. Though a matter can be an atomic matter, we need to understand Hegel as using the term to refer to something much broader. There are chemical matters or "material substances of a particular kind" like H_2O, but a visually green surface may be a directly perceived matter in a painting. So when we speak of "a matter" we do not necessarily mean a matter in a physicalistic sense, since we may speak of the sensory manifold as a sensed matter. We may also use the noun "matter" in the plural.

The final translation decision needing explanation concerns the distinction between *Erkennen* and *Wissen*. It is clear that *Wissen* is higher than *Erkennen*, which is finite knowledge as understood by Kant and Jacobi. "*Erkennen*" as explicated by Hegel beyond its Kantian context comes close to "*wiedererkennen*," meaning the activity of re-cognizing familiar categories (e.g., cause and effect) of the logic in the external world, without yet attaining a Hegelian self-conscious re-cognition of the world as the sensory realization and particularization of these categories. *Erkennen* falls short of true knowing (*Wissen*). It is thus a finite knowing, which is for itself limited by the world it knows.

Das absolutes Erkennen, absolute knowing, is a subject self-consciously recognizing itself throughout the objective world. It is infinite knowing, which does mean the same as "*Wissen*." Mere "*Erkennen*" then means the finite reconnoitering or reconnaissance of familiar markers in alien territory. It means knowing or cognizing as un-self-conscious re-cognizing.[34] Yet it harbors a drive, first theoretical and then practical, to attain coincidence between subject and object, but a drive that has not yet attained fulfillment in *Wissen* or true knowledge. Knowing as re-cognizing does cognize logical forms anew in the outer world—forms already cognized in the logical determinations of our own pure thought. But the thinking subject cannot be forced into complete conformity with the world through *theoretical striving*, and the world cannot be forced into complete conformity with the subject through *practical striving*. For coercion establishes domination or lordship over whatever is coerced. True knowing rather raises the reciprocity of love, the basis of any true relationship with the world, to the level of pure thought.[35]

7. Acknowledgments

I conclude this introduction with an expression of appreciation for those who have assisted me along the way. My first debt chronologically is to Professor Peter Hodgson, who years before the publication of the German edition of the lectures invited me to take responsibility for the English translation at a time when the University of California Press was contemplating publication of a series of Hegel's lectures. I also want to thank Felix Meiner Verlag in Hamburg for providing me with a copy of the German text before its publication in 2001. When I turned to Indiana University Press, I found support and encouragement from sponsoring editor Dee Mortensen and her assistant Laura MacLeod. With proper regard for the importance of this translation, the Press enlisted the critical judgment of three scholars. They all made significant contributions to the improvement of the published version of the English translation. I often profited from their advice, though I bear responsibility for the final result. They are John Burbidge, John Russon, and David Dusenbury. All three commented meticulously on drafts of the translation. Finally, in a few key cases where I deviated from the translation tradition I was fortunate enough to have been able to confer with a native German-speaking philosopher, Professor Bernd Buldt of the Indiana University–Purdue University Fort Wayne Philosophy Department.

Notes

1. My *Introduction to the Study of the Logic of Hegel* keyed to the present *Lectures on Logic* is available for interested students online from the National Social Science Press (http://www.nsspress.com).

2. Georg Wilhelm Friedrich Hegel, *Vorlesungen über die Logik (Berlin 1831)*, in *Vorlesungen, Ausgewählte Nachschriften und Manuskripte, nachgeschrieben von Karl Hegel*, ed. Udo Rameil and Hans-Christian Lucas (Hamburg: Felix Meiner Verlag, 2001), vol. 10.

3. G. W. F. Hegel, *The Science of Logic,* trans. A. V. Miller (Atlantic Highlands, N.J.: Humanities Press, 1969).

4. G. W. F. Hegel, *Phenomenology of Spirit*, trans. A. V. Miller (Oxford: Oxford University Press, 1977).

5. G. W. F. Hegel, *Hegel: The Letters*, trans. Clark Butler and Christiane Seiler, with commentary by Clark Butler (Bloomington: Indiana University Press, 1984), p. 258.

6. "We may give logical determinations out to be . . . definitions of God." See below, p. 87.

7. The science of logic, "when thus thought out into its purity, will have within itself the capacity to *determine* itself, that is to give itself a content, and that a *necessarily* explicated content—in the form of a system of determinations of thought." Hegel, *Science of Logic*, p. 63.

8. G. W. F. Hegel, *Logic: Part One of the Encyclopaedia of the Philosophical Sciences (1830)*, trans. William Wallace, with foreword by J. N. Findlay (Oxford: Oxford University Press, 1975); *Philosophy of Nature: Part Two of the Encyclopaedia of the Philosophical Sciences (1830)*, trans A. V. Miller (Oxford: Oxford University Press, 2004); *Philosophy of Spirit: Part Three of the Encyclopaedia of the Philosophical Sciences*

(1830), trans. William Wallace and A. V. Miller, with introduction and commentary by Michael Inwood (Oxford: Oxford University Press, 2007).

9. Udo Rameil, "Einleitung: Hegels Logik Vorlesungen im Sommersemester 1831," in Hegel, *Vorlesungen über die Logik*, p. xvi.

10. Udo Rameil, „Zur Konstitution des Textes," in Hegel, *Vorlesungen über die Logik*, p. 231.

11. Hegel distinguishes between the empirical order in the history of philosophy, in which Heraclitus precedes Parmenides, and the logical order, in which Parmenides precedes Heraclitus. See Clark Butler, „Empirical vs. Rational Order in the History of Philosophy," *Owl of Minerva*, vol. 26, no. 1 (1994), pp. 31–37.

12. For what anecdotal interest it may have, I published a commentary on the *Science of Logic* in 1996 before having read the 1831 *Lectures on Logic*. See Clark Butler, *Hegel's Logic: Between Dialectic and History* (Evanston: Northwestern University Press, 1996). Upon translating the *Lectures* I found them to be less developed in places than the *Science of Logic*, but did not find them to introduce new logical categories or to constitute a revision in any significant way of his understanding in the original *Science of Logic*.

13. Hegel, *Vorlesungen über die Logik*, pp. xlix–l.

14. Hegel, *Vorlesungen über die Logik*, p. xviii.

15. G. W. F. Hegel, *Lectures on the History of Philosophy*, trans. E. S. Haldane and F. H. Simson (Atlantic Highlands, N.J.: Humanities Press, 1968), 3 vols.

16. Hegel, *Logic*, §86, addition. Karl Hegel refers to paragraphs in the 1830 edition throughout in parentheses without page numbers. I follow him by referencing such paragraphs in brackets without page numbers. The problem with giving page numbers is that there are many editions which readers may use. I do not want to suggest that annotations are, for example, tied merely to the Wallace translation as introduced by J. N. Findlay. There is an earlier English edition in which page numbers are different. There is also another widely circulating translation in English by H. S. Harris et al. Furthermore, these lectures are likely to travel around the world in English rather than German, and international readers may refer to translations of the *Encyclopaedia* in even other languages, including of course the German. Since there are many bracketed references to paragraph numbers in the present translation I prefer, following Karl's usual practice, not to burden all of them with page numbers and thus link them to a single edition of Hegel's *Logic*.

17. Hegel, *Phenomenology of Spirit*, p. 1.

18. Hegel claims that the science of logic systematically treats *"the* determinations of thought" (*Science of Logic*, pp. 63–64, my italics). The system of the determinations of pure thought may be *implicitly* complete in any act of thinking. It then is *explicit* in the *Science of Logic* as a text only if the final thought determination or logical category—what Hegel calls "the absolute idea"—never proves incoherent. The category of Substance proved incoherent in Spinoza's *Ethics*. But Spinoza himself could not know that the absolute under his description of being the Substance was incoherent. Analogously, only some successor to Hegel would know that some further thought determination beyond the logical absolute idea does not merely particularize that idea empirically in the philosophy of nature and spirit, but rather constitutes a new and more coherent logical category. But

this important question of interpretation cannot be pursued here in a translator's introduction. I have discussed it elsewhere. See Butler, *Hegel's Logic,* pp. 288–292.

19. Regarding the popular "romantic" philosophy of feeling stemming from Jacobi and continuing in Jakob Friedrich Fries (1772–1843), Wilhelm Martin Leberecht de Wette (1780–1849), Friedrich August Gottreu Tholuck (1799–1877), but first and foremost in F. E. D. Schleiermacher, see Hegel, *The Letters,* pp. 254–258, 537–544; and G. W. F. Hegel, "Review of K. F. Göschel's *Aphorisms,*" trans. Clark Butler, in *Miscellaneous Writings of G. W. F. Hegel,* ed. Jon Stewart (Evanston: Northwestern University Press, 2000), pp. 401–429. Hegel, though disagreeing with Jacobi, was much more indulgent with the grand old man than with Jacobi's younger followers, who were rivals to Hegel himself. He writes in a letter, "Beyond personal pain, Jacobi's death has . . . overtaken me. . . . We feel ever more abandoned as, one by one, these old branches which we have beheld with admiration from youth on die. He was one of those who formed a turning point in the spiritual development not only of individuals but of the age, who were pillars of the world in which we represent our existence" (Hegel, *The Letters,* p. 443; cf. pp. 304, 318, 321, 331, 358–359, 364, 431). But Hegel shows contempt for Fries's metaphysical appeal to a mere empirical fact of consciousness in an 1811 letter (Hegel, *The Letters,* pp. 257–258). Regarding Schleiermacher, Hegel traced the Schleiermachian mere feeling of absolute dependence on God very early to Jacobi's false reduction of reason to feeling. See G. W. F. Hegel, *Glauben und Wissen,* in *Aufsätze aus dem kritischen Journal der Philosophie, Sämmtliche Werke,* ed. Hermann Glockner (Stuttgart: Friedrich Frommann Verlag, 1965), pp. 388–389.

20. *Phenomenology of Spirit* (1807), *The Science of Logic* (1812–1816), *Encyclopaedia of the Philosophical Sciences* (1817, 1827, 1830), and *Philosophy of Right* (*Die Rechtsphilosophie,* 1821).

21. Hegel, *The Letters,* p. 475.

22. "I do not know how to satisfy your wish to obtain a copy of a notebook of my lectures on the science of religion. You will more easily obtain this through connections with students among whom such notebooks are circulating, though they do so without my knowledge and — according to the few I have had occasion to see — not always exactly to my satisfaction." Hegel, *The Letters,* p. 543.

23. "Karl Hegel was born on June 7, 1813, in Nuremberg and died on December 5, 1901, in Erlangen. He was the eldest son of the philosopher Georg Wilhelm Friedrich Hegel and of his wife Maria Helena Susanna von Tucher. After finishing his schooling and university studies in Berlin and Heidelberg and returning from an extended voyage in Italy (1838–1839) he at once found employment in the Prussian school system. In 1841 he became professor of history in Rostock. In the years of the 1848–1849 Revolution he was politically active as Editor in Chief of the new *Mecklenburgischen Zeitung.* In 1856 he took a newly created teaching chair in history at the University of Erlangen. Here Karl, married to Susanna Maria von Tucher, became the 'first true historian in the modern style' (T. Kolde). With his *History of the Constitution of Italy* (1847) he suddenly came to know fame, and with his further research works and the publication of his twenty-seven volume *Chronicles of German Cities* he entered the first rank of German historians and became the internationally highly respected 'Hegel of German Cities' (R. Fester)." Helmut Neuhaus, "Karl Hegel und Erlangen." Faculty of History, University of Erlangen, 5 December 2001.

Online at http://www.geschichte.uni-erlangen.de/aktuelles/hegel.shtml (accessed 9 September 2007, my translation).

24. Arthur Schopenhauer, *Parerga and Paralipomena*, trans. E. F. J. Payne (London: Oxford University Press, 1974), vol. 1, pp. 96, 144-145.

25. Hegel, *Science of Logic*, p. 32.

26. "The system of logic is the realm of shadows, the world of simple essentialities freed from all sensuous concreteness." Hegel, *Science of Logic*, p. 58.

27. Thus to translate "determinate being" as "determinateness having being" (*Bestimmtheit zunächst als seiende*—p. 97 below) is like translating "a human being" as "humanity as being" in preference to "humanity as being instantiated." It is to refer to an individual human being by referring only to universals.

28. "Review of K. F. Göschel's *Aphorisms*," in Hegel, *Miscellaneous Writings*, pp. 420-421.

29. A fuller but still brief case for a nominalist interpretation of Hegel that is consistent with his texts appears in Clark Butler, "Hermeneutic Hegelianism," *Idealistic Studies*, vol. 14, no. 2 (1985), pp. 121-135.

30. See below, p. 2.

31. See below, p. 144.

32. *Merriam-Webster's Online Dictionary*, s.v. Matter, 2c. Online at http://mwl. merriam-webster.com/dictionary/matter (accessed 9 September 2007).

33. See below, p. 145.

34. See below, pp. 213-214.

35. See below, pp. 172, 177.

Lectures on Logic

Introduction to the Lectures on Logic

Preliminary General Concept of Our Subject Matter

(§19)[1] We shall first consider here the attitudes adopted by thinking toward its object in general. The science of logic has as its subject matter, *thinking*, the *pure idea*. Thinking is the ground within which the logical idea, what thought in truth is, appears. Every science has its own subject matter. As far as the subject matter of logic is concerned, it is at first sight like the subject matter of any other science, much as botany has as its subject matter plants, and so on. Yet the subject matter of logic is higher than that of any other science. Thinking is higher than space and time. It is by thinking that we separate ourselves off from the animals. Just as heaven is higher than earth, so thinking is higher than our vegetative nature. Thinking is not simply one object alongside others. (§20) Thinking does not arise alongside the mental activities of sensation, will, and so on, but is rather ever present within them and is all-embracing. Yet as a subject matter it is nonetheless difficult. Unlike botany, physics, or mineralogy, logic has nothing to do with sensory intuition. The activity of tasting or feeling is sensory, while thinking soars above of any sensory object. With the onset of thinking, all mere seeing and hearing must pass away. In thinking we surrender our firm hold on all the representations of sensory objects with which we are familiar. All such representations must be put aside as we take up the pure element of thinking.

Geometry unlike thinking contemplates objects in space. It does not focus on space itself. It considers something spatial—though as geometricians we do have space itself within the scope of our view, right there before our very eyes. But something sensory about space still remains [as that from which geometrical objects in space are abstracted]. The ancients held that geometry was an introduction to philosophy. For in geometry one has to do, not directly with sensations, nor with any interest

---

1. That is, starting from §19 in the *Encyclopaedia*. See G. W. F. Hegel, *Logic: Part One of the Encyclopaedia of the Philosophical Sciences* (1830), trans. William Wallace, with foreword by J. N. Findlay (Oxford: Oxford University Press, 1975), p. 25ff.

of inclination, but with lifeless products of abstraction from sensation. The mind is much exercised in holding fast to such simple objects.

The subject matter of logic, however, is still more abstract than that of geometry, and is indeed known for its difficulty. We are not used to moving about in such rarified stratospheres and must acclimate ourselves to them. We must hold on tight and persist as we steer our poor vessel off into the vicinity of such abstractions. What is involved here is the strain of negation, of putting all sensation off to the side and of keeping our own bright ideas to ourselves. In doing so we must truly strain. Only then will we come to behold the true subject matter of logic, which in this regard is most certainly a difficult subject. We lack any way of bodily laying hold of it. It is as if the very ground of our ordinary consciousness had fallen away beneath us. Yet what is difficult when one is not yet used to the matter becomes easy with practice.

What comes first in our approach to logic is the historical side, what kind of origin logic has had—logic and along with it metaphysics, for the two sciences coincide. The origin of logic is no different from that of any other science. Determinations come forth in the conscious mind that, in logic but not in geometry, have not been extracted from the senses, and that belong rather to the thinking subject. If we take the simplest of sensory judgments—for example, the rose is red—what lies before consciousness is in appearance totally sensory. Yet the *is* in this judgment is already something of a different and non-sensory nature. There is nothing sensory about *being*, it is already something quite different.

Further, the rose and what is red, as we find them before us in sensation, are one, while it is I who introduce difference or division between them. What lies ready at hand is simple and undivided. It is I who differentiate and divide—I am the source of judging [*urteilen*] and of the act of dividing [*ein Teilen*]. This judgment belongs to me as to the one who apprehends [what is simple by introducing division]. But what is more, if I say "red," the predicate expresses a universal characteristic that at once belongs to blood and various other objects. Yet what I have before me is only a singular red, this determinately red thing. Yet this same red also assumes the character of universality which at once belongs to me [insofar as I have abstracted it from what is singularly red].

But one is no more able to single out color in general in contrast to any singular color than to refer to the animal in general as opposed to referring to this dog or this elephant. The elephant in general, the dog in general, the species does not objectively exist. The genus is something still more general, which once again falls to me as subject. If I speak of cause and effect, saying for example "The house is toppled by water," what I see by my senses is the water and afterwards the toppling of the house. Yet the determination of the one as cause and the other as effect is not a sensory determination, but is a determination belonging to me. Only the successive happenings in time are sensory. Careful inspection shows that, along with sensory objects and interwoven with them, logical forms arise that are quite alien to them, that are not sensory objects. Such forms have been as extensively classified as the species forms of plants and animals, and they moreover have been classified for themselves rather than for any external purpose. The *complete classification of these forms* is logic and, along with it, metaphysics.

Only at the very end of scientific education do we reach the point of observing these logical forms. For the sensory realm is more stimulating to us. Reason in its theoretical form lies in assimilating to ourselves whatever is external, in procuring for ourselves the content of objects. As human beings we start out in poverty and wish to enrich ourselves with the whole content of the world, with a drive to win for ourselves all the abundance that can be found in the world itself. If we say "white" we lay hold of the content of something that appears in ever different objects. Our cognitive drive is to make external objects our own. As human beings we are the activation of thinking. I am this very activation. Thinking expands by its inner instinctive tendency into everything objective. Yet at first we lack all awareness of thinking, it has not yet become an object for us. Just the reverse is true of sensory objects, which are what first appear to us as objective, and which we then assimilate into our own subjectivity. By the [pre-conscious] instinct of thinking we ourselves have introduced the form of universality in the proposition "The rose is red." We still know nothing consciously of the universality present in this proposition. Universality does not lie immediately in my consciousness, it is not yet an object for me. Yet we ourselves are thinking, and what we must now do is to make it objective to ourselves, to posit it out here for our consciousness as an object, just as conversely we transpose sensory objects into ourselves from the outside. The strain of reflection here is greater than in observing a sensory content that is already itself an object.

The thought forms have been observed and classified, especially those of the logic of the self-concept [*Begriff*]. Aristotle has already classified for us the logical forms belonging to subjective logic[, i.e., the logic of the self-concept as distinct from the objective logic of being and essence]. Logic has thus gained currency as a science that has reached completion, and until now we have on the whole added nothing essential to it since Aristotle. The essential foundation of logic also belongs to Aristotle, and this is what today circulates as the usual school logic. Yet it has fallen into contempt, on the one hand quite justifiably but on the other quite without justification. Aristotle proceeded from observation, summoning forth the entire universe in a parade before his mind [*Geist*].[2] He went through the general principles [of nature], he gave

2. *Geist* will be translated as "mind" when the reference is limited to the intel-

consideration to the plants and animals. The physiology of the animals—regarding their walking, their waking, their sleeping—as well as the human mind and spirit—regarding sensation, seeing, hearing, memory, fantasy, the nature of the state and of the will: in all this he went observingly to work, speculatively treating everything he observed. He laid down experience as the foundation, and then passed over from it to the thinking concept. He observed and classified the forms of thought in the same manner as he classified the species forms of nature. But he went no further than that. He thus never reached the forms of rational thinking or of the self-concept as such. The Aristotelian forms are rather those of the understanding [*Verstand*]. Not even in his reflective ponderings did he go after these forms of rational thinking. And even if he had done so he would not, in his time, have been able to give birth to the speculative self-concept.

We must all familiarize ourselves with such forms of the understanding as Aristotle brings forth—they are forms of thinking, abstract forms and one-sided laws. Yet if they are to be of service to true thinking, we must not interpret them so separately from one another, [as Aristotle does,] since they would then be only forms of untruth, finite forms. They would then be only so many different sides of concrete truths, and so would be one-sided. We must tear them out of their one-sidedness and bring them into their interconnection. It is because of such one-sidedness that logic has fallen into contempt, and with good reason.

The form of identity considered abstractly for itself, for example, is an empty abstraction, but in connection with difference it is most important and most essential. It will be said "Everything is identical with itself," "A = A." Or, to express the law of identity negatively as the law of non-contradiction, "Nothing can be in contradiction with itself." That is a fundamental law of thought. If we apply this law immediately in the realm of singularity—"This plant is this plant, this animal is this animal"—it is a completely one-sided determination; [when taken] formally identity is abstract. Yet difference must also exist within identity. One says that all finite things pass away, that their very essence is to cease to be. Self-negation is their nature. We say "What is finite is," but this law already contains a contradiction insofar as we apply being to what is finite. Finite things consist precisely in being contradictory. "Nothing contradicts itself" is thus a poor excuse for a law of logic. Every irrational action is upon itself contradictory, bad states go under because they are contradictory. One can even say "God is contradictory," since he embraces self-negation. I feel need, which negates my self-concept. The feeling of non-being in need is a

---

lect of an individual or of the species. It will be translated as "spirit" when it refers to objective or absolute spirit, or when a contrast to nature is intended.

drive. Activity always proceeds from *need*. God embraces activity, and activity posits alteration, it posits something that is within itself other than itself, something imbued with power. In all activity there is *difference* and at once *self-identity*, for I am identical with myself in what is different from myself. This difference [of determinations belonging to what is self-identical] is found everywhere in consciousness, for I have consciousness of something other than myself, and in that other I am nonetheless at once identical with myself. Hence identity, difference, and contradiction are in everything. So just as I can say "Everything is identical" I can equally say "Everything is contradictory."

Spirit as mind can withstand self-contradiction, while natural things fall to the ground through their self-contradictions, in that something other than each such thing develops upon it. In heaven and on earth, in spirit and in nature, nothing can be found to be merely abstractly self-identical. As an example, consider the syllogism "All men are mortal, Cassius is [a] man, and therefore Cassius is mortal." This syllogism is allowed to pass as valid, but it is defective: "all men" means "each and every single man," and "All men are mortal" is presented as an empirical proposition as in "All metals are electrical conductors." The terms "all men" and "all metals" presuppose empirical awareness of each and every individual. Thus I must have already known it to be true of Cassius that he is mortal in order to be able to assert "All men are mortal"!

Logic considers forms alone. True forms require true content. Form determines content, for the essential form of every content is the idea at the end of the science of logic. The absolute form, the self-concept, the idea, is the true content. If forms reveal themselves to be purely formal and untrue in their content, they are *one-sided* forms. The law of mere self-identity is thus defective, which is why logic in the form of school wisdom is an object of contempt. False categories like this do not arise in concrete thinking and life, and have no greater validity in logic and philosophy. Though absolutely indispensable, they are in themselves defective. Still, one must be able to give an account of them, as to why they are false and absolutely indispensable. We, too, in our science of logic shall lay hold of these familiar forms. But we shall come to know them only as moments of the true form. This true form can be a fully rational logic only insofar as it is a logic in which thinking has won the dignity of being the basis of truth. In the remark to §19, the idea is said to be the totality of determinations. The true science of logic is difficult because it does violence to the understanding. It comprises what is speculative and yet at once embraces what is the easiest of all. Ease lies in *simplicity*. Because we are thinking beings, thinking pervades everything of which we are aware. Yet logic poses a difficulty in other respect, in that its all-pervasive determinations are so very well known that it is not considered worth the trouble to occupy oneself with them. If we truly investigate what these determinations are, we strain to hold them fast each for itself. In addition, once we examine them carefully, they turn out to be quite different from what we initially allowed them to be. Everyone, to be sure, naturally has hold of some logic. We think immediately, and to think we have no need to study logic. We even brag about having no need of such study. Yet thinking is already a worthy subject to come to know. We thereby learn the extent to which what we think is true.

Given the *utility* of logic, we become masters of natural logic by thinking. Yet thinking and having thoughts are different. The object of our study in these lectures is to gain knowledge of thinking, to know what we as thinking beings are. A human being is *spirit* [*Geist*], and to come to know what lies therein is our highest achievement. Whatever a human being is, we are truly human only insofar as we know who we are. A human being bears within him- or herself a right to such knowledge, but the actual possession of what is one's right is still something else.

There is no unnatural *artificial* logic, it is said, but *conscious* logic without a doubt can exist. We receive pure thoughts into our heads, thoughts which are true. We learn how to hold fast to what is universal, and it is by doing so we receive our education and learn how to lift out what is essential. Considerations of utility must not be scorned. We must come to know what is true for itself rather than for external ends, it is said. Yet the other side of the matter is again utility. God sacrificed himself on the cross within the natural world for the sake of the world of individual human beings. Thus what upon and for itself is most excellent also proves to be most useful.

(§20) We come to approach our subject still more closely as we now consider *thinking*, which belongs to consciousness. We human beings think, the animals do not. Thinking is called a mental power, a faculty. Embracing feeling, representation, imagination, the faculty of thinking taken as a whole is known as theoretical mind. Beyond theoretical mind lies the will, the faculty of desire. Thinking at once falls to intelligence, to which representation and intuition also belong. Thinking is said to be but one mental faculty, one activity—one *among* others. Each power is taken to be independent, and the soul is imagined to be what holds such and such faculties within itself. The soul is taken to be a kind of external medium [*Umgebung*] in which every faculty independently operates for itself on its own account. When such representations are used we speak of mental *powers,* and relate them to one another through determining each to be tacked on as *also* present. What we have here is an only external compounding. Our immediate consciousness is held within [the limits of] such categories.

We also represent mind as a *one* in which everything is contained. If we inquire into the relation between these activities, it must be said that to be human is to think. But what is thinking, what does it do? It is nothing apart from what is universal. Thinking produces the universal, and it is by doing so that thinking is thinking. If it is said [with Kant] that thinking forms concepts or brings manifold representations into unity, such a statement is superficial to the extent that every representation, every sensation, is already *both* one *and* upon itself a manifold. The earmark of thinking is rather the form of the universal which it produces. This earmark first makes its appearance in *assertions* and *definitions,* and it requires for itself *proofs.* We cannot simply appeal to representation in establishing what is said here of thinking. What is to be said here is only the introduction or preliminary to the science of logic. What we adduce here is more properly historical, affording only a representation of the science. In the science itself it will be seen that the universal for itself, on its own account, is necessary, that the other forms revert back to it, that it is what is true. The universal is the product of thinking, but [in this preliminary exposition] the universal form is taken up merely empirically. We represent thinking to ourselves as an activity. As an activity thinking is the *universal in its activation.* The universal is the form by which something is thought. Thinking is active, and the result of its deed is what is thought, regardless of the content by which thinking is affected, on which thinking imposes universality. The subject, the *thinking* subject, is the *I.* That the I is essentially the thinking subject may at once take us by surprise. We represent to ourselves the I as proliferating in particular determinations, in this range of knowledge, we represent it as this wholly concrete I. Yet what exists out there for us to take up [as its abstract essence free of any particular content] is merely the I, the thinking subject.

Thinking, having concepts, seems far removed from us, but it is in fact what is closest at hand. In thinking I remain absolutely at home with myself. I am myself this thinking. This close proximity of thinking, this immediate oneness of thinking and myself, also impresses itself on us. We represent thinking to ourselves as separable from the I, but it is in fact what is most present in it. If we say "I go," "I am suffering," "I am pleased," the I remains ever present in these determinations [*Bestimmtheiten*] of my state, of my interest or will. I can thus be determinate in multiple ways. Now I feel, now I don't, I now instead will, and so it goes. Yet in all these determinations I remain as the common thread to it all. Put differently, I *accompany* all these representations[, as Kant has it]. "Accompany," however, does not say enough: I am entirely invested in these representations.

Yet I am not merely the common thread among all these determinations. A determination held in common is a bad form of the universal by which diverse things are compared as similar. Comparison is an external reflection on things that does not belong to the things themselves. So the I is not merely common to all things by comparison, but is rather absolutely these things all at once and all taken in only once. Yet I am also, in my self-abstraction from things, merely universal, and as such I am on the contrary free of every one of these things. The mere I is not only intuiting, feeling, and so on, but is also at once none of these. If feeling, intuition, belonged to my very nature, I could not be without it. The I stands in its freedom above all of these things. I posit myself absolutely as simple self-reference. The I is a pure thought space, which like sensory space can be filled in an infinitely various manner. The I is thus perfectly simple, bearing reference only to itself, and freedom of thought lies precisely in this simple self-reference. Thinking in its determinateness is the [concrete] universal, but I can also abstract from everything. The I in this self-abstraction is completely empty, which is what among the East Indians has passed for what is most high. In this emptiness I am this completely unitary individual, I negate everything and exclude all. Just so is infinite singularity present in the I, which once again also contains absolutely concrete determinateness. But in saying "I," in invoking this absolutely singular being of mine, I say directly the opposite of singularity. For everyone says "I" in reference to him- or herself. The word "I" which I say means everyone. The I, in this its singularity, is at once completely universal.

I am the thinking subject. The I illustrates the self-concept by existing throughout for itself alone, merely on its own account. Thinking is the universal taken as active. The universal is first what is abstract. By a "concept" we usually understands a determinate representation of the imagination. But in the science of logic the concept is something completely different, of which the I provides an example. This singular subject is immediately united with the I. Only as this singular thinking subject does thinking lay hold of truth, and its product is whatever is thought, the universal. The I is thus most contradictory, being completely universal and at once perfect singularity. From where we now stand [before the onset of the science of logic], the claim that I and thinking are completely identical can only be based on an appeal to representation. Logic is the science of truth. What is purely abstract is totally lacking in truth, and singularity considered abstractly merely for itself is untrue.

On the distinction between sensory objects, representations, and thoughts. In common parlance "representation" and "thought" are interchanged promiscuously. But the difference is a matter of high importance. Religion is on the whole held within representations, while science *thinks* representations. First comes what is *sensory,* and it will be said that what is sensory falls to the senses. But how are the senses determined? How is what is sensory so constituted that it lies within senses? A sensory object is determined as immediately *singular.* I have a singular sensory intuition only at this determinate time, at this moment, absolutely situated in time and space, and this intuition is immediately determinate. The simple character of whatever is sensory, as likewise the simple thought determination of what is sensory, is singular in its immediacy. I, like any sensory object, am also singular, but the singularity of the I, unlike that of a sense object, is mediated by universality. I am singular only insofar as I am mediated by universality, just as the I is universality only as mediated by singularity. The I exhibits singularity raised to the level of pure universality. What is sensory, by contrast, shows only abstract singularity. But a human being as a person, as an agent of action and willing, is what, from its beginning as sensory, has raised itself, within the I, to the level of universality.

The object of sensory intuition is a manifold that is richer than mere *sensation*. But the manifold activity of combining that results in the intuiting of such an object is itself singular. The manifold character of the determinations is separate from them. In intuition we have the *object of intuition* in a single *one*, and the combination of singular determinations likewise always occurs in a singular manner. *Representing* the object of intuition is something still further. In sensation the object, assuming it is an external object, exists in interconnection with our own corporeal nature and external being. Representation, unlike sensory intuition, is taken up for itself, without the immediate reference of such intuition to one's body in its given external environs. For I can have an *image* of an object without standing immediately in front of it, without physical contact with it. The representation resides essentially *within me*. The I as the simple universal is the self bearing reference solely to itself. Thus if a manifold of intuition lies within me as a simple being, that manifold sensory material comes to be simplified by me. Insofar as this material enters into me, it must enter the I reduced to a point, and this point affects the sensory material with its own simplicity. We find this already to be the case with images. In the external intuition of objects I myself am more externalized than I am with the representations of imagination. The image of an object is always more indeterminate than the sensory intuition of it. Within representation individual points are no longer as determinate as they were within external intuition. Further, the image lies within me, within the universal space of representation belonging to universal time, something I carry around within me [while changing my location in sensory space]. Representations are more simplified than objects of sensory intuition. Their form is simplicity itself, universality itself. Representation is thus more spiritual than a sensory object. Two things to be distinguished in representation are its form and content. Its content is twofold: sensory content and thought content. Quite generally, the form of representation resides within me. Representation, and thinking even more so, epitomizes. They are compendium-like. For example, I represent to myself a battle which, within sensory intuition, is completely infinite, is of the most infinitely manifold character. But the representation of being a battle is totally compendium-like. The battle in its existence, as *immediately* represented, is not as simple as it is in [subsequent] representation.

To cite another example, I know blue as a particular color by sight. But as completely simple as my representation of blue is, the color blue exists amid an infinite swarm of other objects. If I leave everything other than blue aside, blue cannot exist merely for itself, in an isolated state, without contrast to other objects. Here we become active in analysis and composition. This activity of analysis and composition begins in representation as an activity of simplifying and generalizing what is particular. Here our own conscious activity of negating or abstracting finds its onset. Here we find the activity of representing [by images] generally. A representation is isolated and is simple [relative to what it represents] within its isolation. A representation may stem from without, from the senses, or it may stem from the mind [*Geist*], but is it not yet the self-concept even if it may still be labeled as a thought. I unite separated determinations of an object, e.g., of a flower, in my representation, in my image of it. What we have is the unifying of a manifold. Such unifying acts of representation proliferate. There are many acts of uniting. Philosophy lies merely in sheer acts of unifying manifolds. But at this stage, in representation before the onset of philosophy, external determinations come to be bound together conjunctively by an "also." As belonging to a subject they come to be recounted one after the other, but the subject itself is, as it were, the rigid self-same point to which they all belong. Our representations of the properties do not bind themselves to one another on their own. Rather, they remain isolated over against one another. They come to be bound together only externally, in a third thing. The chief characteristic of representation is that the references which two things bear to each other in representation lie within a third thing. The understanding posits essential referential relations, referring to terms such as cause and effect, but has no insight into the necessity of the relation. Religion is full of representations, but again it lacks insight by a self-same subject into the necessary relation of the determinations as one after another they come to be recounted. Any insight into such necessity is lost on representation as such. Thinking is simply something else than representing. To thinking as such belongs whatever is universal. The forms merely lying upon our representations are the very content of thinking. Thinking is their activation. Thinking has to do merely with the forms as such. The question arises as to the worth of these forms. Thinking [is, in its product,] purely universal. Repre-

sentations are given as determinate and in isolation alongside one another. Thoughts are as universal as representations, and yet a referential relation enters into thoughts. The mutual reference of cause and
effect is a thought. Through the positing of the one the other is also
already posited. So likewise with the whole and its parts. These determinations necessarily bear reference to each other. The two determinations, holding forth in their independence even while bearing reference to each other, distinguish the understanding from the self-concept.
Thinking is what is universal.[3] Sensory intuitions and feelings are singular. Yet a determination such as singularity at once exhibits universality. For all things are singular, singularity is shared by them all.[4]
Singularity is thus not separated from universality. Thought is itself
and yet reaches out into what is other than itself.

Language belongs to us as human beings, and so bears the mark of
thought. Thus language prevents us from saying what we can only intend saying. What is within me—what I alone hold as merely my opinion—is peculiar to me, belonging only to me. If I say "That is my opinion" I think others do not share the same opinion. For my opinion
[*Meinung*] is only mine [*mein*]. From this Plato distinguished[5] δόξα or
opinion from ἐπιστήμη or knowledge. Yet when I openly speak my
opinion what I utter can only be universal. If I say "This point here!"
this point is at once all points, everywhere in the world. If I say "now!"
now is every moment of time. If I speak, say, or will "this!" as something totally singular, it is everything, for everything is a singular
this. Whatever is singular becomes, as soon as we utter it linguistically, something universal. We help ourselves out with names, but
nothing could be more arbitrary. The name lacks any [necessary] reference to the person named. When I say "I" I mean this absolutely
singular individual, but what I thereby succeed in referring to is rather
every individual. It is said of feeling that it is something ineffable, that
it is throughout merely something peculiarly mine. But of all statements that is the most meaningless and lacking in truth. I determine
what is singular, this or that, by universal determinations which can
each be shared with other things. What is singular and what is universal are thus quite inseparable, and here lies the nature of whatever
is concrete. There is nothing true in what is singular as such, just as
there is nothing true in the universal as such, since both are only
empty abstractions. As we think and philosophize abstractions no

3. That is, to think is universalize, to generalize, the singular or particular determination into a universal as the product of thinking.

4. That is, all things are singular, but when thought or predication attributes
singularity to them it makes them into something universal.

5. Compare to Plato, *Meno* 98a; *Republic* VI, 509d–511e; *Republic* VII,
533d–534a.

doubt arise, but it is precisely the job of [the science of speculative] logic to come to know the true nature of abstractions, to come to know that whatever is abstract is thereby empty of truth.

(§21) We now come to *thinking*, to what it in general is. We have already called it the activation of the universal. Thinking [in its reflection on an object] belongs to the conscious mind. We speak, in connection with thinking, of reflection, of thinking something over. We at once harbor representations of law [*Recht*] or of the state, we think about it, and by thinking something over we believe we fathom its essence, what is essential or true in it. This prejudice of the ancient world[, namely the prejudice that by reflecting on something we get to its essence, which is the first position of thought toward its object,] has now become shaky, as in more modern times everything else has been attacked and even overturned [by the second, skeptical position of thought toward its object]. Among the ancients it was never doubted that by thinking something over we come to know it. Philosophy, it has been said, comes to know things from the ground up. But the position that has now [in the third place] become current is that we hold to be true what, on the contrary, *immediately* reveals itself, what arises without further reflection. [This is the third position of thought polemically reasserting immediate truth against skeptical Kantian attacks.] But we have said that thinking has a product, which is none other than the thought which it thinks, the universal. This means that the universal is actually present within the matter at hand, it is the universal inhering within the matter itself, its inner universal. But with this position of thought toward its object we revert to the ancients: one arrives at the true matter at hand only by an activity of thinking it over and of producing the universal.

(§22) The further determination of thought [beyond ancient metaphysics, is the second position of thought toward its object in Kant's critical philosophy, which goes beyond the ancient naive optimism about finding the universal ready at hand]. It consists in holding that thinking effects an alteration in the object of thought over against its sensory show. Relative to what by that sensory show we first supposed, this show comes to be altered by reflection [*Nachdenken*]. Genera and species are uncovered, all of them something universal. The law of falling bodies, of movement, is something universal. What we have directly before our eyes is by contrast immediate. Subsumption under the species alters what is immediate. We strip away what is sensory, and lift out the universal. The forces of nature are likewise universal. The alteration underway here we call *abstracting*. It seems absurd, if what we want is knowledge of external objects, to alter these external objects by our very [abstractive] activity upon them. Quite absurd to want to come to know things as they are [in themselves] and yet alter them, thus receiving things into our knowledge only as altered. The alteration consists in the fact that we separate off what is singular or external, and hold the truth of the thing to lie in what is universal rather than in what is singular or external. Quite oddly, for Kant it is by altering things that we are persuaded we secure their inner truth.

(§23) The true nature of things arises in our consciousness by way of thought. I receive the object into myself, but the true nature of the object is a product of my mind [*Geist*]. As a thinking subject I am present in the object, and precisely herein lies my free relation to the object. On the one hand, I entirely forget myself to occupy myself merely with the nature of the thing. But, on the other hand, the true nature of the thing is produced merely by the activity of my own thinking. That is the connection between the nature of the thing and my own essence.

"To think for oneself" is a redundant phrase. For no matter what one thinks, one is thinking for oneself, just as one eats for oneself or drinks for oneself. But the phrase "thinking for oneself" has also been used in reference to so-called original persons who have come up with something no one else has ever produced. Originality is highly rated, but from originality what is to be derived is only peculiarity [*Besonderheit*].[6] What is true is universal upon and for itself. What is peculiar, if it is only peculiar, is of negligible importance. Homer affords an intuition of things as they must be, but the poet himself in his idiosyncrasy does not intrude. Whenever something is solid, its peculiarity vanishes. People speak of the arrogance of philosophy and knowledge: man has eaten of the prohibited tree of the knowledge of good and evil. This separation [of oneself from the rest of creation in the conceit of having exclusive self-knowledge] is, to be sure, the root of sin. What preceded this separation was only a state of unconsciousness, of oblivion. Man alone can fall into evil. What he ought to be he must first make himself be by overcoming evil. This separation is indeed the root of evil.

In knowing I come to be for myself. Insofar as I am I, I am completely free. I can become evil in that I can abstract from what is just, from what is ethical [*sittlich*], and set myself in opposition it. I can abstract from everything, so that I am left with no essential content. That I so posit myself is abstract *conceit,* and everything for me is then conceit. I am this self-conceit, but only insofar as I remain stuck in self-abstraction. Knowing encounters this opposition, but the same activity which passes this self-separating judgment, which introduces this division, also holds court over it, over the same division. Knowing then once again enters to heal the division. Which means: a human being has eaten from the tree of the

6. *Besonderheit* is normally "particularity," but with a negative connotation it becomes "peculiarity."

knowledge of good and evil, and only thereby has become human. A human being was persuaded that, in eating it, he would be the equal of God—the height of conceit. Subsequent confirmation of this was attributed to God: "Man has become like one of us."

A human being is spirit, consciousness, and with human knowledge [*Wissen*] he is at once the knowledge of the opposition between the human knower and the natural created world which, apart from us, is devoid of knowledge. Insofar as this opposition brings in the will, it is the opposition of good and evil. Reconciliation, when it occurs without opposition, is natural reconciliation. The animal becomes what it ought be, and it does not stray from the natural law of its being. A human being, however, comes to be good by virtue of his freedom, by his free will. But this opposition [of good and evil] contains their reconciliation. The form which reconciliation takes here lies in what we have already pointed out. By thinking objects I arrive at their truth. In thinking objects I am free insofar as I think them, and thus at once have hold of their content. Here I abandon my prior self-conceit and enter into the matter at hand by thinking the object, and such thinking then itself belongs to the matter at hand. The above opposition is here raised up beyond itself, and reconciliation is thus at hand. Arrogance lies in holding on to something peculiar to oneself. Modesty consists in receiving for oneself the matter itself which lies before oneself. True modesty consists in not insisting on what is one's own, in not insisting on one's peculiarity, in not remaining stuck in one's own idiosyncratic ideas, but instead in willing only the matter itself. As we look only at the matter itself, nothing peculiar is present.

Feeble-minded modesty holds itself clear of the matter itself, and such modesty directly passes into arrogance again. Conscious of its own merit, modesty then forgets to forget itself, while when we hold ourselves within the matter itself we forget our peculiarity. In knowing we are free, we remain firmly lodged in thinking. In philosophy we have to do with the matter itself, and with the surrender of self-conceit. Aristotle held that we ought to make ourselves worthy of knowing the matter at hand.[7] This matter, this substance, God, truth, has being upon and for itself.[8] We must make ourselves worthy of raising ourselves up to the level of that matter. We make ourselves worthy when we leave our peculiarities behind. We enjoy dignity by taking up residence in the content of knowledge, in what is substantial, and such dignity is quite the contrary of arrogance.

7. Compare to Aristotle, *Metaphysics* I.2, 982a4ff., 982b19–32.

8. *Anundfürsichsein* has usually been translated as "being in and for itself." My preference for "being upon and for itself" is explained in the translator's introduction.

(§24) Thoughts understood as what is thought may be called *objective*. This seems to be a contradiction, since thinking thought is subjective. But the terms "subjective" and "objective" are used in very different ways. When I say that thinking is "subjective" [in the positive sense], I mean by "thinking" my freedom, my universality. But we also say [negatively] that something is only subjective, such as an opinion, an assurance, where one means peculiarity by "subjectivity." Pure subjectivity is the I,[9] this single one in its pure universality. On the one hand, thoughts are subjective, but are objective only insofar as I [as subject] have hold of them [as objects]. On the other hand, objective thought occurs where the content of the thought is the very matter at hand itself—it means that this matter is objective on its own account. This matter is also what matters to me. This objectivity is invoked spiritually as well as non-spiritually, since what is spiritual has in appearance something unessential about it [which conceals the matter at hand which I must come to know].

Logic, it can now be seen, coincides with metaphysics. However, the matter at hand is chiefly thoughts. But one understands by "logic" thinking only insofar as it is subjective form, while by "metaphysics" one understands an applied thinking, a thinking which extends over the objects held in representation. Metaphysics thinkingly contemplates God, the soul (rational psychology), and the world (cosmology). It is therefore a thinking of objects. We may indeed call it applied logic, though it is very different from the applied logic of the usual textbooks. The distinction between thinking and its objects falls by the wayside, for we now have objective thoughts, i.e., thoughts which themselves are the matter at hand. One *thinks* the matter, one does not think *about* it, but we are rather lodged within it, in the matter itself. Objective thoughts are thoughts which constitute the content itself, they are what is substantial. Logic is thus content, and with that it coincides with metaphysics.

Among the forms of logic the self-concept, judgment, and syllogism [*Schluss*] are likewise apprehended. It seems that these forms belong to the conscious mind, and in one respect that is right. For one says "I form for myself a concept of some matter." The same thing that I have in my consciousness of the matter truly belongs to that matter itself, it is its substance. This implies that the self-concept has a certain content, but that this content is also to be the content of the matter itself. The predicates that arise in judgment are not added to the matter; rather the matter at hand has these predicative determinations upon itself. In judgment I distinguish between subject and predicate, and this division is something subjective, it is [subjective] form. But this division occurs in the judgment of finite things. The object has the property, but is also

9. *Das Ich* will be translated as "the I," not as "the ego."

separable from that property. Things are thus their own judgment in the realm of the finite, for their properties are separable from them.

Anaxagoras was the first to say that *nous* rules the world,[10] not personal thinking, but rather the activation of the universal, determinate development toward ends, realizing its goals. If one says "God by his wisdom rules the world," God is thereby in the world, not outside it. We will see that things themselves are concepts, judgments, and syllogisms—these are forms of *nous*, of universality. The animal is something universal, but without realizing it, it is universal only for the human mind. The laws of spirit are universal essentialities, and the essentialities of what itself is objective.

(§25) The entire interest of philosophy revolves around the fact that I have a concept of this object because I know what is universal in it, which is what is abiding. Individual animals die off, the universal species remains. To be sure, the universal is present in what appears to the senses as something singular, but the species present in the individual remains and preserves itself despite the death of the individual. When we say "There is an object present, the very matter itself," it is we who speak who are the subject. The opposition established here between subject and object is of the greatest interest to philosophy. Contained within this opposition is the determination of *truth*. Yet we must distinguish philosophical truth from ordinary truth. Ordinary truth lies in the fact that our [subjective] representations agree with an object, that representation has the same content as the object. In representation, the content of the object becomes more general than it is in the object itself, but the essential content nonetheless remains. Our representation ought to correspond to the content, and that is truth in the ordinary sense. In other words, truth is something *I* possess [in my subjective representations]. The question as to whether the objects themselves have truth—which is truly of philosophical interest—does not even arise. If we express ourselves more precisely, all we can say is that the representations are *correct*.

The rule by which the representation is judged [in theoretical judgment] is the object with which it agrees or does not agree. The object lays down the law to which pliable thinking, in its representation, adapts. But in practical life we have one unbending aim, one obligation [*Sollen*], one plan. When we build a house, it is we who establish the rule[, i.e., the blueprint by which matters are measured]. Things are not themselves the rule, but rather must conform to our chosen representations. Matters are correct when we make them adapt to our chosen rule, to our representation.

10. Anaxagoras, Diels fragment 12, in *Selections from Early Greek Philosophy*, ed. Milton Nahm (New York: Appleton-Century Crofts, 1964). For Plato on *nous* see *Phaedo* 97b; for Aristotle on *nous* see *Metaphysics* I.3, 984b8.

At the same time as we pursue diverse interests like house building, as human beings we ought to regulate our practice by the [moral] law. The doings and strivings of human beings do not lay down this law, and so in morality matters are quite the contrary of what occurs in the pursuit of such diverse interests. Here an ambivalence enters. The moral law must be true in itself, and our practice must correspond to it. We can thus say of an action, morally speaking, that it conforms to its aim, which is what makes it a true action. And so we effect a transfer of truth over [from our subjective representations, e.g., in choosing to build a house,] to what is objective, and rightfully so, since whatever is objective in our action ought to correspond to the moral law. We have, to the one side, our own objectivity, our own immediate being with its impulses, and it is by subjecting them to moral education that we are to become what we ought to be. Off to the other side, there is another objectivity[, the moral law,] which relates itself to the objectivity of our impulses.

We now generally have hold of both something objective[, i.e., impulse] and something subjective, i.e., thought. [By the ordinary concept of truth,] the external object provides the rule in theoretical pursuits, while what is mental [*das Geistige*] lays down the rule in practical pursuits. Truth in this second higher sense also has two sides: one the one hand, what is objectively real, and, on the other hand, its self-concept as such. In the case of truth in the ordinary sense, the only question is whether we have hold of it. In the case of higher truth, the other to which the house or my action is to conform is its self-concept, and the question is whether the objective reality conforms with its self-concept, whether it is what it should be. Truth occurs when a real object [whether an external object or an action] conforms to its self-concept. What is bad is then something untrue, since it is opposed to the concept of what it ought to be. An action which fails to conform to its purpose is a bad action and fails to be a true action, where before [in the truth of something real] the thought was objective under the determination of being the self-concept.

The *ideal* occurs where the thought and nothing but the thought is realized. What is *ugly* is only an accident of one or another sort, as when the self-concept of being human does not alone pervade a human being but exists alongside illness, grief, passion, and so on. In whatever is *beautiful*, reality completely determines itself beginning from within and then moving outward.

We shall come to know such higher truth more closely in the *idea*, where the self-concept is at once reality. What is true is the idea. In the idea there are two determinations: thought and reality, thought and the object or being. Abstractly viewed, we have an opposition of thinking and being, and the idea is the unity of the two. There are thus two sides, and the only question is the relation between the two. It is a question of their unity, of the kind of unity that is found here. That is the great question of philosophy, which has principally occupied the interest of our age. If thought determinations are finite, they are untrue. Truth generally is whatever is infinite. Truth is found wherever reality corresponds to the self-concept. Thus the self-concept has hold, in reality, of nothing beyond what is its very own. That the two are other to each other is mere show. The self-concept intuits itself in reality, it is for itself in what is real, it is other than itself but is at once one and the same as itself in the other.

I have a plan for a house as soon as I record whatever I wish to do, but this plan is fully contained only in the house itself by which the plan is carried out. Infinity lies in such a correspondence between the plan and its execution. The self-concept in this correspondence lies beyond itself, it is no longer merely for itself but finds itself within an other, in diverse appearances. And yet even in this beyond the self-concept is at home with itself and has thus returned within itself. If I relate myself to something other than myself, I am finite. My sight comes to an end in the object seen, and in visual sight I thus comport myself as a finite being. But in thinking I comport myself as an infinite being, since I remain throughout by myself in my object. If what is real corresponds to its concept it is infinite, and that is *affirmative infinity*. Insofar as thought determinations are finite they do not conform to truth, which is infinite.

The plain relation of what is real to its self-concept is either finite or infinite. If what is real is other than its self-concept, the relation is finite, and the determination of thought by which we apprehend what is real is itself only finite. But this finitude of thought determinations may be taken in two ways. By the first way, they are, as thought determinations, something merely subjective and in their object they meet with their end [*End*] which makes them finite, which stands over against them as a negation of them. By the second way, finitude[, instead of being an external limitation on the thought determination,] enters into the thought determination itself. Thought determinations bear finitude upon themselves when one such determination finds its limit [*Grenze*] in another thought determination [rather than in its object]. The content of a thought determination can have its limit in another thought determination, much as a cause has its limit in the effect, much as a volume of space has a limit [in an adjacent volume].

We have, then, thinking and being, the self-concept and the object. We have said that truth lies in what is objective, which gives us both the self-concept and its object. A higher matter for our consideration than the *object* as distinguished from the thinking of it is the *relationship of the thinking to its object*. In considering how we think, we note that we first think in a totally naive manner. Thinking is present in all my representations because I myself am present in them. We then naively assume that by thinking we learn what the truth of a matter is. The first mode of philosophizing was this naive mode. The truth of the matter came to be taken up in thought quite immediately [without distinguishing our thinking of it]. The presupposition was simply that we arrive at the truth by thinking. In this first mode of philosophizing, the opposition between thinking and objectivity has not yet been thought. Such was the path followed by ancient philosophy. The ancients did not make explicit that thinking is different from the matter itself, from the object thought.

According to the second position [or mode of philosophizing], thinking and the object are considered to be different, so that we simply fail to reach the object through thinking. Rather, we at once take up the object quite as it is in itself, without thinking it. If it is said that the subject must conform to the object, the mode of philosophizing is empiricism. But if it is said [with Kant] that thinking is a development of forms internal to thinking itself while the object itself remains external to the forms [without the forms conforming to them,] quite another separation occurs between thinking and the object.

The *third* mode of philosophizing is a return to the first path of the ancients, but now with a reflective consciousness of our own thinking, and of the alleged fact that thinking in general, the subject, is immediately connected with its object. The subject does not exist without immediate knowledge of the object, and it is only by thus knowing the object that consciousness attains to truth. But according to this immediate knowledge [in Jacobi], both determinations—the subject with its immediate object—are limited to a single object, to God. In immediate knowledge thinking and God as the object thought are inseparable. These positions of thought we must now go through one by one. What holds interest in our present time revolves around these relationships.

A. The First Position [of Thought] toward Objectivity

(§26) Spirit has been thought. What spirit is in and for itself has been alleged to be known only to thought. The world, what it is in its essence when it is abstracted from external sense perceptions, also came to be contemplated *thinkingly*. There was in antiquity confidence that thinking could not fall into error once it strode forth for itself and on its own account . On the whole this was the procedure through all the [empirical] sciences, even in natural history and the doctrine of nature. Kinds, species or laws, powers were contemplated in these sciences, and were brought together by reflection. The content of thought was supposed to correspond to appearance. This content was to be the essential content of what exists. But what exists upon itself has its inessential side. Yet what exists is not left in its immediacy, but comes to be grasped in its universality. Thinking is thus present in all the sciences.

As innocently as one proceeds today in the empirical sciences, philosophy in antiquity has proceeded just as innocently with its objects. We shall see [in section B.II, below,] the nature of what Kant in his critical philosophy called *experience*. Philosophy in antiquity differentiated itself from the other sciences, from the empirical sciences in particular, only through its objects. The objects of the empirical sciences are finite. Philosophy also had its objects, whether they were found in our consciousness or were apprehended by sense perception. Yet these objects were each to be the whole, they were each to be the same universal all-encompassing object. The absolute object is *God,* over against which the world passes as something accidental. Yet the question comes back again as to whether the *world,* by virtue of its matter, is eternal. Beyond that, the world is space, a complex of infinitely numerous things. The world is only these disparate existing singular things. In philosophy the world is viewed as the whole and becomes the universal object. Another object of philosophy is the *soul.* It was obvious [to classical metaphysics] that the soul was an object of an entirely different order than the world. Such are the objects which philosophy has elected for itself, and through them philosophy distinguished itself from the other sciences.

(§27) Philosophical thinking can either be authentic speculative thinking or it can be a thinking that holds itself within finite determinations, either a thinking of what is true or a thinking of what is finite. In the latter case it is a thinking that lacks all truth because it is determined by what is other than it itself, because it does not go back into itself but goes beyond itself to what is other than it. We shall first consider thinking with respect to this second, *finite, deficient side.* Philosophizing, which has the totality for its object, has comported itself in a finite manner. The objects and thought determinations that the other sciences have are finite, but philosophy is to have totalities for its objects. If the thought determinations of philosophy are not absolute, they fail to correspond to their object. The consideration of infinite objects according to finite thought determinations is the philosophy of the understanding. The understanding insists on finite thought determinations, so that philosophy becomes merely the understanding's view of reason's objects. [Classical] metaphysics received its complete development prior to the [Kantian] critical philosophy. The earlier philosophies were merely fragmentary, with much of what is speculative mixed in with the rest. But metaphysics, and Wolff's metaphysics in particular, has developed finite thought determinations. This philosophy has now passed away, but the thinking determined by it is still present. Our most immediate reflection contains only categories of finitude. Laws, forces are all thought forms, but the question is whether these thought forms are to be taken up in their finitude or in their truth. *Naive thinking* can be true, it can be speculative, but [in classical metaphysics from antiquity on] it has been so uncritically. It has had no consciousness of the thought forms which it has used and by which it has fallen into contradictions, so that it has since been remarked that this is not the way in which we reach the truth. The predicates which are given to objects are thought determinations. From §33 and from the following [paragraphs] on, the thought forms of metaphysics are pointed out. We can leave them aside here. If we wished to go into them in a more detailed manner, we would have to go into the entirety of metaphysics.

The first general branch of metaphysics is *ontology* [§33], τὸ ὄν, the metaphysics of what is. The ontological determinations of essence, being, unity, manyness, substance, and phenomenon on the whole make up the Aristotelian categories. In his *Metaphysics* Aristotle goes through the same categories, the categories concerning whatever is [ἃ κατεγορῖται περὶ τῶν ὄντων]. The special, more concrete branches of metaphysics have treated, first of all, the soul[, i.e., *rational psychology*, §34], but merely according to the thought of it, without empirical psychology in which what we know from sensory experiences about the activity of the soul is taught. Spirit is the organization of all our doings. Its activities belong to it as such. By the "soul" one understands rather a thing, *ens*. We inquire into the seat of the soul. As something bodily, spirit steps into what is spatial. The third branch of metaphysics has treated the world, *cosmology* [§35], the theory of nature, natural history, and so on. Along with this branch the determination of the freedom of the soul is also treated. In cosmology the world has been treated only by abstract thoughts. Yet the world can be considered in its truth only as *nature,* by which the world is nothing abstract but is rather something actual, an essential being. But if we wish to consider the world, we must take it up through its activities and external expressions. The philosophical approach to the world is the consideration of it in its necessity. What is concrete . . .

[A text fragment is missing here in the German transcript.]

. . . then [we have] *rational theology* [which is the fourth branch of metaphysics, §36], reaching as far as the light of reason. Proofs have been given that God exists and abstract determinations[, i.e., divine attributes,] have likewise been apprehended as belonging to God alone.

(§28) In §28 [of the 1830 *Encyclopaedia*] it is pointed out that in metaphysical reasoning our procedure will first be to have a subject [of predication]. In knowledge, its predicates will then be enunciated. It is to be seen which predicates belong to the object which serves as the subject of predication. Predicates imply universal determinations. It is presupposed here that, if we wish to know an object, we must think it. Reflection brings forth thoughts, and the present naive metaphysics presupposes these thoughts—they become the content, the essence of the matter itself. There is as yet no mistrust, no doubt, but instead only sound human conviction. What is deficient in this naive procedure is that, though its thoughts generally contain truth, it is a further unanswered question as to how these thoughts are internally determined, how thinking develops in a more exact manner. In this naive procedure, such thought determinations have been taken as valid predicates in isolation from one another, as containing truth in their mutual isolation. For example, is the world finite or is it infinite? One or the other comes to be taken as a predicate that expresses something that is for itself true on its own account. Or, to cite another example, we may say "The soul is simple." Is a thought such as simplicity a determination which is true for itself on its own account? That is the further unanswered question [in classical metaphysics]. The *one* or the *whole* is a true determination taken in this way for itself—it has been taken up in a completely naive fashion. What was looked into here was only whether such predicates belong to the objects [rather than whether the thought determinations contained in the predicates were in themselves true]. That is the first mode of reflection, and on the whole we are right in adopting this mode: it is a question of this or that determination correctly belonging or not belonging to the object. The question is whether a judgment of this kind is correct: "Matter is composite," "The world is finite," "God is necessary being," and so on. But the further question is whether such predicates are true on their own account. Plato already said that it is necessary to contemplate the objects themselves, and that in doing so one goes beyond the objects in their sensory form. We can cite countless philosophical theories, but nothing is said thereby as to whether the content given in the predicates is in itself true. This external consideration of the correctness of theories is left behind in a philosophical consideration of the truth of the content. When this content is considered for itself on its own account, it is considered *thinkingly*. If I say "God is the cause of the world" the truth[, i.e., correctness] of what I say will be granted, but in saying it the true relation of cause and effect is not exhaustively determined. For a cause by itself expresses only a finite and at once untrue relation. Should we speak of what is true in causality, we must leave to the side such untrue relations. Awareness of this is obtained through the science of logic.

There is nothing bad in determinations like *force*. Rather, we simply mean that these determinations belong to the subject of which they are predicated. But, once again, we must look into these determinations themselves to see if they are themselves true, and this leads us to a critique of such thought determinations. Everywhere I go I bring with me my determinations of thought, and bring them forward even without being conscious of them. I do so quite instinctively, until I am brought to the point of attending to them. But with that I come up with a contradition. In mastering the situation, I thus come inwardly to know these thought determinations as I become fully acquainted with them. Judgments like "The paper is white" are quite correct,[11] but their predicates lack truth. The thought determinations must be investigated to see if they are true.

(§29) Such predicates are of limited content. If we want to call in representations to bear witness to the limitations of our predicates, such representations are abundant when we speak, for example, of God or Spirit. What we find is that those simple predicates are not adequate to that abundance of representations. If I say, for example, "Spirit is simple," we have the totally empty determination of simplicity. Simplicity is inactive, lifelessly abstract, as when we say "Space is simple." We thus find the predicate "simple" to be inadequate to represent God. That "God exists" is the very least that can be validly said of him. This sort of predication has contributed to discrediting such naive metaphysics. If we apply to nature abstract predicates such as [appear in the judgment] "Nature makes no jumps, but rather advances by degrees," very little is said in comparison with the great abundance of nature itself. Predicates like "just," "good," to be sure express an affirmation, but they are also limited determinations. God is such and such, but with that what he is is not exhausted. Beyond that is the fact that these predicates contradict one another. If we proceed merely on the basis of God's justice, we proceed against his goodness. Or if we proceed on the basis of his goodness, we proceed against his justice. God is further all-powerful. If I pursue a determinate aim merely of my own, I proceed against divine power, since over against divine power any aim of my own must remain indeterminate. Yet if I say that God in his wisdom has created free beings, I at once say that he has created [the real possibility of] evil. Here again a contradiction arises. Such predicates at once show themselves to be of limited content. The Orientals[, e.g, the Hindus,] give their God infinitely many names, each expressing a particular determination or relation to the world. But "infinitely many" is once again something inexistent. These predicates belong to but one subject. They stand in community only through that subject, which is their bond. Beyond their respective determinations, they coincide in this subject. If I say of God "He is eternal, good, wise," these three determinations are not connected with one another by themselves. Were they to be connected in this way, his goodness would have to inhere in his justice, and so forth. But these are accidental predicates of that subject. By contrast, when we say of a human being that he or she "has bowels," "has nerves," or "has mus-

---

11. "The paper is white" is correct in getting at a fact, but the question remains as to whether the statement gets at it under a fully coherent predicative thought determination.

cles," we have the feeling of speaking of one and the same thing in its function and activity. These predicates are not so very much merely side by side as to have their connection only in the subject of which they are predicated. Rather, they are directly connected with one another. The one cannot be without the other, since each is the same total living being. They are connected with one another among themselves. But in the case of non-organic things, we see an external relation of one thing to another. Gold has its different properties, and in the most minute particle of gold these properties remains the same. It has its properties, and the properties in this set are found over and over again side by side [in different particles of gold]. No matter how small the particle of gold, the set of its inseparable properties remains ever present. Yet we have no insight into any necessity of their inseparability, we merely have faith in it. But when we also say of spirit that it is willing and that it is also thinking, the properties of spirit are similarly enumerated side by side like those of gold.

(§30) Such are the objects of [special] metaphysics: the world, the soul, and God, each a totality. Spirit, too, is a totality within itself, a whole which is at once an infinite realm. These are the objects of reason. The representations we have of them lay the foundation in this naive metaphysics. Such representations are the standard by which we judge whether the predicates apply or not. The representations of God and of the soul are merely presupposed. A representation is something subjective. The present age has a different representation of God, as also of justice, from that of any prior age. But it should be spelled out just what justice by its thought determination is, just what God is, and so on. Often etymology can be called into service. We often say that all human beings have one representation of God or justice, but this does not prevent anybody from having another representation. Thus all science has a contingent presupposition, just as the geometer begins by postulating this contingent representation of a point or of a line.

(§31) These representations of metaphysical objects at once appear to afford us a firm grasp. God, spirit, and the world are something determinately fixed within me by a particular representation. We could not philosophize if we did not have, as a foundation, such a fixed representation. But the question is whether any such representation has itself a fixed foundation. This supposition comes into question as soon as we ask "What is God?" We give predicates to God, and our representation of God at first receives a fixed determination through this predication. But the nature of the objects of metaphysics is only now to be spelled out. When I ask "What is God" or "What is spirit?" the very sense of the question is that the given representation is not enough for me, that I am not satisfied by it. No matter what is, its thought determination must first be indicated to me. In judgment, it is not until the predicate arrives that the nature of the subject is spelled out. If I say "God is eternal," "God is omnipotent," my representation of God is extended beyond what is given in the subject. Going beyond merely what is given in the subject, I contradict what I first presupposed in invoking the subject. The representation contained in the subject does not suffice for me, and so I carry it out further. It is not until the predicate arrives that we acquire knowledge of the subject from which we began. The absolute is often understood as merely abstract. But what the absolute is, or what God is, comes to be expressed through thoughts and their further determination. So it comes to be said in the science of logic that God is being, and then further on that he is essence, that he is the self-concept, that he is the idea. This is the form we give to our logic. We may thus make God into the subject, but the subject is what God is only if what we posit in the predicates comes to be the case. That is the matter before us, and whether it is called "God" or "the absolute" is of no consequence. By its subject-predicate form judgment is one-sided and hence false. If I say "God is eternal" I succeed in getting at something, but "eternal" fails to express the nature of God, and to that extent my statement does not get it right. God is an entirely different sort of concrete being from what is expressed by any such limited predicate. In philosophizing we have to put all imaginative representation to the side. Representations constitute something fixed in our consciousness. If we were to try to rid ourselves of all fixed representation [and not just put them to the side], we would nonetheless again have a representation, namely, the representation of finding ourselves floating atop something quite bottomless.

(§32) Classical metaphysics became dogmatic. Skepticism has set itself over against such dogmatism. Skepticism has considered the representations of our ordinary consciousness, of our ordinary assertions, as it has likewise considered assertions which refer to metaphysical objects. Skepticism attacks all such assertions and shows them each to contain a contradiction: dogmatism philosophizes by exhibiting a statement [Satz] that immediately licenses the opposite statement. "The world is infinite" and "The world is finite" are examples. Dogmatism pronounces one of the two opposed statements to be true. Stoicism, for example, has pronounced the truth to be thought, where its opposite is what is sensory. The metaphysical dogmatism opposite to Stoicism has thus said that the principle behind every human disposition and action is sensation. Dogmatism asserts that one of the two statements is true— one is true, the other false. Either the principle of all truth is thinking or it is sensation. The two principles are different, and either the one or the other is valid. It is around such opposed metaphysical dogmas that all controversy in philosophy has turned. The supposition of the understanding [Verstand] is that if the one is true, the other is false. That is the finite [contradictory] faith of the understanding. For it has been found that both statements can be proven, and with such proofs consciousness has found itself in contradiction. This *contradiction* has called forth *mistrust* and *doubt* about thinking, and a disavowal of metaphysics generally. This disavowal lies at the basis of the second position of thinking [in relation to objectivity]. For such abstract predicates [as thought and sensation] do not correspond to the concrete content of that living totality. Those predicates are dead, purely simple, and empty of all self-movement. Spirit, however, is within itself living self-movement, while the rigidity of all such abstractions resists such movement.

B. The Second Position of Thought toward Objectivity

The history of philosophy beholds the transition to this second position more closely [than we do here]. This position harbors a mistrust of thinking, the conviction that it is impossible for thinking to get at the truth. It thus separates thinking off from the truth, and indeed off from objectivity in general. This separation comes in two versions: *empiricism* and the Kantian *critical philosophy.* Empiricism asserts that one gets to the truth only through sense experience as such. Our thinking must orient itself around sense experience, so that thinking is sidelined. The critical philosophy considers more closely than empiricism what "experience" means. It contemplates what is perceived in opposition to thinking. It sets the two determinately over against each other, and tries to show by thinking itself, by its own doing, that thinking is incompetent to apprehend the truth. The uniting of thinking and experiencing for Kant yields appearance, whereas thinking [by itself] makes totalities like the world, the soul, [and God] into its proper objects. But in so doing thinking no longer has experience of anything, as it falls into a labyrinth of representations and contradictions. This is the second position, which on the whole is the principal standpoint of our time. With this second standpoint is connected a third standpoint, that of immediacy [as in, e.g., Jacobi]. According to this third standpoint, thinking serves only to bring true knowledge into a state of confusion and thus is generally incompetent.

B.I. Empiricism

Empiricism is of the greatest antiquity. The skeptics, in particular, called themselves empiricists. They were quite conscious of having to do only with appearances. Yet true empiricism is modern empiricism, which comes to us from England (Locke). We are all natural born empiricists. We all perceive by our senses, we all rely on sense perception. From [metaphysical] thinking we all return in relief back again to empiricism, which proceeds polemically, ferreting out what is true in our experiences. The contradictions in which metaphysics lost its way have precipitated this return to sense perception. The onset of mistrust in *a priori* [knowledge] resulted in this pure empiricism. The devil, miracles, magic, and superstition were allegedly all mixed in [with metaphysics]. Those caught up in superstition have indeed set out from thoughts of a general nature. Superstition has indeed made use of [metaphysical] thinking to vindicate itself. The desire which now asserted itself was to consider nature and its laws merely for themselves, and from this the grand principle of empiricism has proceeded. One can also get to empiricism starting from the spiritual side. As magic and witchcraft embrace a capricious side of our humanity, so there has been a quite different arbitrariness prescribed in the political rule under which human beings live out their lives. Empiricism called again into question the issue of the divine right of kings at a time when it was previously said that the monarchical principle was above all criticism. It is against this monarchical tyranny of accident and arbitrariness that empiricism asserts itself. We have entered into the same inquiry with respect to what the peoples of the world have allowed to pass as [international customary] law, and as internal state law. In empiricism the need arose to give validity to the wealth of our representations over against [metaphysical and political] abstractions. However, the endless extension of [empirically based] disputation has made us to realize that by empiricism we just might end up demolishing everything. We have it in our power to make everything totter,[12] and here has arisen the need for a firm hold on something.

What I am to believe I must myself have seen or perceived with my own eyes, or at the very least others must have perceived it. Thus it must reveal itself to me to be present [in what is perceived]. Nature has been made the [metaphysical object] of much reasoning, and what is present in nature has been inferred from abstract principles. In opposition to this, *empiricism* [§37] said that whatever is present in sensory objects must be perceived, that it is perception which gives credence and which supplies the content of belief. Here lies the principle of subjective freedom [in individual judgment]. Philosophy, like empiricism, knows only what is. What is true for philosophy is also actual, and at the same time only what is rational is truly actual. Whatever is bad in its existence [without being bad in concept] is null. Philosophy is concerned with what is, and has this in common with empiricism. It is far easier to say what ought to be than to say what is. If truth is to lie in what is, to state the truth is more difficult than to say what ought to be. We begin by passing judgment on something [by the standard of what it ought be]. What is false in a thing is thus quickly found, but it is more difficult to discern the genuine article.

12. Hegel appears to allude to the Reign of Terror in the French Revolution.

(§38) Empiricism and metaphysics share experience in common. According to representations which it itself presupposes, metaphysics likewise has its ground in experience. It proceeds from representations [grounded in experience]. But we must distinguish the *sense* perception [on which empiricism is based] from *experience* [in Kant]. A perception is but a single representation. In general, nothing singular qualifies as an experience. Perception is feeling, internal or external intuition. Experience belongs to the form of general representations and statements.

Empirical science, the science of experience, distinguishes species. The laws of nature and of spirit belong to experience. Experience [of this sort] is something universal. Its triumph lies in recognizing the universal in the singular. The forces of nature are something transitory and singular [in their various expressions], but in experience they come to be apprehended as universal. The universal comes to be fixed [in the mind], and the apprehension of it is thinking. When one has apprehended the universal in an event, one has at once accorded to the event its legitimate rights. So [the essence of] what we call "experience" lies in universality. This notwithstanding, universality in the form assumed in experience is not supposed [by empiricism] to have validity for itself on its own account. The validity of experience [according to empiricism] is not to be based on thinking or the universal. The fact that an electrical force exists in general, for example, is not to be based on the fact that the force develops [as a category of logic] in this particular way. For its universal content would then be discovered and proven merely by thinking. In empiricism the two sides of universality and particularity are so positioned as to deny that the particular has the universal for its basis. Rather, the believability of the universal content is to rest solely on perception. It will be said [by empiricists] that thinking has no place here, so that experience and thinking come to be set in opposition. But in order to discover something universal one must already believe in its existence. Kepler started out with the belief that reason, the universal, had to exist in the planetary system. Experience enjoys certainty by the immediacy of its existence with the object. The object is such and such, and I, the subject, know it certainly to be so. Something external, an object of my experience, has being; and in that it falls within me, it is identical with me. A consistent empiricism, which throughout lays something sensory down as its foundation, leads to a denial of everything supernatural. Naturalism, materialism proceeds from what is sensory.

In the *Kantian philosophy* what is singular has been isolated from form, which has been cast into relief. Regarding the two forms of *universality* and *necessity,* it has been established that they are nowhere to be found in ordinary sensory perception. We have absolutely no such perception, for example, of the *all.* We so limit "the all" as to say that what is meant by it is only all things of which we know. But someone who says "All men are mortal" is not merely saying that all men we know of are mortal. What is meant is rather that man is mortal. We call this an induction, but it can never be complete. So we see that we cannot obtain universality by perception. As for necessity, it is the totality back into which the system of essences returns. All universality, when cast into relief, belongs to the self-concept. In perception as such we have no necessity, but have only what is side by side in space, and before and after in time. What is singular, however, is not isolated, but is connected [with what is beyond it]. Yet the interconnection in perception is purely sensory. It is not necessary. In space, everything has its place side by side [with other things]. Thus, in inner space, we have a multiplicity of representations all side by side. And so it is also with time. First something is, and afterward it is no more. We get close here to cause and effect. But what presents itself to perception is merely: now this is, but afterward something else is. However, that the succession hangs together as cause and effect is not given in perception. The interconnection of cause and effect lies outside time. For something is a cause only insofar as it has an effect. They are inseparably bound up with each other. Their unity lies outside time. In sensory appearance, to be sure, the one comes after the other, but this appearance is already foreign to the interconnection of cause and effect.

So *universality* and *necessity* are not found in sense perception [§39]. From their absence in perception the conclusion has been drawn by empiricism that they have no truth, but are only a matter of habit, of my own distinct nature, of what is necessary to me, a necessity always limited to me. What is in question is thus only subjective necessity. Universality is thus only a purported universality. Laws of jurisprudence thus appear to be accidental. Hume came to this view. A follower of Locke, he drew the right conclusion as to the Lockean substance that we fail to perceive. We perceive neither cause nor effect. Law and custom are supposed have validity for themselves. They are supposed to be universal, but universality is given a different interpretation by the skeptics. Law and custom are supposed to belong to the nature of spirit. But these skeptics then said that law and custom [to be valid] must show themselves to be present everywhere, so that any place where they are not found represents a miscarriage of law and custom. If we consider existence empirically, we do not see by experience that freedom, for example, is a universal property of human beings. But with that the [universal] right to property is attacked. It is said that property is only a habit introduced at some time or other. In religion there occurs the very same manner of proceeding. There are lots of religions. When experience is called to bear witness as to the constitution of religion, it teaches nothing determinate in the matter. Neither in religion nor in the matter of free will is anything fixed by experience. This is the system of philosophy that passes for [modern] skepticism. It has assumed that experience is the foundation of all that is true. An important conclusion that follows is that all violence and lawlessness are grounded in experience, in what is factual. Humean skepticism is opposed to fixed principles. He made perceiving into the foundation. Ancient skepticism rather taught, against the Humean view, that perception is mere appearance. Things are and at once are not, for they are variable. The ancient skeptics exhibited appearance in the place of being, and in this respect modern skepticism is quite the opposite.

What we call "necessity" becomes, in the empiricist system, nothing but subjective necessity. But within empiricist perceiving, which wants to have nothing but contempt for thinking, thinking nonetheless enters as sense perception becomes experience [in Kant]. Species, laws—they are all universal. Composition [or aggregation] is also a universal category, but is the worst of all categories. For composite things remain quietly outside one another, and lack the unity which any living being must have. Thus empiricism, in an entirely unconscious manner, conceals the [logical] categories and yet makes use of them, but without knowing what it is doing or even wanting to know. Philosophy has for its object nothing other than what is. But the experience of empiricism prefers the very worst of thought determinations. This is the reflection [on empiricism] made by the *Kantian* philosophy.

B.II. The Critical Philosophy

Kant starts out from Humean skepticism. He notes that universality and necessity do not exist in sense perception or sensory consciousness, and so must be found elsewhere. It is presupposed in the critical philosophy that these determinations of universality and necessity *are* present. They are not to be found in sense perception, but *they are there.* So goes the critical philosophy. These determinations must then be found in thinking. Thinking is their source. Whatever we know we ourselves have affixed [to sense perception]. This is the philosophy that brought forth a revolution in Germany, the philosophy that changed the standpoint [of all German philosophy], and from it all further development has proceeded. This philosophy remains the basis of philosophizing today, so that the result of the Kantian philosophy has thoroughly penetrated education.

With this advance what is called "thinking for oneself" is associated, consisting in the fact that every individual wants to produce something peculiar to himself. It has thus come to pass, and continues to occur, that ever since this Kantian philosophy has penetrated German education each individual wants to produce something new for himself. Yet what one produces that is allegedly "new" is typically something very old that falls beneath the critical philosophy. Often philosophical systems that are chronologically later than Kant contain nothing more than the Kantian philosophy itself, and what they contain that goes "further" [than Kant] is still for the most part a return to the old metaphysics.

The great merit of the Kantian philosophy is to have directly called our attention to the fact that use of categories by thinking proceeds without ever even being noticed. It is important to take cognizance of this Kantian standpoint, especially in order to realize that everything that gives itself out to be something beyond Kant is nothing but the Kantian philosophy itself accompanied quite inconsistently by neglect of the critical use of thought determinations.

(§40) Within our knowledge there is a sensory content, and a general relation to such content. The Kantian philosophy asserts that universality and necessity are as much a fact as sensory perception, and it is this fact that the Kantian philosophy seeks to explain. Hume explained universality and necessity as habit. In the Kantian philosophy, however, they are explained differently. Our own consciousness is active in bringing forth these determinations. All our determinations—such as ground and consequent, cause and effect—are determinations of universality. In the Kantian philosophy these determinations are taken to have their source in the I. They belong to the *spontaneity of thinking.* Not to the caprice of the I in particular, but to the spontaneity of the I in general. They are, in other words, something of one's own doing, something that determines the sensory material.

I have before me a sensory perception, in fact many such perceptions. One sensory perception I call ground, another effect. It may occur to us that the fact that I posit these sensory perceptions and no others must ultimately be due to some outside cause. But these determinations of cause and effect have their source in my own activity. The fact that I apply these and no other determinations must have its ground outside the sense perceptions themselves. This system of philosophy is known as *subjective idealism.* If I say "Here are substances, subsisting essences," the truth of my statement is purely ideal, something belonging to me, to my thinking. There is nothing real in this statement that could be set in opposition to idealism. According to subjective idealism *I* am the one doing this. To use the Fichtean term, I am the source.

It seems as if *I* could "posit" at will, as if I one-sidedly produced for myself my own world. In just such a manner is subjective idealism understood. Yet my activity is [externally] caused to determine the world to be thus and not otherwise, or as Fichte tells us, there arises [in the world] a *resistance [Anstoss].* I become conscious of this my own determining, of my positing of these relations, in a material whose ground lies outside me, in what has *being in itself.* However, I know nothing of this external ground and resistance. I only know of what is sensory, and of my own thought determinations. Outside them, however, there is a beyond that I do not know, and that offers resistance to me. That of which I do know is purely my own production, but that through which my production [of what I know] occurs is the unknown, it is what is *in itself.*

Within what is called *experience,* sensory [content] and thought determinations come to be distinguished. Upon seeing an electrical phenomenon I say it is an expression of a force. The force is a thought determination, it is what is objective in the sensory content. Beyond this thought determination is something completely singular [and non-universal], like the expanse in which the electrical spark becomes visible to me. This singular localized expanse in sense experience is subjective. What is objective is the universal force. Thought determinations, "concepts of the understanding" as they are called, contain whatever is objective.

(§41) It is said that this objectivity of a force once again falls to the side of subjectivity. The [objective] principle of my will is my own [subjective] practical reason. To this extent the [objective] concepts of the understanding are [also] subjective. What is objective, however, is whatever is universal and necessary, and yet even this is lodged in my own subjectivity. To be "objective" means first of all to be only what is universal, true, ethically customary [*sittlich*], and so on.

What is objective are the concepts of the understanding, though they are at once in another sense subjective. These concepts have been subjected to criticism. Stirring instinctively within us, they must be held fast, and we must come to know them. It is in these concepts that we place the greatest worth. However, they prove illusory until we have exact knowledge of them. Kant's critical philosophy seeks to uncover this knowledge. Experience has, as Kant says, [two] *components* (the expression is poorly chosen): what is sensory and what is universal or objective, with the latter belonging once again to the thinking subject.

(§42) *Three stages* are to be distinguished: a. theoretical [reason], b. practical reason, and c. the reflective power of judgment.

[B.II.]a. The theoretical faculty

[1.] Knowledge in general. We have here something *sensory* and what is *thought.* Whatever is sensory immediately belongs to *feeling* in general. I feel something to be hard. The determination of hardness affects me. Or rather my eye is affected, and so it also goes with taste and smell. It is quite the same with inner feelings, revenge, anger, inclination. With the inner feelings there is no need to draw attention to the fact that we are dealing with sensation just as much as when we deal with external sensations. Such affections make up what is subjective.

[2.] A second stage [in knowledge] is intuition. Whatever is contained in my feeling I intuit. What I intuit is external to me, and it moreover consists in things that are external to one another, and in that respect the object of intuition is spatial. What I intuit is also in time as well as space, since my feelings come one after another. This successiveness is not immediate as I am affected by sensation, but holds separately from it. Hardness affects me, and what is hard is then something spatial. Spatiality and temporality do not belong to the sensory *content.* They make up what Kant calls the *form* of whatever is sensory, the form of intuiting. He says they are *a priori* forms of intuiting. It is an active intuiting that introduces them. Or, to put it otherwise, what we are affected with by sensation comes to be tossed into the forms of space and time, but their being tossed into these forms is our doing.

Of whatever is hard it will be said that it is outside me. In intuiting I already turn inward, since I posit this content of what is hard as external to me. A metaphysical question then arises as to whether space and time are outside as well as within me, but we leave this question to the side. Space and time are for Kant to be forms of intuition. Space and time bear upon themselves the very universality of forms of intuition. They are left to be filled with content no matter how that content may be determined. Space is universal continuity, the quiescent [state of] things side by side. Time is also continuous. That is one side of the matter. We know our feeling to be immediately in space and time. This immediate universality of space and time is supposed to be an *a priori* form.

[3.] Standing over against these spatial and temporal forms of intuition are the *categories* or *concepts of the understanding*[, the third stage of knowledge]. The forms of space and time exhibit abstract *manifoldness* itself. Space lies in the fact of things being outside one another. Time is simply a thing's continuous passage beyond itself. This manifoldness has being merely for me as a completely simple non-manifold being. It is into this simple being of the *I* that the manifold of feeling and of space and time are tossed. I am thus what is simple, a self-identical I. I am this being that relates itself only to itself. This being of mine is at once the simple being of consciousness. It follows from this, since the manifold must enter into me as simple, that the manifold will be forced together, compressed. The manifold undergoes simplification, and this activity of simplifying it is thinking. What is simple within my consciousness is the concept, the *thought determination in general,* the *category.* To simplify is to bring things belonging to a manifold into relation with one another. To relate the many means to bind them in a one. And that is simply a story of my own doing, which is called "original binding." The binding is "original" because it is unconscious.

I am this simple being. Simplicity here means relation, a bond. This relation is determined in manifold ways. Different manners of simplification arise. The determinate manners of simplification are the categories, the thought determinations, the concepts of the understanding. It is of infinite importance to be alert to this, and awareness of it belongs to the most common of educations. The determinate ground of concepts of the understanding lies in the fact that cause and effect, for example, are inseparable, the one coming after the other in time. If I say "This is the cause and that the effect" I posit the indivisible unity of both. This inseparability [of cause and effect insofar as neither can be without the other] is, when positively expressed, their identity. The ground for this is the original identity of the I, which is originally identical with itself.

The I gives itself out to be the source of the categories. As the I *unconsciously* acts on the sensory material, it is this totally simple being. That material comes to be viewed as an object that I have projected beyond myself. If I say "elephant," "cause and effect," and so on, I give expression to this sensory material in objective form. The activity of relating thus has two sides—the I and whatever is objective. As I contemplate mind, I think of it as engaged in representing, in thinking. I grasp the determinations of mind in one or the other of these two ways, either from the perspective of the representing thinking self or with regard to its object. To consider mind as *conscious* is something quite different from viewing it merely as the thinking I [in general]. If I consider my mind as conscious I am conscious of an object. Consciousness lies in the fact that it is a conscious relation of me, of my activity, to something else, to the object.

The different relations that I entertain with objects are the Kantian categories. There are, as stated, two things here, my activity and the fact that the objects as such have being for me [in my consciousness]. The Kantian exposition describes the course of knowing, but it at once takes in the different relations of thinking, and of mind as conscious. In other words, his exposition comes to include mind as conscious. What we call "concepts of the understanding" were construed by Aristotle as if they derived from what is objective [rather than from my activity]. According to Aristotle a category is what is said of whatever is. [With Aristotle] we imagine whatever is to be external, but it is already [unconsciously] a thought. The determinations of whatever is that follow are further determinations of thought. Here in Kant's critical philosophy, however, thought comes to be represented [consciously] as a relation to what appears as objective.

We must on the whole hold to the claim that knowing is a thinking in its determination of feeling, of intuiting. Categories are thought determinations, and are manifold. The I is totally simple, entirely lacking in determinations. It is taken in a totally abstract fashion, in its indeterminateness. The categories, however, are determinate thoughts, determinate modes of activity, but we have [within ourselves] the indeterminate I understood as the source of whatever is determinate. Yet the question now becomes: how do I pass from the indeterminate to the determinate? How does this transition make its way from the universal to the particular? To ask "How does the animal [in general] come to determine itself as a totally particular animal?" is to ask that very same sort of question. It is just so with the I. This question is of infinite importance.

In the Kantian philosophy the answer to this question could not be easier. Kant in fact passes over the question, since the determinations of thinking are taken empirically from the different forms of judgment as they present themselves in [classical] logic. To judge is, to be sure, to determine. The determinate manner of judging is determinate thinking. Yet what Kant found ready at hand [in the table of judgments] was taken purely from observation. The Fichtean philosophy proceeds from the *I*, as in actual fact the Kantian philosophy does also. Yet the Fichtean philosophy does so deductively, so that the necessity [of the transitions] by which thinking goes through the series of determinations is exhibited. Fichte's philosophy rises to the immense challenge of coming to know the necessity of the progression. Kant brought his categories together externally. The Kantian philosophy also demands proofs, but it leaves proofs already by the wayside in its first beginnings.

One speaks of *transcendental* [deduction]. Thought determinations come forth in consciousness, bearing their respective names. The artificial terminology that in fact comes forth in the Kantian philosophy is of course dispensable. We find in Kant the transcendental unity of consciousness. What is *transcendent* is whatever goes beyond consciousness, beyond, for example, the understanding in its determinateness. Thus mathematics is transcendent if it goes beyond pure mathematics in its immediate form, where objects are left in the realm of the finite. Transcendent mathematics goes beyond the understanding, as for example when the circle, the curved line, is observed to consist in infinitely many straight lines, which are at once infinitely short in length. Yet however these short lines may be represented, as straight lines they remain essentially different from the curved lines [that define a circle]. What is transcendent is thus totally contradictory.

In metaphysics what is "transcendent" is what goes beyond the finite, as when, in [dogmatic] metaphysics, reason passes onto infinite objects about which it can say nothing. What is "transcendental," as the term was used by Schelling in calling a branch of his philosophy "transcendental idealism," is rather what can in fact be reached by transcending the finite. The possibility of transcending the finite is provided by the I itself in the unity of consciousness. The Kantian philosophy passes on to a [transcendental] infinite. The source of this [transcendental, objective] infinite lies in the I, pure unity, a [subjective] infinite, a pure equality of self with self in which all difference is absent, hence which comes to an end in no limit, in no relation to an other. The I, directed to apprehending something objective that is at once infinite, is thus the true source of that infinite [as an objectified expression of itself]. If what is objective is now to be apprehended as the infinite, it is allegedly demonstrable that nothing remains in it to require a further ground. This is what was meant by Kant when he called his philosophy "transcendental." Designating his philosophy in this way has the purported result that one ought not to attempt transcendence by going after [unknowable] objects of reason. For the [infinite] I is the source from which such transcending [of the finite], in order to reach the infinite, springs.

(§43) The categories belong to thinking as such. Mere sense perception is raised to the level of what Kant calls *experience* by the categories, which make up what is objective in experience. Regarding the categories taken for themselves, the criticism comes to be made that such concepts belong to the subject, but that within the subject itself they require some material content in order to have any value, so that consciousness may be filled with some content. When the categories are taken merely for themselves, thinking and its determinations become empty. The categories are objective, but what is objective in them belongs to thinking, and so has objectivity only within the subject. It will be readily recognized that whatever is "objective" in this sense belongs to thinking. Such idealism lies in asserting that whatever is objective, since it is found in our consciousness, is ideal.

Yet whatever constitutes what is *real* in experience is only a determination of feeling, and is at once admitted to be itself subjective. This yields *subjective idealism.* We can thus say that whatever is real proceeds within the limits of such [subjective] knowing. The chief question is whether such "knowing" is true knowledge. The answer to this question [in the critical philosophy] is that experience, in such subjective knowing, does not provide us with the truth. We do not know, in such knowing, what is insofar as it lies both upon and for itself. Rather, we have only subjective knowledge. Whether the categories exhibit upon themselves truth is not investigated by Kant. In the Kantian philosophy thinking cannot get to the truth, since the thought determinations are only finite. What is known by them is purely finite. In the science of logic we shall be leaving the [Kantian] opposition of objectivity and subjectivity entirely to the side. It remains the firm conviction of humankind that by thinking the truth can be known. To be sure, such thinking [as lays hold of truth] is itself subjective, but it also penetrates to the very heart of the matter, insofar as thinking does not stay put and behave in a finite mode.

(§44) The categories [according to Kant] cannot be determinations of the absolute. Yet the absolute ought to be known. To really know [*erkennen*] is to scientifically know [*wissen*] something as it is in its own determinateness, according to the necessary connections it has upon itself, according to the necessity of those interconnections. It is in this that determinate scientific knowing consists. By the [Kantian] categories we fail to apprehend the absolute, but there are two interpretations to this failure. Either the absolute cannot be apprehended in thought through anything finite, or—as comes to be conceded by some[, e.g., Jacobi,] in connection with Kant—sense perception falls within thinking. The absolute, however, is simply not the sort of thing that can come to be perceived [by the senses], and this is why the Kantian categories [which apply only to sense perception] do not suffice to apprehend it. Beyond the subject there remains, in total abstraction from it, the object simply as such, since what we know about it are in part only feelings and in part categories, which are all determinate and which all belong to the subject. The indeterminate being which remains yonder is the thing in itself, which allegedly cannot be known. How this other is constituted [in itself] is unknown, for how it is constituted [for me] is my doing.

Let us agree with Kant that, over against the subject, there stands an other. Yet nothing is in fact easier than to know *what the thing in itself is*. It is something objective, it is not the I, it is something different from me, but in all this it remains empty of all determination in itself, it is *totally abstract*. Moreover, this abstract thing is totally universal, where whatever is universal is understood to be a product of thinking. This worthless residue [*caput mortuum*] of a thing in itself is thus a creation of my own reflection, something still left over after all determinate objectivity has been subtracted from it. The thing in itself is the universal, it is what is abstract. We may say that it cannot be known. For to really know is to know [*wissen*] an object scientifically according to its own determinate content. If the thing in itself is to be indeterminate, if it is to lack all determinate content for me, I can know it no more than I can see color on a totally white wall. We shall see later that what lies in the background of what is beyond the finite, what lies beyond the finite, is itself determinate. But there is nothing in the thing in itself for human reason to ferret out. It is untruth; it is not the truth we seek. This is what emerges at the present stage in the Kantian philosophy, in which everything is laid out as subjective. Yonder is something in itself, a beyond, something totally empty. We shall show how empirical knowledge fails to be true, not because it is subjective, but because of quite another reason. For its categories are merely categories of what is finite.

(§45) The [Kantian] categories are finite thought determinations. They require material, and are in themselves empty. It is with this requirement of a material stuff that their finitude is posited. These categories make up what is generally called [in the critical philosophy] "the understanding." Here a definite distinction between the understanding and reason arises. *Reason* is the *capacity for* [our relation to] *the infinite,* for the unconditioned. (Whatever is finite relates itself to something else and is thereby conditioned.) This view of reason is, on the whole, correct. Put negatively, reason lies in thinking what is non-finite. It has the infinite for its object. It is activity, indeed infinite activity, and its object is likewise the infinite.

What is the "the infinite"? The "unconditioned," the *"non-determined."* It is whatever is identical with itself, whatever is equal to itself. Whatever is simple is in this sense [abstractly] "infinite," since it is related to nothing other than itself. What is infinite in this abstract sense relates itself to nothing that is other than itself. This [self-]identity is the original unity of consciousness. This self-identical being comes to be cast in relief [in Kant's critical philosophy]. It is said that this self-identical abstractly infinite being is no longer contained in determinate categories, that it no longer has any sensory material for its object. Rather, thinking wills for itself an infinite object, it makes itself into this object, into the end. For this object is to be equal to itself, to be the infinite and not to be anything determinate. This self-identity is in truth affirmation, and is at once an abstract negation, in which all determinateness is negated. This standpoint, which [in the critical philosophy] goes by the name of "reason," must now be held fast. What is unconditioned is taken [by reason] to be what is essential or truly absolute. Empirical knowledge, from its side, is valid only for appearances. The content of experience fails to be adequate to the I, to abstract self-identity, since empirical knowledge is always determinate. The thing in itself is made [by reason] into the object.

(§46) Yet a need to know the thing in itself asserts itself. As soon as the thing in itself becomes determinate through the categories we think it in a determinate manner. The categories are subjective. The thing in itself, however, is once and for all external to the categories, placed beyond and outside them. Should I wish to determine it, that determination belongs to me. The determination does not belong out there to the thing in itself.

The above contradiction arising in the attempt to know the thing in itself may now be seen in a more precise application. Representation has hold of objects, not merely the thing in itself, but more determinate universal objects such as the soul, the world, and God. The question for knowledge is now: what are these objects in themselves, in their truth? We have empirical knowledge of the activities of the soul, we have sensory perception of the soul. But what is the soul in itself? We have already seen that [an answer to] this question is rendered impossible by the presupposition that *what is in itself* is indeterminate. Yet we have here [in the soul, the world, and God] determinate objects, and with that determination is present. This is a totally abstract contradiction. One wants to know something as it is in itself, but that is a contradictory demand, for what is in itself is indeterminate. This contradiction pervades the entire exposition. To be sure the contradiction does not come to be stated this abstractly, but it is still at the basis of the whole exposition.

(§47) The consideration of the *world* [in the critical philosophy] is of special importance—consideration of the antinomies. But let us first attend to the *soul*. The soul has been taken up by metaphysics under rational psychology. It was first pointed out, in rational psychology, that I already find myself as conscious in my own consciousness. This conscious being, which I find myself to be, I transform into thought determinations. Such is the procedure of the former [dogmatic] metaphysics. But now the critical philosophy asserts, regarding this metaphysics, that experience itself affords thought determinations. Yet we have no right to translate or transform this experiencing into [pure] thoughts. By the *soul* we understand a thing which is really mind in an embodied form.[13] Human beings and the animals have souls. Yet human beings also have mind, but mind assuming the form of natural life is the soul. The soul is subject to natural conditions. Mind, however, is not in nature, but is the activity of self-abstraction from nature. The soul is mind in its immediate being.

In consciousness I find myself, it is claimed [§47], in these four empirically given forms. [1.] I find myself as the determining subject. I am the ground, I am the concrete one who wills, who is active. 2. I also find myself as something *singular,* something abstractly simple. This simple I is the foundation of all my manifold determinations. 3. I also find myself in experience as self-identically one and the same in every manifold of which I am conscious. I have, prior to any given time, done that, said that, sensed that. All this belongs to me. I am one and the same in all such manifolds. I behave as seer, as thinker, as one who represents. I am always one and the same—just so do I find myself. 4. I find myself to be a thinking being distinguishing myself from the natural things outside me. Already my own body is outside me, outside my abstract self. These are the four points to which the I refers—this I which all by itself singly sets itself over against its bodily being as also over against external sensory things. To be sure, we can know these four determinations from sense perception. Classical metaphysics, however, has not stood still with these forms as forms of sense perception, but has rather transformed them into categories. Upon closer examination, the subject falls under the category of singularity, etc. Singularity is a metaphysical category, but we may leave this aside and first take singularity as given in sense experiences. From such empirical knowledge one is to infer pure thought determinations that subsist for themselves, and that is what the former metaphysics did.

[1.] The first principle [of rational psychology] is that the soul is a *sub-*

13. In this Kantian context, *Geist* is translated as "mind," not as "spirit."

stance that corresponds to what I find in experience. I know myself to be an active subject. 2. The soul is a simple substance, it is singular, the abstract relating of self to self. 3. I am one and the same in all manifolds. I am numerically [self-]identical, numerically one, having remained the same throughout. 4. The soul differentiates itself, isolates itself within itself, but at once stands in relation to what is spatial. All that has remained more or less unchanged [throughout dogmatic rational psychology].

It is unjustified, Kant now says, to substitute these four just cited metaphysical categories in the place of the proceeding four empirical determinations. Precisely this was already Hume's observation as regards empiricism in general, namely, that categories are not really encountered in sense perception, and to this extent the critical philosophy holds no further special interest. Yet to the critical philosophy goes the merit of having freed [speculative] philosophy from the metaphysical use of the categories of the understanding regarding the soul—from the categories of *simplicity, immateriality,* and so forth. Whatever is simple is dead, not self-moving, whereas spirit[14] is full of rich content, infinitely active. Abstractions like simplicity applied to the soul fail to contain the fullness of spirit. Spirit is essentially whatever is active. This activity essentially falls on the empirical side, and yet the different activities must be taken in their interconnection. Spirit is within itself a system. Its manifold activities must be brought back to unity, but this unity must not be the merely abstract unity of simplicity.

This simplicity has been connected with the *immortality of the soul.* It has been said that only what is composite is exposed to destruction. What is composite can fall apart, as when I dissolve a musical piece into individual notes from which the harmony of the whole is absent. What is simple, however, cannot be destroyed. Kant, on the other hand, appealed to an [empirically] present simplicity, a simplicity subject to modification. For example, degree (temperature) is a simple determination, but is subject to the greatest variation. Red is simple, but can become more or less intense. It is always this same simple red. Accordingly, as Kant tells us, if the soul or consciousness is laid out as something simple that is no proof of the immortality of the soul. Consciousness can be subject to variations [in intensity] and can sink into unconsciousness, as in sleep. The sensation we have of the remaining stubs of [amputated] members still qualifies as consciousness, but in degree is only one step removed from consciousness at its very weakest. Such simplicity is a good counter-example to the [classical metaphysical] category of simplicity. The real interest of the immortality of the soul goes quite beyond merely abstract simplicity. Spirit is more concrete in its simplicity.

---

14. The switch from "mind" to "spirit" for *Geist* is to indicate that Hegel is shifting to a critique of Kant based on his own perspective.

The main point is that such abstract metaphysical categories are one-sided, and are insufficient to grasp anything true, precisely because there is no truth to them. Such simplicity is an abstraction without activity—a one-sided and untrue determination.

(§48) At this point Kant's critical philosophy takes an interesting turn. If reason now takes the *world* to be its object and moreover wishes to know it, it knows it only by the fact that it thinks it. Yet, in this thinking, reason falls into contradictions. For the thought determinations [when taken as determinations of the world as a whole] contradict one another. These determinations, however, remain absolutely necessary [to the world insofar as it is thought as a whole]. Kant might well have viewed rational psychology in the same manner [in which he viewed rational cosmology], for it is important to show how the abstract determinations of the understanding fall into contradiction, how in fact they negate themselves. Kant called the contradictions that arise as we think the world *antinomies*. The contradictions consist for him in opposite assertions about one and the same object. From such opposite assertions Kant concludes that the content of the world in thought cannot belong to the world as it is in itself, that the world insofar as it has this content is mere appearance. He thus presupposes that the world in itself is free of contradiction. Yet the human mind can fall into contradiction. Contradictions do in fact belong to it. Yet mind, spirit, is infinitely higher than the world, so that if contradiction should be considered a defect, i.e., something beneath the level of spirit, spirit must nonetheless bear its own responsibility for it. In the realm of spirit the categories themselves bring with them contradiction. The categories are upon themselves defective. Kant traced the defectiveness of categories to the fact that they are subjective, that they fail to reach the thing in itself. However, here [in the science of logic] the opposition of categories is no longer apprehended as a subjective opposition to being in itself. This opposition is instead apprehended so that the categories stand over against one another [rather than over against being in itself], and indeed so that *each category contradicts itself*. Here we first enter into the quick of the matter. This insight into [self-]contradiction marks an essential advance. Such an insight is lacking in [dogmatic] metaphysics.

Kant proceeds by unmasking statements with respect to the world [as a whole]. He exhibits different sides of the matter at hand, and shows the contradictions that arise when one thinks these different sides of the matter. He has brought forward *four antinomies*. Yet such contradiction is not limited to these four items. For, as the ancient skeptics already showed, contradiction can be exhibited in *everything*. Contradiction is to be seen in every logical category. It is upon themselves that the categories each come to the end of their rope, meet up with their finitude. They each meet with a negation by which they are cancelled and raised to a higher level.

We cannot go into any closer detail regarding the antinomies. We point out only the following: the world is in space and time. It at once impresses itself on thinking that *either* the world has had a beginning [in space and time] and will have an end *or* it is infinite in space and time. Further [for things to exist in] space consists in [their being] abstractly outside one another. Matter consists of the many, and thus consists in [many beings] outside of one another. Yet now one may ask whether matter is divisible to infinity or not. If not, we get to the *atoms*. If matter is infinitely divisible, everything material that we come up with is composite. As often as I divide a material object, the simple one is [again] negated in that object, so that the thought determination of composition is taken as foundational.

We can also ask whether space consists of spatial points, and time of temporal points? In each case the same pair of opposite replies arises. We can further ask whether there is freedom in the world. Persons exist who make an absolute beginning, who are absolutely free, and so on. Yet Kant says that both sides[, i.e., free will and universal causality,] are necessary. Just so does the world as much have a beginning as it has no beginning. It can as easily be proven that matter is divisible to infinity as that its ultimate principle is the atom. Kant carries out his proofs in his own way. He says these are no courtroom "proofs" by which, through circumstantial grounds, one would lend only plausibility to a conclusion. The proofs here are not the kind of sophistry in which a ground exists that dissipates when posited over against another ground. A proof within one antinomy quite generally contains nothing illusory, but rather is party to a necessary opposition.

Yet Kant's proofs here are contorted *apagogical* [indirect] proofs. The one [opposed] determination is as necessary as the other. We say of space and time that they contain points. We willy-nilly suppose limits in space, and a limit in time is also a point. Like the *now*, the point is, as a limit, completely simple. So there are limits in space. That is the one assertion. The other assertion is that the [ever present] now is limitless, that it is *continuity*. I have in space a point, hence the negation of continuity. The point is in space, and yet is itself at once something spatial. For it is connected [as, e.g., near or far] with other points in space. The point constitutes no absolute [non-spatial] abyss in space. The skeptics said that the point is a false representation, that it is nothing. To be sure, the point is only something supposed by the understanding. No one can show a point to anyone, though it is in space, and therefore is spatial. It is by the inability to exhibit points that the skeptics highlighted contradiction in geometrical definitions. The point is difference, it makes for a border, but it is at once no difference, no border at all. Extension cannot be separated from points, since once extension is separated from them they make no sense at all.

The same is true with the now. As soon as I say "now" it is no more, it has become something other than itself, a flowing line. The same is true of the beginning of the world. A beginning is a limit in time. To be sure I can posit a limit, as when I say "a hundred years from now," and so on. Yet time absolutely hangs together as a continuity. We also suppose limits in space. The end [to which something comes in space] is a limit, but space is limitless. The two opposed [thought] determinations are necessary to each other,[15] and that is an important thought determination in its own right. Every opposed determination lifts itself into its other, into the determination opposite to it. Every concept is something concrete that contains within itself diverse determinations, and thus contains an antinomy.

The ancient Eleatic dialectic concerned itself in particular with matter, space, and time regardless of whether they are limited or not limited. Space and time are continuities, but continuities in which there are always differences. The two determinations[, limitless continuity and discrete line segments,] are inseparable, which is a contradiction. Yet we know that spatiality and matter exist, whereas a contradiction cannot exist, or so says the critical philosophy. Purportedly this contradiction falls within our subjective thinking. Here we run up against the fundamental law according to which what is contradictory not only cannot be but likewise cannot even be thought.

Yet what is allegedly impossible here, namely, thinking contradiction, is exactly what turns out to be the case. We think contradictory [determinations] as lying within one [being]. Mutually exclusive determinations are present in one being. Discreteness and continuity belong to space, to time, to matter. Insofar as such opposite determinations belong to one and the same thing, contradictions indeed exist. But such contradiction falls only within thought, Kant tells us, not within the world. The world cannot contradict itself.

Yet how can we contradict ourselves? Would not our self-contradiction refute any claim of mind, spirit, to being higher than nature? In any case, self-contradiction is not resolved by the fact that it is in the mind. The self-contradiction is still in the mind, and it would be of far greater interest to really resolve it there in the mind than in nature. The true resolution of contradiction in the mind is the dialectical moment. The con-

---

15. For Hegel, this is to distance himself from the classical metaphysics which Kant critiqued, in which opposed determinations, e.g., the discreteness and continuity of the world, are established in separate classical metaphysical proofs.

tradition consists in ever resolving itself [dialectically],[16] but at once in always arising anew.[17]

Every drive, every longing, every [act of] willing by the mind is a contradiction. I have a need, I *am* in need. That is negation and at once a contradiction. Everything I do is directed to resolving that contradiction, to reestablishing peace of mind. The *satisfaction of need* is the resolution of the contradiction.[18] What is dead contains no contradiction. But the critical philosophy contains no resolution of this contradiction.

(§49) The third object of reason is *God*, who should be known and thought. Proofs of the existence of God have been offered. As human beings we have faith in God. We think, and we think our relation to God. We want to know the necessity [of this relation]. Human beings want to ground their faith. Whatever could be known through the *natural light* of reason was allegedly taught by natural theology. Yet natural theology did not get very far, since in thinking our relation to God it assumed the standpoint of the *understanding*. Here is how thinking [guided by the understanding] has proceeded. We represent God to ourselves, but cannot say that God is perceived or intuited. And so must it rather first be proven that *he exists*.

The standard used in judging a representation [merely as such] is that it not contradict itself. It will thus first be proven, therefore, that our representation of God is not upon itself contradictory. In representation God passes for being what is most high, but height is but an expression of quantity. God passes, further, [in the usual ontological argument] for the most perfect being, a being without defect, containing no negation within itself. So there is no contradiction in him. Rather, since contradiction is absent, in God there is only harmony with itself, pure reality, no limitation. That is what the understanding makes of God. God is *pure* reality, i.e., limitless and at once indeterminate. Yet "being indeterminate" is nothing but abstract [self-]identity. God is the highest essence. Yet if that is where we remain stuck, his essence is but a matter of indeterminateness.

Finite things each have a finite essence. The [divine] essence of es-

16. That contradiction consists in ever resolving itself may imply that thought cannot rest with a contradiction in an indirect proof context. Hegel's claim that we can think a contradiction could be taken to mean, not that we can simultaneously think something to be both A and not A, but rather that in trying to think of something as both we end up only thinking of it alternately as A or not A.

17. Again, there is ambiguity here. That contradiction always arises anew may mean that past contradictions are repeated, or that every new resolution of past contradiction leaves something out in its new identification of what is inclusively absolute, so that something relative is said to be non-relative or absolute.

18. This may be taken to say that to be conscious of need is to place one's essence in a satisfaction contradicted by one's existence.

sences is totally abstract, a worthless residue [*caput mortuum*]. Yet natural theology goes on nonetheless to say that this essence includes everything. The essence is to be concrete, to include everything, but that
turns out to mean that it includes everything only in its [infinite]
truth. For if it included finitude as such it would include negation. For
negation is finitude.

Beyond that, God has attributes. He is good, all-powerful, wise. Yet
that is already a limitation [in God]. The decrees of divine justice are
lifted through divine goodness, through grace. *Abstract justice* consists
in the fact that whatever is finite [*das Endliche*] comes to an end [*ein
Ende*]. What is finite deservedly goes under. Merciful *goodness* is the
contrary [of abstract justice], since it upholds what is finite even
though it ought to go under. Those divine attributes are already in
themselves diverse. Each is a particular attribute. What is more, they
limit one another. In order to put these divine attributes at a distance
[from God in himself], since God is supposed to be what is most real
[and thus free of contradiction], it is said[, e.g., by Leibniz] that we
must take such attributes only in the eminent sense, e.g., not as *human
justice*, but as totally *real justice*. Yet such justice then becomes totally
abstract. When these determinations of justice and goodness are taken
determinately, each is what it is. The eminent sense of "justice" is the
nebulous sense, indeterminate sense. This criticism [of natural theol-
ogy] was never stated by Kant. Being stands opposed to possibility.
God is a thought object, and ought not to be something merely subjective. He ought to have independent being for himself on his own account. The issue comes down to one of thinking and being. What is to
be effected is the unification of both. But in this second Kantian position of thinking [in relation to] to objectivity presently under consideration, it is the separation of the two that is laid out.

(§50) There are *two paths to unification*. Thought as pure thought is
the thought of God. One can pass over from being to thinking or from
thinking to being, and this gives two paths for the unification of being
and thinking. [In natural theology] the beginning is first made with
being. There are two sorts of proof of God's existence: on the one
hand, the cosmological and teleological proofs, and, on the other
hand, in the third place, the proof highlighting the second type of
unification, transition from thinking to being, i.e., the ontological
proof. These proofs are now widely rejected and are clearly defective.
Yet it is easier to know that something is defective than to know what
is true. However, when we recognize the defect with any definiteness
we also come to recognize therein what is true. Here [in the introduction to the science of logic] it is only possible to stress what is most important. For the science of logic in all its branches is nothing but the
process of the above transitions, the transition from objectivity to sub-

jectivity and back again to objectivity. The transitions themselves essentially fall within the science of logic itself.

A Further Remark [on §50]. Sound common sense will never allow any transition from what is empirical to thinking to succeed. If we start with being, the world stretches out before our eyes, and from the world thinking would make a transition to God, to pure thought, to the fact that *God* comes to be taken up beyond the *world*, over on the side of *thought*. This transition comes to be made thinkingly, and constitutes a *conclusion*. So from the world God is inferred. These arguments have come to be criticized. We have an intuitive acquaintance with the world. The world assumes in our consciousness the shape of an aggregate of contingent determinations. Further, we so determine the world as to recognize purposes in it with regard to living beings, since a living being needs air, water, food to survive.

Yet the satisfaction of such needs is not at once posited along with the positing of a living being. These necessities belong to the living being, to the very *concept* of such a being, to its very nature, but they do not exist merely through the existence of that nature, they are [in their contingent existence] independent of that concept or nature. Yet these independent existents [of air, food, etc.] go together [with a living being's own survival]. The world is so constituted that human beings, animals, and plants in fact do survive in it. That is the teleological relationship. A living being requires the necessities of life, and life necessities (in order to be such necessities) need living beings, but neither has necessary being through the other. Therefore there must be a third element. Ordinary common sense thus raises itself up to [recognize] a higher divine essence that has instituted [this relation of the world to the satisfaction of need]. This is the usual teleological proof attempted by commonsense. The proofs of God's existence are nothing but descriptions of common sense trying to raise itself up beyond from the world, or thoughtful pointers for doing so.

From finite being infinite being is inferred. Yet it is said that there is no bridge between the finite and the infinite, that there is rather an abyss between them. From either of the two it will be said that it is impossible to infer the other. We might say that there is a leap in going from the finite to absolute existence. That is the main criticism that the Kantian philosophy gives: in the Kantian philosophy it is observed that one climbs up to God in the theistic proofs from our empirical representation of the world. Starting out from the world, one then concludes that an absolute divine essence is upon and for itself necessary. Against this inference it is alleged [by Kant] that we are not entitled to grant that absolute essence to which we move. For what we have before us is but a collection of finite beings. Reason thus becomes transcendent, advancing on ground where there is no longer any solid sensory perception beneath it. It leaves all solid ground behind. There is no pure thought to be found in sensory perceptions. But something else is made out of such perceptions than what they in fact are. Yet, according to the theistic proofs, it is only by transforming sense perceptions into thoughts that we get at the truth. The critical philosophy asserts that whatever is made out of sense perceptions [while leaving them behind] is not proven by them. [In the theistic proofs] truth always lies in what is thought insofar as it differs from objects of sense perception. Yet merely for itself [apart from objects of sense perception], what is thought lacks all validity.

The world leaves us unsatisfied. Nothing temporal satisfies. For whatever is temporal is mutable, contingent, and absolutely dependent. Thought demands a fixed point, and in this world there is none. So we climb out of this contingent [sphere] to thought, to a necessity which is what it is not only upon but also for itself. Here is the climbing in question, this passage beyond the world. Human beings will simply not allow themselves to be robbed of this ascent, [allow] this *passage* beyond the world to be taken away from them by the Kantian critical philosophy. Let the critical philosophy bring whatever objections it will against this ascent. To think God is to pass beyond the world. To apprehend this act of passing beyond the world is still something else. The apprehension of it is to be attained by what are known as proofs of God's existence. But it is furthermore a fact that, in such expositions of passage beyond the world, the passage itself, as it actually exists in the mind, is not given an entirely correct exposition. The form under which the passage is brought is not correctly laid out. The understanding infers the one thing from the other, where both exist. It is said: "This line is equal to a second line, and the second is equal to a third," and one then concludes regarding the first and third lines that they are also equal. Just this sort of deductive inference is what is expressed by the theistic proofs. It is a matter of saying that, because the contingent world exists, God therefore also exists. But this obliges us to concede being to the contingent world in our proof.

We thus have two beings, the finite and the infinite. Insofar as we leave behind the world as it is, it is said (as Jacobi also says) that the finite world lays the foundation (bottom of page 59).[19] God's existence is

19. If the term "foundation" is understood epistemologically in the theistic proofs, Hegel may be taken as inferring in this paragraph that the term must also be understood ontologically, that to avoid circularity the world must have a being independent of God's being. But in his science of logic the contradictory independent being of the world is unmasked as a passing moment within the infinite divine being. The German text's reference to p. 59 in the 1830 *Encyclopaedia* is to a passage in §50 which reads, in the Wallace translation: "the world, which [in the theistic proofs] might have seemed to be the means of reaching God, is explained to be a nullity. Unless the being of the world is nullified, the *point d'appui* for the exaltation [of God] is lost. . . . It is the affirmative aspect of this relation [between

portrayed in the theistic proofs as being justified by the sensory world, and as dependent in its justification upon it. Such is the position, twisted all out of shape, which we encounter [in the cosmological and teleological arguments]. For in fact it is God that is the absolute ground. To be sure, [in the science of logic] the matter will eventually lay itself out in this sense. What will be said in the sequel is that raising [the finite relative ground into the absolute ground] corrects the false stance [of grounding God in the presupposed being of the sensory world]. So we start out from the being of the world of accidents in the theistic arguments and infer another world. We ourselves say, however, that God is the true being, the ground of all. The relationship between the finite and infinite worlds is thus immediately inverted in the science of logic. In this [new] transition [from God to the finite world] the false, twisted show of the [first] transition [from the world to God] thus vanishes. If we start out from the world of accidents and infer [another world], our manner of proceeding can be expressed as follows: because the contingent world is, God *is*. Yet that means that the contingent world by itself, the world that has fallen to our lot, the world as it appears, a world that is upon and for itself null, in no way belongs to true being. This world is a being that is as much non-being as being. We thus quite simply state that its being is purely and wholly one-sided, and that its value in no way exceeds that of non-being.

Whatever is necessary *must be*. In lifting [the finite world up into infinite being] the self-negation of the finite world is essential, but this self-negation does not appear in the classical theistic proofs. Insofar as this contingent world is, we have in this world only its affirmative side of being and not its self-negation, and that is what is one-sided in the classical proofs. The real conclusion to be drawn is that what is contingent does not have its ground in itself, but has it solely in something else. The mere fact of its being there [*Dasein*] is but a nullity, and this nullity presupposes another being, a necessary being.[20]

The transition [beyond this world] is thus not from something affirmative to something equally affirmative, but rather is a transition from something upon and for itself null. That is the true sense of this transition, which contains the negation of its starting point. In *Spinozism* the same misunderstanding arises. It is said that Spinozism embodies both pantheism and atheism. According to Spinoza there is but one sub-

the world and God], as supposed to subsist between two things, either of which is as much as the other, which Jacobi mainly has in his eye when he attacks the demonstrations of the understanding."

20. Hegel's meaning may become clearer if restated in the language of contemporary formal logic to say that the world's independent being is not a *premise* but a self-negating indirect-proof *assumption*. See Clark Butler, "Hegel and Indirect Proof," *The Monist*, vol. 75, no. 3 (1991), pp. 422–437.

stance, and everything worldly is purely accidental. Truth is substantial. Of course that will not be enough for us, since God is a substantial subject, the substantial spirit, substance as spirit. We imagine that Spinoza confuses God with a finite natural object, since he says that the substance of the world is God. On the one hand, that statement is quite correct, since God is present in the world—God is omnipresent in the world. But if what is worldly contains what is substantial, God is made out to be finite. But the same false conclusion, that God is finite, can be extracted from the proposition that he is omnipresent, since he is thus also present in whatever is finite.[21] The same one-sidedness of thinking here recurs. If we say God is outside us, that he is outside the world, and that he lets the world subsist as a real and actual world, we to be sure end up with a finite God. Yet the sense of Spinozism is that whatever is worldly is mere appearance out there for our sensory perception, but such perception is not true thinking. If God is in the world, his power is also in it: God is what negates the finite. In God what is finite falls to the ground, but what falls *to* the ground passes *into* its ground, and in its ground it is raised up again. This worldly being as being outside one another is merely negated, and thought in its one-sidedness is also raised up in this unity of the finite and the infinite.

In Spinoza's system, God alone *is*. What is other than God is a being that at once is not a being, and so is show. Thus it cannot be said that Spinozism is atheism. It is rather the exact contrary of atheism, namely, *acosmism*. The world is no true being, there is no world. Rather, God and God alone is. It is not to their credit that people say that Spinozism is atheism. In the unity of God with the world, the world is thought of as not true being. Those who say that Spinozism is atheism find it less off-putting to say that God has no being than to say that the world is not. They rigidly continue to insist that the world has a reality, that a finite being is a true absolute being.

[So beyond the *form* of the theistic proofs] the critical philosophy is concerned, in the second place, with the *content* of their starting point. Here the question concerns our starting point. From the contingent world we either proceed in the [cosmological] theistic proof to necessary being upon and for itself. Or we proceed [in the teleological proof] from adaptation to an end in the arrangements of nature. The world is an aggregate of contingent existents. Yet adaptation to an end also occurs in the world, and is laid out in individual detail. Raising the finite up to the infinite therefore has the sense of laying hold of activity as activity directed to universal ends. But here the critical philosophy remarks that, although

---

21. Note that to say God is omnipresent is to say that he is in part present in what is finite, but not completely present in it unless we take Hegel to mean that at depth level the infinite is the ground of the finite.

we do note adaptation to an end in the world, we also note much that is not adapted to any end. If, for example, we posit a living being to be an end, over against it stands an infinitely great extent of non-adaptation to any end. In other words, countless living beings evincing life in seed perish without ever having attained their end! The entire misery of the world is likewise a non-adaptation to the end of self-preservation and of the good. Such is the testimony of experience. Yet the true conclusion of the [teleological] argument will nonetheless refer us to a divine essence that is active by the [providential] pursuit of an end. But what is contained in this true conclusion is different from what was contained in the [assumed] starting point of the subsistent being of the world, which is now laid to rest. The raising of the finite into the infinite now acquires a quite different sense: it is the raising of the finite up into thinking, which goes after what is universal.

However, this content according to which God is upon and for himself necessary being, that he is the cause, that he directs everything according to ends, does not yet correspond to what we [in Christianity] represent to ourselves as "God." Further determinations are necessary to complete the representation we have. From the side of our experience [of God] these theistic determinations remain incomplete. In point of content there is a limitation in these determinations [of God in the classical theistic arguments], a defect. We would really have to make up for the defect by asserting a world of spirits, of an absolute, infinite spirit. Thus truth, spirit scattered as endlessly as light is scattered throughout all heavenly bodies, would be the true starting point, while the raising [of the finite to the infinite] would then be the truth of these countless spirits which, as many, are at once each finite and limited. This truth is the one and absolute spirit. One would thus already have had spirit as the starting point, but only as limited spirit. However, this true transition [from finite spirit to absolute spirit] finds a place in philosophy. The truth of ends in the finite sphere is the absolute final end. As active, as end, this raising up [of the finite into the infinite] thus begins with the finite but goes on to the universal insofar as this universal strips away the initial forms of mere finitude and thus becomes [manifest in] immediate being.

(§51) The other path is the reverse, the so-called *ontological proof*: the beginning is made with the thought of God, with a subsequent transition to his being. In the first path being is common to both sides[, i.e., the contingent world and God]. What is stripped away in this being [as not belonging to God] is only its limitation, its finitude. What we have now, however, is the more abstract contrast, not of being to being, but of thinking to being. I have an abstract concept in my head, and now the question is whether it contains any truth. Being is the worst of abstractions. Thinking is also an abstraction, since it lies only within a subject of thinking. It is in the thinking subject that thinking is actual. What is actual is thinking by the subject. But given the abstraction of both thinking and being, there is much that can be said back and forth. The representation of God is alleged not only to be a representation, but to be a representation of a *being* that is independent of our thinking.

This path of the ontological proof was unknown to the ancients, but has been introduced by Anselm of Canterbury, by the scholastics. The simple criticism raised by Kant is that thinking and being are different. From the fact that I have a representation of something finite it does not yet follow that it has being. But Kant's observation is quite trivial, and was doubtlessly already well known to all philosophers. And, insofar as it was already well known, it can be the ground of no new objection to the philosophical principle [that the infinite self-concept includes its abstract being]. A representation or concept is finite should being stand over against it, since it is something particular, meeting up with its end in being. As has always been well known, merely given my representation to myself that I have a hundred thalers in my pocket, it does not follow that a hundred thalers are in my pocket. That is no doubt correct, just as it is also correct that there is no difference in content[, as contrasted to form, between an infinite concrete concept and its abstract being]. Kant says that being adds nothing not already contained in the [finite] concept. Yet a finite representation, its finite content, loses its one-sidedness if being corresponds to it. If I say "a hundred thalers," they are a mere abstract representation. It is a further fact, lying beyond that abstract representation, that the hundred thalers exist. Thinking and being are different [in form, but not in content, within the infinite concept], but insofar as something is known to be merely represented it is finite. Yet it is not, in the science of logic, a question of the finite concept, which is already well known to differ from its being, but of the true infinite concept.

Anselm, Spinoza, Descartes have said that God remains identical whether in concept or in being. God is what is most perfect, and only what is most complete contains this unity [of the infinite concept and its being] in total fullness. It is this unity [in its fullness] that is what is most perfect. However, this thought of God also has a defect, which is that it is *represented* as a presupposition [rather than being dialectically constructed by the science of logic]. It is said that we represent God to ourselves as the most perfect being. Yet this most perfect being is at once the self-concept [treated in the third branch of the science of logic]. Whatever is most perfect must include being within it. If it did not include being, we could posit an even more perfect being that would include it. What is further at issue is to show that the self-concept bears upon itself the self-movement by which it raises its own one-sidedness up beyond itself [into unity with being], that the self-concept determines itself as being, and thus that being itself lies in raising up its own one-sidedness and passing over into the self-concept. The self-concept thus reveals itself to be the truth of being, just as it in turn shows its truth to lie in the idea, i.e., in the unity of reality and the self-concept. Whatever is bad in the world fails to correspond to the self-concept of the world, and so is finite. Yet to be God is to be infinite.

Being, however, is a poor abstraction. It is the poorest of them all, the simple relation of self to self, immediate and immutable. It is possible to have an equally bad representation of the self-concept, but it will still be our belief that being belongs to the self-concept [without being formally identical with it]. The self-concept contains the oneness of self with self, which is the moment of its immediacy. That moment also belongs to being, except that the self-concept is not limited to the one-sidedness [of the immediacy of being]. With regard to Kant's criticism [of the ontological argument], it is essential to hold on to what it does and does not accomplish. It fails to be shown in this criticism that there is any truth to thinking in itself. Insofar as thinking and being are different [in content], thinking is not true. The Kantian critique of our intuition of the world possesses the great interest of claiming to exhibit the nullity and finitude present in thinking by itself, but it is really only the nullity of the categories [of the understanding] that is exhibited. Thinking indeed shows itself to be contradictory, but thinking itself is the resolution of these same contradictions, though this resolution is not shown by the Kantian critique.

(§52) The result of the critical philosophy is that thinking never gets beyond abstract thinking. The form of abstract thinking is *abstract identity.* Thinking for Kant posits itself as something objective, something perceived, determined through and through with sensory material. Yet beyond this sensory content, which is known as *experience,* nothing exists but the abstract identity of a thinking that [in the critical philosophy] is reason, the unity of the self-consciousness. Thinking, therefore, merely unifies the material provided by experience. This application of the self-identity of thinking is nothing but the ordering of such material. This order is a relationship, a unity, an external unity of things. This oneness of thinking with itself falls within us, and changes nothing in the things themselves that come to be ordered. This oneness concerns in no way the content of objects, but establishes a purely external relationship between them. Such a systematization of experiences is what reason is supposed to be. It is supposed to consist in those very compositions as are found in our contemplation of nature. Its business is one of classification. The sensory manifold is to be brought into unity.

Yet the further this unification of content proceeds, the paltrier its content becomes. A further more general universality beyond humanity is the animal, still further is the realm of all living beings, while the most abstract unity is then the *thing*. Reason should lead to ever greater unity. Yet the more this unity corresponds to what [in the critical philosophy] is called reason, the emptier it is. This is what Kant's philosophy regards as reason. One may simplify the laws of nature by saying, for example, that they are all cases of natural attraction. Planets, like the rest, are nothing else but the unification [of different observations under the same law of attraction]. Yet the positing of the planets in their unity is empty, since everything can be posited in such a unity. It is precisely particularization, which is what is at stake here, that is lacking. One sort of attraction is that by which a stone falls back again to the ground, and another sort is that by which plants attract the moisture of air. Everything that is living in spirit is likewise [an activity of] attraction. Learning is appropriation, hence attraction. So attraction is the one universal law. Yet precisely for this reason, it is totally empty. Reason as understood in the critical philosophy cannot ever become the organon of truth. Rather, reason is only the canon, the law, the rule. The [Kantian] claim that reason is forthwith incapable of knowledge holds fast to the contrast between concept and reality, concept and actuality [that Kant makes in his critique of the ontological argument]. All representing that lacks actuality is finite thinking just as, likewise, whatever being fails to correspond to its concept is finite being. What is true is what is actual, and what is actual corresponds to the self-concept.

[B.II.b.] Practical reason

(§53) It was especially through Kant that practical reason gained access [to current German philosophy]. Practical reason concerns the will, which is laid out in contradistinction to *intelligence*. Yet to will is still to think. The will is driven by what is universal. Law [*Recht*], ethical life, is the universal. Yet the will as a natural will is a finite, particular will, i.e., desire [*Begierde*]. If what I will is property, legal property, I will the universal, since the law is the universal. May practical reason lay down objective laws for freedom, for being *self-determining*! This is what distinguishes practical from theoretical reason. The pinnacle of what is theoretical, the I, is taken to be empty of determination. What for Kant is said to follow, should reason try to think the infinite, we have already seen. Practical reason is said to determine itself objectively, and in such self-determination lies freedom. That reason in its practical function can be self-determining is accepted as valid. It is commonly accepted as valid because experience shows that to be a human being is to be free in this sense, as confirmed by our own inner perception. This claim can be allowed, but it is a further fact that the will is the universal, that desire proves to be finite and allows itself to be led back to the universal will upon and for itself as its ground.

The principle according to which I as will am self-determining in myself makes a human being conscious that he or she is free, that there is no law for one to recognize other than the law one knows be a determination of one's own will. The Kantian philosophy won general assent to this principle by which the will is within itself absolute. In prior [medieval] philosophizing, the vocation of humankind was in principle stated to be blessedness, but an ambiguity remained as to what blessedness was supposed to be. What it was did not depend on me. It was claimed that we ought to have such and such inclinations toward blessedness, and so on, and that was how morality was established. Our inclinations entered into opposition with one another, and the satisfaction of them depended on a divine will external to them.

Against this view of the human vocation, the one great principle established [by Kant] is that man is *free*. A human being is capable of renouncing everything, and so can never be compelled. Thus a human being's highest satisfaction must lie in freedom, and it is to this that we cling whenever subjected to external force. Freedom is always within a human being's power, and whatever is offered to a human being in whatever respect can only be offered in a manner consistent with this freedom. A human being must find in whatever is presented a determination of his or her own will. This principle quite deservedly won widespread assent to the Kantian philosophy.

If one explores consciousness for something to become the vocation of one's life, what one comes up with is variable and accidental. Yet in freedom, as the vocation I discover for myself, I find a fixed point of attachment within myself that no one else can overpower. In this freedom within me I find absolute satisfaction, a formal satisfaction that spirit finds within itself. I am identical with myself, but in this identity I am self-determining, and these determinations are the laws of my freedom, they are my own self-determinations. This principle is of infinite importance. Yet the truth of the principle comes to be based on experience, on *my* consciousness. There are, however, enormously many experiences, and many people by the experiences they have know nothing at all of freedom. To them it remains to be to be proven that the truth is other than what their experiences tell them.

(§54) However, the question now shifts: I determine myself, and with that there enters a content, but what now is the further determining principle [by which I determine myself]? Or, to put it otherwise, what is my duty? What is moral, what is the moral law [*das Recht*]? The answer to this question depends on the following development: either we lack any criterion of what is moral at all, or that criterion is only that what is to be regarded by us as moral ought to contain no contradiction[, which is Kant's criterion in the categorical imperative]. Yet such a criterion is once again abstract self-identity[, A = A], so I am once more on abstract ground.

It is said that one ought to do one's duty merely for the sake of duty. But the question is: what is one's duty? What is the law of right and wrong [*das Recht*], what is the moral law? Here we find [in Kant] abstract self-identity, and over against this abstract identity lies all that is particular. It will now be said, for example, that we should return property belonging to another person when that property has been entrusted to us. If I do not accept this duty and thus return the property, I contradict the initial presupposition that it is the other's property. Yet contradicting that first presupposition by disowning the duty and not returning anything entirely depends on maintaining the presupposition that the property in question is even now the other's property.[22] However, just how is this further presupposition grounded? And, quite generally, how is [the whole institution of] property to be grounded? The alternative presupposition that no property should exist at all contains no contradiction. So the principle [of the moral law] remains formal, in that self-identity is alone to be the criterion of what is moral, is alone to be the determining ground [of the obligation to return property]. However, any particular determination [such as property] is absent from mere self-identity, which thus can afford no ground at all.

[B.II.c. The reflective power of judgment]

(§55) Kant, proceeding as by sure instinct, introduced [beyond theoretical and practical reason] the third side of matters, the *reflective power of judgment*. It is called the *intuitive understanding*. In everything that is theoretical the understanding has been at work [according to Kant], but in that sphere the understanding has presupposed experience. What we have now, in the reflective power of judgment, is an understanding that is at once by itself intuitive, a self-realizing concept. This new determination [of the object] is contradictory in that the determining is now intuitive[, i.e., produces its own object]. Particularization, singularization, is given out to be something called forth merely by thinking, through the understanding. The self-concept is now self-realizing, bringing forth a reality in correspondence with it. This Kant called the power of reflective judgment, in contradistinction to the power of subsuming judgment where a rule is laid down as the basis and I subsume the particular given object under it.

The reflective power of judgment is a power that does not merely subsume. Rather, what it encounters is its own law standing over against itself[, reflected in the object]. The object is thus to be contemplated in such a way that the particular determination proceeds from the understanding itself, so that the reality of the determination is made to correspond to the understanding. In the power of subsuming judgment, the particular is

22. That is, only property can be stolen.

added externally to the rule: it is a subordination of the particular under the universal rule. The determination comes to the object, to the particular, externally. That is how mechanism universally works. A weight is lifted, something is set in motion. That is an external relation—the universal, whatever is determining, comes externally to what is determined.

In the power of reflective judgment, by contrast, the universal produces the particular out of itself. It does so in fact, according to Kant, in the organic realm and in art. In the organic realm, in the circulation of blood, for example, a *mechanical* model has been adopted [cf. William Harvey]. Yet a living *organism* is not driven mechanically [§57]. Whatever is organic is self-determined. It makes something else of whatever impinges on it [*Anstoss*]. The organs, for example, make foods into blood. In any living organism there is an enlivening soul that awaits our knowledge of it, soul that is itself self-knowing. The principle of movement proceeds from oneself. Just so with the process of life. The reproduction of the members is a living process. The members inwardly determine themselves out of themselves.

Determining and coming to be determined here cease to be two different things. Their unity is the *soul*. In this way mechanical circumstances become free, every part is ensouled, in each part the universal life is present. These limbs, these guts, are the very means of life, but the living soul is active in them as well. All members of the body are continuously regenerated insofar as they preserve themselves. Yet these products are at once productive. Through the parts the whole is brought forth. But this whole is the living soul, and is at once itself productive. Such activity, such conduct, is "purposive activity." We have here a determination by ends. The living organism is its own end. Forever producing itself, it realizes this end which it itself is. Everything is purpose, everything means. The guts are the means, but they also contain the end. The distinction between coming to be produced and producing falls by the wayside, as does the distinction between end and means, cause and effect.

Kant saw that the understanding does not suffice for the apprehension of living beings, and with that we reach the concept of the intuitive understanding. [For Kant] the intuitive understanding is the [regulative] idea of reason. So in the case of what is organic the [non-intuitive] understanding does not suffice [to apprehend it]. The other realm in which Kant proved the insufficiency of this understanding is *art*, the aesthetic realm. In a work of art a thought is present. The work of art is the universal that realizes itself in these [technical] forms, in these features. In these forms we see the soul, its character, we see what the artist represented to himself, but it is the forms themselves that give expression to that soul. Here content and form are inseparably united. Matters are different here from what we find in mechanical artifacts, or in architecture.

The line and angle are forms of the understanding. In the subject, how-ever, there exists something *genial,* the capacity for artistic ideas [§56]. The artist reflects, and this or that representation makes up the founda-tion of his work, but thinking for the artist is an exercise of the power of imagination. The artist builds his thoughts into something sensory which no longer has validity for itself [as sensory], but whose meaning rests upon the artist himself. The [artist's] meaning can be no longer some-thing merely inner, but is out [in the open], entirely invested in the sen-sory form, in reality. Here is the absolute unity [of content and form].

Many, and notably Schiller, have found in the idea of artistic beauty a way out of the [Kantian] philosophy of the understanding. Schiller's great soul took its fill of philosophical ideas. But Kantian abstractions were not enough for him. The good, the true, essentially received for him the determination that it be present, and indeed should be present, as the beautiful, i.e., that it should have being and should be present in reality, in its identity with actuality. To this Schiller gives expression in many a work, venting himself accordingly. These, then, are the two sensory appearances[, the organic and the artistic,] in which an experi-ence of the unity of the particular and the universal is present, in which the living soul penetrates through and through what is material. The greatness of the Kantian philosophy is that through the intuitive under-standing he reached the idea [as regulative]. Yet he did not yet know that the unity of the particular and the universal is not only a truth present in these two particular [organic and artistic] appearances, but that it is the truth upon and for itself, and that within thought, as the idea, it is the one and only truth [§58].

That far Kant did not get. To know this would imply that one realizes that theoretical and practical reason both exhibit one-sidedness, that they are only abstractions, only moments of the truth. Kant said that ar-tificial products as also natural products are each to be judged a unity. But that is our judging, we reflect on them in this way, this is how we appre-hend them. It is doubtless true that this is how we consider them once we are no longer stuck in the mechanical culture of the understanding. But the further question is whether viewing matters this way is or is not the truth upon and for itself. If we know it to be the truth upon and for itself, the subjective standpoint according to which we merely reflect on some-thing external falls by the wayside. We come to know that the two sides, thought and being, do not stand so absolutely over against each other.

(§59) This unity was then extended even further. The good is to de-termine me, my will. But the perennial disunity of the two is also rep-resented. The good as the universal, as the rule, does not have its oppo-site in my will as the universal will, but rather in nature, in the [particular] will that determines by natural instinct. The good as uni-versal is the opposition of the good and the world in general. If we now apprehend the representation of inner unity by which the universal lays itself out as realized in the particular, we also apprehend the thought of the opposition of the good and the world being lifted. The good then functions as the rule for the whole world. Yet if the world has being for itself on its own account, it fails to conform to the good. Everything has its own laws. But now it is represented to us that this disharmony ought to be lifted, that the good should be realized, and that it is God who is to bring about the harmony. As much as this unity is present to our senses in living beings in the natural world, and as much as it is also present in works of art, the same unity is present to thought, in which the good rules as the final end of the world over both living beings and artworks. The Kantian philosophy also reached this highest form of the idea, of the unity of thinking and being, but it then reduced that form of the idea to a purely subjective manner of taking things.

(§60) Thus for Kant "the good" means nothing but our good, the moral law of our own practical reason. We have found this moral law, duty, to be purely formal. Lying within it is a contradiction. On the one hand, it is said that what is true is the unity by which the good realizes itself in the world, by which the world is powerless in the face of the good; while on the other hand it is said that this harmony is subjective, something merely represented, something that only should be, an impotent rule that can accomplish nothing. It is said that this unity of the good and the world is the truth, but that it is a unity that is not, that only should be—and here lies the incongruity. The absolutely final end is absolutely realized in the world, and yet is only realized as something that *should* be, it is only a subjective faith. Yet what that means is that the unity is not, that it does not exist. But it is still the truth. This unity expresses itself in the form of infinite progress. The end is realized, but is not completely realized— which means that it is not realized. That is the contradiction.

We have seen this unity of the good with the world exist in subordinate limited spheres, in the living organism in nature, and in artistic beauty. But it then comes to be said that viewing matters this way is only a matter of our opinion. In the highest spheres, it is explained, this unity is true, but this unity is never a fully present unity—it is forever incomplete, so that the opposition between the end and the world never goes away. Virtue, the good understood as the good of this particular individual in the sphere of finitude, is in ceaseless struggle with the self[, i.e., with inclination]. In the realm of finitude, virtue is admittedly a struggle, admittedly a matter of what merely should be. What holds upon and for itself is still something else again. It will be said [in the critical philosophy] that the unity of the good and the world is only a postulate of practical reason, which is to say that it only should be.

A contradiction surely arises when all is not "going well" with the good. It is said that reason does not know the good to be united with the world. But reason, divine providence, rules the world—in divine providence no externalities and contingencies are to be seen. The absolute final end of the world is not so powerless as to not realize itself. It is true, as we said, that we cannot perceive the end's worldly self-realization [by the senses], and yet the end is not so impotent as to not realize itself. As we look out upon world history [rationally], just so does history look back at us. To be sure, there are particular ends and demands[, e.g., of justice,] that fail to be satisfied in the course of history. To be sure, one can always withdraw[, e.g., from the world's injustice,] into one's own subjectivity. Yet it still must be recognized that what is rational is the unity of the final end with the world.

We have considered this second position [of thought toward objectivity] at greater length because it has completely penetrated the culture of the present age and, moreover, in part still holds its place within it. The forms and shapes assumed by the Kantian philosophy come at us from all sides. As we have explained above, they have their ground in the most abstract of oppositions. What is most interesting are the points where Kant reaches beyond himself. Yet he no sooner gets beyond himself than he reverts back to what we have already explained as untrue.

C. The Third Position [of Thought] toward Objectivity

The third position [prior to the science of logic] reverts to the first [ancient] position. Like the first, it is *immediate knowledge*. But is no longer *innocently* immediate.[23] Its immediate knowledge is now *polemical*, self-reflectively restricting itself to what is totally simple. Immediacy also existed in the first position of classical metaphysics, where God, soul, and world came to be thought straightaway. Just so does thought proceed again here—but this time it does so reflectively, with an awareness of immediacy restricted to one completely simple point. The position is polemical. It results from [a reaction to] the critical philosophy, except that what is last in the critical philosophy, namely, *faith*, now comes to be singled out for itself on its own account [as first]. What sets itself in opposition to faith is the Kantian philosophy itself.

(§62) This assertion of immediacy includes, however, still a further

23. If *classical metaphysics* explicitly absolutizes what is immediate (e.g., Parmenidean being) with an unconscious and thus innocent negation of its mediation by something else (e.g., nothing, becoming . . .); and if *metaphysical skepticism* negates this absolutization of what is immediate as contradictory by highlighting such mediation (e.g., Kant), *polemical belief* reasserts the absolutization of what is immediate by refusing the skeptical self-negation of that absolutization (e.g., Jacobi's return to immediate belief polemically directed against Kant's metaphysical skepticism).

consideration. We saw in the Kantian antinomies that the thinking of the understanding in metaphysics falls into contradiction with itself and is therefore incapable of knowing. So now it is similarly claimed that the understanding could achieve no knowledge of God [as the unconditioned] because its forms are all conditional and limited [§62]. Jacobi, in this respect similar to Kant, made this claim. Yet he set himself vehemently in opposition to Kantianism in its practical branch, which makes its principle out to be duty for duty's sake. The good for its own sake, to which Kant holds fast over against what lies in the inclinations and in whatever is sensory, stands for Kant in opposition to instincts and inclinations. Jacobi polemicized against Kant in this matter and located the validity of all that is virtuous and good in the individuality of each human being. He generally based himself on each individual human being's feeling and customs.

The Lacedaemonians did not reply to Xerxes, as he exhorted them to come over to his side, that their individual sense of moral duty prevented them. They rather replied that doing so would be against their ethical customs [*Sitte*] and habits. They replied that by their ethical customs and habits they at once stood together as but a single individual. The Lacedaemonians had no Kantian morality capable of becoming conscious of itself in duties. Jacobi says that they were ethical precisely because they did not base themselves like Kant on the opposition between inclination and duty. This ethical unity is to be sure an important side of the matter, but the unity in question here is one of custom, education, and culture. It is still part of being a conscious human being that one is aware of the good and of right in the form of the law and duty. Jacobi opposed this one-sidedness [of unity in ethical custom] to the other one-sidedness of Kant, who made the division within a human being between duty and inclination into his foundation.

Yet in the upshot of his thinking Jacobi agrees with Kant. Only his starting point is different. For Kant ends up insisting that thinking differs from its object. Jacobi agreed, justifying his polemic by saying that thinking in the form of knowing is only thinking, proceeding from conditions to further conditions. A cause is that by which I understand its effect. But the cause is itself conditional and finite. For example, if the cause of the lightning is electricity, the question arises as to the cause of electricity, and so on. So we endlessly proceed from one thing that is conditioned to something else that is equally conditioned. And that is what is called "knowledge." Knowing is this procession through a series things that are all conditioned. The last item in the series would be the unconditioned. But we never "know" it, since we only "know" what is conditioned. If we made something other than the unconditioned into the ground of the unconditioned, the unconditioned would cease be unconditioned. Here we have the *mediation* [of all "knowledge"] of which Jacobi spoke. "Knowing" is thus mediated thinking. But along with this comes a representation: reason has a representation of the unconditioned which we cannot know.

So inner scientific knowing [*Wissen*], if it wants to have knowledge [*Erkennen*] of what is true, must behave in an immediate fashion, and that is what has been called *faith* [or belief, in contrast to what Jacobi calls "knowledge"]. The sole presupposition is that "knowing" is a thinking which merely follows the path of mediation only by conditioned objects. That is the presupposed fact. No other "knowledge" [*Erkennen*] exists. There is no true scientific knowing [*Wissen*] other than immediate belief. But Jacobi leaves this claim at the level of a bare assertion.

German philosophy has proven very receptive to Jacobi's simple line of reasoning. The main point [of criticism to be made against Jacobi] is that he does not take up the self-concept of the unity of mediation and of immediacy.[24] Yet the contrast between mediation and immediacy arises within every concept. Being [for Jacobi] is at once completely immediate, and so it remains. [For Jacobi] we gain our assurance from immediate knowledge, which gives itself out as a *fact of consciousness*. But if we look carefully at the matter, whatever in truth is completely simple lacks all mere immediacy. It affords no immediate knowledge at all. Rather, everything that is immediate exists only with and through mediation.[25] The above "fact of consciousness" is thus totally incorrect.

The other main point in criticism of Jacobi is that, just as immediacy is joined to mediation, mediation is throughout joined to immediacy.[26] It is said that to "know" is to proceed from something conditioned to some-

24. Hegel's science of logic, here in the introduction, discovers itself through the history of philosophy itself. The first step consists in embracing the self-negation of classical metaphysics through Kant. Hegel departs from Jacobi's polemical refusal of the skeptical critique of classical metaphysics. Second, the Hegelian science of logic surrenders the contradictory classical absolutization of what is immediate by including mediation in an expanded concept of what is immediate. Jacobi's philosophy of polemical immediate faith attacks Kant from a pre-Kantian dogmatic position which is nonetheless no longer innocent of knowing Kant. Hegel's science of logic advances to agree with Kant, but also advances beyond Kant, reestablishing metaphysics on a post-Kantian basis. His science of logic negates the classical metaphysical negation of the other. It views what is immediate as speculatively reflected in its mediation, as concretely self-identical in and through what is other than whatever is immediate. Hegel's extensive treatment of Jacobi, whose positive philosophy hardly ranks him in the same class with Kant, must be understood in context as a thinly veiled critique of a school of thought which was influential into Hegel's Berlin period. This school was represented by Schleiermacher on the faculty of Berlin University, where Hegel taught.

25. To give a possible example, the evening star as immediately given turns out to be what it is by the mediation of being the morning star.

26. To pursue the example in the previous note, the evening star which medi-

thing else that is equally conditioned. But such "knowing" is only *finite knowing*. However, immediacy is also found in such finite knowing. What is mediated proceeds only by passing over into immediacy as other than it. That is what is one-sided [in Jacobi's view of immediacy and mediation as each isolated from the other]. Just as Kant fixes on the subjective over against objective, Jacobi fixes on immediate oneness. "Knowing" as finite knowing is a thinking that attaches itself only to what is limited.

(§63) The affirmative assertion in Jacobi is that truth exists for us, that we know of God immediately. Our representation of God and our certainty with regard to him reside precisely in us. With respect to questions of right and ethical customs, he says the same thing, namely that they reside in us. Their presence in us he calls "reason." This simple knowing is called *faith*. We speak of looking and seeing [*Schauen*], we know what we know by looking and seeing. The truth is known, for Jacobi, in the same way. The method is very convenient. Every effort of investigation is spared. Knowing God can also be called intuiting him [*Anschauen*], and the form of immediate knowing is again present. As Cicero says, nature has implanted in us certain instincts of friendship and love. In much the same manner we can also speak of the instinct for knowing God. This is quite correct, but the one-sided assertion is then made that reason is but a simple, *foundational knowing* devoid of any self-movement.

We believe in God immediately. To say that I believe this or that usually means that I have reasons to believe it. But in order to have certain knowledge, more than having reasons is required, namely, immediate intuition. The object of knowledge lies there before me in immediate consciousness. I myself am present in this consciousness in the act of sensing, intuiting, and the object thus falls within my sensory consciousness. I in my act of intuiting am identical with the intuited content. The content is as certain as my own self is. Jacobi says that we believe that we each have a body, we believe that sensory objects lie before us—all that is an immediate certainty. We know it all directly by intuition. The belief here in question is supposed to be immediate knowing by reason. Having faith and knowing are usually set over against each other in philosophy. But [for Jacobi] what I have faith in I "know." It is only a question of the type of knowing. The contrast between having faith and "knowing" is empty for Jacobi, referring only to the fact that in faith knowing fails to be mediated. Philosophy [as developed in the science of logic] does not oppose Jacobi's assertion that reason, spirit, has knowledge of God. It cannot occur to philosophy to wish to contradict the content of such propositions. Human beings, being rational, do harbor within themselves that higher sphere in which resides the know-

---

ates the morning star is mediated by the immediately given morning star precisely by not being the morning star as immediately given.

ing of God. This is straightaway the principle of human freedom [from a purely conditioned existence].

(§64) So what does immediate scientific knowing know? It knows God, the infinite, the unconditioned. Of God we have a representation. Furthermore, in the ontological proof the conclusion that God exists connects in thought or representation the universal, taken not only upon but for itself in being for its other, with being. According to the Kantian principle, the thought and being of something are different. But in immediate knowing [for Jacobi,] they are inseparable and thus identical. They are so very identical that they cannot be drawn apart.

What holds for Jacobi here in this matter of thinking and being also holds for *Descartes*, the philosopher who once again introduced genuine free philosophizing into the European world. His first proposition is "I think, therefore I am." Thinking for Descartes is also the I. But if we leave the I out, we have only thinking and being. Now the pure thought [which thinking thinks] is God, with which being is bound—the being of God is inseparable from the thought of him. Descartes spelled out the connection by which thinking, intuiting, or whatever we call it, is a simple unity within itself, and by which that unity is at once being. Mere being is abstracted here from all the mediation by which the simple unity of being with thinking in fact[, i.e., concretely] exists. So thinking and such being are inseparable. Moreover, Descartes' proposition "I think, therefore I am" is not a deductive argument [*Schluss*], since the second statement ["I am"] contains something beyond what is given in the first ["I think"]. But the proposition still contains the inseparability of thinking and being, the identity [of thinking and being despite the distinction between them]. Descartes[, proceeding beyond the unity of our thinking and our being,] also lays out the thought of God as our thought, as our representation, and as united with his being. But where he does this in the ontological proof he also brings mediation to the fore. What is deficient in his ontological proof, however, is that the inseparability of thinking [the thought of God] from being is left as a presupposition. In this respect, his claim contains nothing new[, nothing beyond Anselm].

(§65) The peculiarity of Jacobi's point of view, we have seen, is that for him mediated "knowing" taken in each case in isolation goes through a chain of things that are conditioned, so that what is "known" depends on "knowing" something else. So what is mediated is not understood as dissolving into immediacy. What is peculiar [in Jacobi] is the quite exclusive assertion that only *immediate knowing* contains truth. This, we say, is the polemical side of the matter as posited against mediated "knowing." With that an exclusive either/or disjunction of mediation and immediacy is posited, without any middle term. This is the understanding speaking. What is truly rational is neither the one nor the other, but is the both/and, the one as well as the other. But let us for now leave this aside.

Jacobi says that we all have knowledge of God, that this knowledge resides within us immediately as a fact of consciousness. [Not being philosophers,] most have never traveled up and down the byways of metaphysics or proofs. It is surely true that the human understanding is conscious of God without ever confronting the mediation of proofs—just as we eat, drink, and digest without knowledge of anatomy and physiology. The other question, however, is whether this immediate knowledge does not already essentially contain mediation within itself, whether it is immediate only through mediation. Digestion, for example, is upon its own showing a process of mediation. I pick up food, I prepare it, I swallow it down. That all consists in mediating the immediately given food. Something other than digestion stands in relation to digestion. A process of mediation is present there.

The question now is whether the sort of mediation that exists in proofs of the existence of God, in the law [*Recht*], in questions of ethical custom [*Sittlichem*], is to be excluded when it comes to our faith in God's existence. In Jacobi it is really a question of the same abstractions of mediation and immediacy as appear in the science of logic. We shall have to look into the logical categories of mediation and immediacy. All inquiries lead back to logic. Knowing [as faith] is determined for Jacobi as immediate knowing over against finite mediated "knowing." Yet both are called knowing. It is a question of their opposition, which lies in the determinations of immediacy and mediation. To be mediated is to pass through an other—the mediation of something is the canceling of itself in favor of its other, immediacy. It turns out that immediacy and mediation are unseparated and indeed inseparable.

We find even in experience that immediate faith contains mediation within itself. Some have tried reducing metaphysics to *psychology*. There are many ways of shoving philosophy—the contemplation of the determinations on which philosophy upon and for itself depends—off to the side. We know by experience many, many things immediately, but we ourselves are *conscious* of knowing them only by the mediation of our immediate knowledge. Mathematicians know immediately what relationships hold in the triangle, in other words they know them by heart. But we know very well that going and passing through proofs have preceded such immediate knowing. As human beings we have a large number of experiences in life by which we know things immediately. Such knowledge is an immediately given result mediated by the experience of life. We know very well that such immediate knowledge is a result of life.

(§66) It follows that the immediacy of knowledge absolutely results from mediated knowing. The parents as viewed by the children are immediately given. What is immediate is whatever we start out from, but then it is just as essentially mediated as it is immediate. I am now immediately in Berlin, but this fact is mediated by the fact that I have either traveled here or was born here. "I am" expresses the same immediacy, but then falls back again into mediation. The point is really quite trivial and is generally known, although certain individuals who are overly educated nevertheless align themselves against it.

(§67) The immediate knowing of God, of customary ethical life, originally exists in seed within the human spirit, as a potentiality. This immediate knowing is brought to consciousness only in a mediated way through education. The more abstract side of education is the spirit's inner [world-historical] development taken in general. It is here a question of fact, a matter of experience. In baptism in the Christian religion, an essential condition is that what lies upon itself within the child comes to develop within him. In Plato this development takes the form of *recollection*. He says that nothing comes to us by being introduced from the outside, everything is only recollection. To state the essence of the matter, our souls before their transfer into our bodies enjoyed divine intuition. That intuition has now [in this life] become unconscious, but our souls recall it once more to themselves in their encounter with the objects of this world, which contain something of what they earlier intuited.

People have spoken of *innate ideas* [which are found in Plato]. In particular *Locke* has polemicized against them. According to him, everything a human being knows comes from *experience*—the very opposite of innate ideas. But the very expression "innate ideas" is already misleading. The sense of the expression should be that certain ideas properly belong to the human spirit. But innate ideas are then refuted by the objection that all human beings would accordingly have to have the same innate ideas. That would be correct if "innate" were understood in its natural sense. But what is innate in a human being does not necessarily emerge as a *natural* development; rather, a human being must himself bring forth this development within himself by his own activity. Whether a human being realizes his or her vocation as a human being or fails is a matter of free will. But whether a human being ever actively exercises free will is essentially conditioned, since it is mediated by the education and culture of his or her time. Just as the fact that one has such and such opinions is mediated by one's culture, so whether one actively attains to that last and most extreme of abstractions[, namely free will,] is also a result of the culture at hand.

(§68) Whatever we are we are immediately. But our immediate being is mediated. But beyond this general relationship of mediation and immediacy lies a still closer relationship. The knowing of God and of things divine is a fact of human consciousness, and such knowledge comes to be stated as our rise above what is sensory. To rise above something is to leave it behind and to pass over to something else. In so rising, then, we end in faith in what is divine. Since the path of faith consists in rising above what is sensory, its path is one of media-tion: rising above sensory being precedes the result of faith. One gets to a second thing only insofar as one starts out from a first. A human being exhibits natural knowing [*Wissen*] and willing, and this begin-ning is the ground by the mediation of which we pass over into faith in God. Faith results from this rise. Sensory knowledge and willing come first and then mediate the belief in God.

(§69) Let us now go into the content of immediate knowledge more precisely. Consider the mere content of such knowledge, as in its acqui-sition by a human being. This acquisition in its existence, as a fact, con-tains mediation. The fact contains, we have seen, mediation for itself on its own account. But when we take this content of mediation for itself, we have something abstract. We leave out part of the whole. The con-tent of immediate knowledge is the representation of God, which is im-mediately connected with his being. The content of this knowledge is said to include the claim that the representation of God essentially in-cludes this being. God can only be represented as enjoying being, and that is the content of this immediate knowledge. The mere thought of God by itself is not true, but becomes true only through the determina-tion of his being. Or, inversely, if being is taken for itself on its own ac-count, it, too, is nothing true. The thought [of God] is apprehended in its truth only as being, while being is true being only as divine being.

What is already present here is the *idea*,[27] which stands opposed to the determination of immediate knowledge [§70]. The content of the immediate knowledge of God and its representation gains its truth only from its connection with being, which likewise gets its truth only by being connected with God—in other words, being is nothing apart from being mediated. Each *is* only through mediation by its other. The truth is only both determinations in their inseparability.

If we speak of diverse determinations and wish to say merely the same thing of them all—namely that their inseparability *alone* is true—we of course assert their mediation by one another. But this sort of ab-stract assertion of mediation is empty of all thought. What our abstract assertion in fact says is the opposite of the non-empty proposition we are trying to state. If we hold in consciousness only the one side, [only the inseparability of the determinations,] the other side of the matter, what the diverse determinations themselves each express, is at once denied. This one-sidedness is readily taken up by the understanding, and the refutation of it emerges in our consideration of even the most trivial of particular determinations. Here philosophy has to do battle only with the abstractions of the understanding. In §71 and the fol-

27. The idea is treated in the concluding sections of part one of the *Encyclopae-dia*. See Hegel, Logic, pp. 280–96.

lowing paragraphs, still further general determinations based merely on such a *foundation of immediacy* are set in relief.

(§71) For Jacobi it is the fact of consciousness that is to pass as the truth. If something is a fact of our consciousness, *it is so,* and we should therefore stick with it. That is the principle. The assurance is given that I find such and such in my consciousness, and so it is established as a fact. Yet this does not imply that what I find in my consciousness is present in *my* consciousness alone as an idiosyncrasy, as something peculiar to me. Rather, what I find in my consciousness is said to belong to the very nature of consciousness, i.e., to the consciousness of all human beings generally. Or, more correctly put, it belongs to the self-concept of the consciousness.

But we immediately notice, in this connection, that such an allegedly immediate claim needs to be proven, that it must be derived from the nature of the consciousness. Rid yourself of such mediation and you spare yourself the proof. However, anyone surely has the right to reply "But this is not a fact of my consciousness." One proof for the existence of God that used to be strutted out was that all the peoples in the world believe in God. What immense authority must now be enjoyed by humankind for any individual who would have a different conviction! Freedom, however, aligns itself against the authority of the greater number. What I believe is my own business. This proof was thus abandoned because it failed to find any basis in the nature of spirit [*Geist*] generally. Many individuals and peoples are known who have no representation of God at all. But this appeal to all the world's peoples is nonetheless worth more than me appealing to my own individual consciousness.

(§72) The other consequence [of appealing to the consciousness of the individual or a people] is that all superstition and worship of false gods comes to be explained as true worship. None who pray to the steer or monkey base their worship on reason and grounds. But their immediate consciousness of the validity of their belief is the same as occurs in all religions. With that the whole foundation of morality is raised up. The evil man finds such and such drives and inclinations within himself, and so believes they are right. They are a matter in his opinions which, insofar as they are believed, are thus explained to be justified. To be sure, we must respect the beliefs of every human being, but what is essentially in question is the content of belief. It is said that even among the heathen there have been good human beings. That is no doubt true, but the question is how right and wrong are grounded in religion.

In more recent times any arbitrary interest of action is often made into its very purpose. *Irony* extends over everything, as one allows any assertion at all to pass as valid merely insofar some individual feels a need for it. But I cannot accept this result and allow anything to pass as valid if my *own* empty self-certainty is what is ultimate, and if it alone gives its legitimate stamp of approval to everything. That is the point of [Jacobi's] immediate knowing: nothing is essentially determined for me [independently of my arbitrary will]. Even those who have not reached awareness of this ultimate ironic principle nonetheless have that very irony as their underlying principle.

(§73) But those same people, following Jacobi, say that something is immediately present in our self-consciousness that irony cannot touch, namely that we know immediately that God *is*. But we have no wish to know *what he is*. Whatever he is, is first introduced by his purpose. But knowing a purpose of God, hence knowing what we call a divine attribute, would be a form of knowledge. It would be determinate knowledge. We can lose our way in declamations about truth and God, but we do not want to know what such divine attributes are. My subjective activity alone remains to give determination to this thing without content. The Athenians dedicated an altar to the unknown God. The present immediate knowledge gets no further than those Athenians. For nothing is known of God

(§74) Immediate knowing seems to have cast away all limitation, all mediation, and yet its immediacy is a limited one. Even the infinite is limited if it is singled out all by itself, since it has, beyond it, the finite as its limitation. If I apprehend what is general and what is particular, each for itself, what is general is still only one of two determinations, so each side in the contrast turns out to be particular. That leads to an important reflection, an inversion about which the understanding knows nothing. Because the immediacy is so one-sided, its content is finite. What by its content is general is made by this form of immediacy into something abstract. If immediacy is to fall to God, all mediation will be denied of him. God is thus indeterminate, purely equal to himself alone, purely abstract. God, apprehended merely as immediate, is merely equal to himself. But if we go on to say that God created a world, that world is already something other than him, which has being only insofar as it is posited by him. However, even though that world in time comes to be raised up [in the Incarnation] beyond this otherness, the world as other than God nevertheless has been posited, and that is a limit [upon God's mere immediacy]. God must be grasped as mediating himself merely with himself in his other, determining himself with himself. God is known only as *spirit*. Immediacy by itself makes the universal a mere abstraction. Philosophy has to refute mere abstraction—what is abstract has no truth to it. All mediation is left out in [abstract] being. But it is not the nature of the finite merely to be by itself. What is finite necessarily has a relation with something else outside it. A living human being is also conditioned, bearing reference to an other, and so is also mediated. Spirit [as consciousness] is likewise conditioned, namely by being conscious of something else. Consciousness is the being of spirit as conditioned.

Spirit in truth lies in mediating itself with itself. If we stop with what is finite, it is conditioned. The finite is mediated. If I now say "The finite has being," I pronounce it falsely to lack mediation, which is untrue. By "is" we express immediacy. There is no alteration, transition into something else, in "is." All alteration is cancelled in the "is." The understanding is the apprehension of something merely determinate, so that it is taken up only in its relationship to itself. The thing is thus made fast. Yet no finite content stays fixed, everyone falls subject to alteration. Contained in the Kantian antinomies is the principle that the understanding contradicts itself. This is also the principle of immediacy, which essentially lies in the understanding.

(§75 and the following) It is presupposed by Jacobi that [finite] knowing proceeds in the second realm of mediation, in the realm of what is conditioned, and that this is the only kind of thinking there is. But his presupposition is false. For still another kind of thinking exists, which the science of logic illustrates. What is true is this third realm [*das Dritte*] about which immediacy [or immediate knowing, the first realm,] knows nothing; God is both true as immediate, but he at once transmutes himself into mediation. This is the eternal process.

(§76) If we compare immediacy [or immediate knowing] with the former[, classical] metaphysics, Descartes says that being and thinking are inseparable: *cogito ergo sum*. The same assertion is also expressed in Jacobi's immediate knowing. But the inseparability of thought and being is not merely immediate—since thinking is true only by the mediation of being, while being is true only by the mediation of thinking. As Descartes already says, we know immediately[, i.e., innately] of the thought of God and of his existence. [Jacobi says that] we know immediately of the existence of external bodies, and it is in this that sensory consciousness consists. But there is also mediation in such consciousness. If I know a sheet of paper, I know this sheet only by the mediation of my consciousness.

(§77) But now consider the differences between the two points of view [of Descartes and Jacobi]. In the first place, the point of view of modern philosophy[, unlike Jacobi's point of view,] started out and proceeded quite *innocently*. The Cartesian philosophy originated in the principle of the inseparability of being and thinking, and then proceeded to knowledge of a more developed sort. Descartes began to philosophize freely, simply by thinking, and by thinking objects he apprehended them and held them in thought. He is in this respect the true founder of modern philosophy. Yet his philosophy, in its execution, is [contrary to Jacobi's in that it is] solely a philosophy of what is finite. He holds in mind two thought determinations: *thinking* and *extension*. Whatever is extended is material. Thinking, for him, is thus so limited that it never gets beyond determination by whatever exists naturally as something material. Descartes became stuck at the level of mechanical being[, the mechanical being of nature]. Yet from there he proceeded to knowledge of a wider sort that did not restrict scientific knowing [*Wissen*] to the principle by which mediation is allowed no validity. What God is we cannot simply know [*erkennen*]—here in scientific knowing the demand for mediation immediately arises. This second difference between the two thinkers is that we cannot [according to Jacobi] know [*wissen*] of God in any determinate or necessary fashion. For Jacobi we proceed [in "knowledge" as *Erkennen*] in the usual manner, dealing only with what is finite. That is also the result of the Kantian philosophy: we know only *appearances*—whether appearances have being or not does not come into question. The manner of "knowing" remains entirely the same throughout. The abstract determinations [of appearance] have no hold on the content of knowledge. The empirical sciences of the finite come to be pursued in this very way. But Jacobi's standpoint of immediacy dispenses with all the considerations of method [which preoccupied Descartes]. Yet we must nonetheless carry on with the sciences of theology and morality. If we wished to proceed by Jacobi's principle, the entire dogmatic content of theology would be reduced to the bare proposition that we immediately know [*wissen*] that God is. Yet it will still be admitted that God has deigned to reveal himself to us. But from this Jacobian standpoint we make no attempt to know [by what is finite—*Erkennen*] anything that is true of God. Because we are not to *philosophize* [as contrasted to having a bare philosophy of immediate intuition], no method is acknowledged. For method strives after a true procedure for thinking—which is nothing other than true philosophizing, knowing something [truly]. Such philosophizing is tossed aside. But in that we cannot really remain stuck in immediate knowing, we proceed in an entirely uncritical and unphilosophical fashion, with neither rule nor measure, with no science of what we are doing. Philosophy is in particular tossed aside because it cannot really rest content, as Jacobi prefers, with mere assurances. Philosophy cannot be based on merely giving assurances, on imagining that human beings merely speak out of moral feeling [*Gemut*], that they merely speak feelings [*Gefühl*]. The question of philosophy that must be put to a human being with feeling is "Is the feeling [*Emfindung*] true?" By the principle of immediate knowing, however, one just allows it to be true without further inquiry.

Either we have immediate knowledge [*Wissen*] or we have knowledge along with representations that mediate it. This Jacobian disjunction assumes that there is no third type of knowledge. But a third type most certainly exists, i.e., knowledge that contains mediation every bit as much as immediacy. God is simple identity with himself, and that is the moment of non-mediation. But he is equally mediation of himself with himself through what is other than himself. Everything contains the moment of mediation, whether mediation within what is finite or a thing's mediation through itself, with itself [in its other]. Yet Jacobi pre-supposes that either one or the other holds, but not both.

The above standpoints are thus the three standpoints [preceding the science of logic] about which the interest of present time revolves[: the appeal to innocent immediate thinking, to skeptical mediated thinking, and back to immediate thinking polemically directed against skeptical thinking]. The interest of philosophy itself is to know the matter at hand as it upon itself is. *First,* the *naive metaphysics* [of the ancients] lacked all consciousness of the criteria, categories, or thoughts by the use of which such philosophizing naively moved about. The result was the contradic-tions in which such thinking came to be caught up. *Second* comes the separation of thought and its content, the standpoint according to which the content and thinking are two quite different sorts of things. Thinking [from this second standpoint illustrated by Kant] is incapable of winning the depth that comes by entering into its objects. Rather, it remains here on the one side [of appearance], while something else stands over there on the far side. A gulf comes to be assumed between thinking and its ob-ject. The incoherence of it at once lies in the fact that thinking, since it is subjective, is explained as untrue, as not being of anything that is true. The other over yonder, which has being in itself, is something empty, and so we determine it to be merely this abstract being. The *third* standpoint is once again[, but polemically and reflectively,] the unification from which naive philosophizing proceeded, [according to which] thinking and being are immediately one.

(§78) The presuppositions of this third standpoint are now to be given up as we enter the science of logic. What is to be given up is the immediacy of knowledge with mediation set over against it. [This op-position] is but an arbitrary assurance [on Jacobi's part]. Indeed *all* presuppositions are now to be given up. In the science of logic these thought forms will be examined in their totality. Immediacy and me-diation, being and thinking—all these thought forms will be thor-oughly examined. In Jacobi's reasoning they are only used without being examined. As Descartes already said, *de omnibus dubitandum est*—one must start out from doubt, in fact from despair. Doubt ex-presses rather an external circumambulating, an uncovering of con-tradiction and the unrest of contradiction. To be sure, this unrest and contradiction are what drive us to philosophy. Ancient skepticism was not merely a doubting but, so to speak, a despairing which harbored the complete misery of the human spirit. This skepticism had as its re-sult a total stilling of spirit, *ataraxia.* Skepticism proved above all that nothing is fixed, so that no one is licensed to invest him- or herself heart and soul in anything. For everything lacks being to the same degree that it has it. If everything is fixed, if everything is frozen fast, by the same token nothing within me can be brought into motion. Skepticism comes to a stop in the abstraction of *nothing*. An introduction to philosophy can indeed be effected by showing that everything contains within itself contradiction. That would be a joyless path to take, but it would also be quite superfluous, since this negative [skeptical] side is already present within the science of logic itself.

[More Exact Concept and] Division of the [Science of] Logic[28]

(§79) The expression "laws of the thought" in the science of logic is really a misnomer. When we speak of *laws of the will*, they are only [external] laws, assuming that the particular [impulse] stands opposed to the universal will according to the very concept of that will. When we consider thinking as it is upon and for itself, it is not subject to any external laws, but is self-legislative. Logic is to be considered in these lectures from three consecutive points of view, which are not to be viewed, however, as parts of a whole. One cannot limit consideration of logic to merely one of its sides. The *first side* which it presents is the abstract, understandable [*verständig*] side.

The *second side* is dialectical or negatively rational. Immediacy and mediation are the two thought determinations corresponding to these first two sides. The understanding sets up these two thought determinations as separate, but it is still something else to exhibit the second determination as negative, to show that these thought determinations of the understanding are not so very fixed, but rather are finite, transitory, a confounding of these very determinations and of the understanding itself. The *third side* of the logic is the speculative or positively rational. It brings the first two determinations together in their unity, unseparated from each other.

(§80) The *understanding* holds each determination fast. I hold the finite over to the one side, and the infinite over on the other. For example, the cause is held on the one side, and the effect on the other. The understanding is one-sided, and it thus presents a false apprehension of things in opposition to philosophy. The understanding holds fast to one thing, and must give it validity over against its other. A man who thinks he must hold his destiny fixedly in mind is a man of the understanding who holds to one thing, and who does not allow himself to be distracted by any of the other good and excellent things along his path in life. We employ the understanding in dealing with all our concepts in determining them

---

28. As its last paragraph shows, this section, which is presented as a *preview* of the science of logic, may be better understood as a *review*, after reading the whole logic.

fixedly, in defining them. But if we limit ourselves to the understanding, we only have hold of the series of determinations as it appears in the logic of the understanding, which only gives definitions [or defining determinations]. For example, to be a cause is merely to be such and such, and to be an effect is simply to be yet something else. In this way we can easily transform the logic of *reason* into that of the *understanding*.

(§81) What is dialectical is the passage of such determinations into their opposites. Passage to a thing's opposite is commonly viewed as the result of hunting about it externally to find its opposite. But true dialectic is the determinate apprehension of something according to the determination to which it is destined. True dialectic peers into such a definition as is provided by the understanding and contemplates what is contained therein, whereupon it results that, without anything being brought in from the outside, the definition by its very content contradicts itself. This does not occur by comparing one determination externally with another. It rather transpires simply within the first determination itself. That is what Plato and the ancients called contemplating something upon and for itself. It is one thing, for example, to see many an external thing, each of them striking this or that person in the eye. It is quite another to contemplate beauty by its very self-concept, to contemplate the good upon and for itself, and so on.

The Platonic dialectic is mixed [in with this dialectical side of the science of logic]: in part objects are contemplated as they are upon themselves, and in part the contradiction in objects as they are upon themselves is brought forward through something else which is likewise fixedly held in view. The end result, then, is, that we no longer have anything fixed in mind. At this point the whole thus remains negative. *Socrates* in particular sought to exhibit contradictions in conventional principles and opinions, and to challenge people to deeper insight. The dialectic is the *immanent* [self-activity of the object of thought] going beyond itself, but this activity remains within the scope of the original determination itself.

The ancient skeptics in particular practiced this dialectic, in which a particular application[, namely a counter-example,] is set in opposition to a general assertion. But theirs was an external dialectic. However, the real dialectic of the general assertion is immanent in that it has come to show contradiction within the self-concepts themselves. Such immanent contradictions go though all the sciences. *Modern skepticism* is very different from *ancient skepticism*. Modern skepticism[, e.g., Hume,] believes it has hold of the truth in whatever is sensory, while ancient skepticism showed how whatever is sensory is precisely for that reason untrue. The end result with which the ancient skeptics came to a stop is *nothing*. But they took this result to be *abstract nothing*. However, this view of the result is one-sided. To put it simply, the result is admittedly nothing, but it is nothing of a certain determination [e.g., something bright], and with that is a *determinate nothing* [i.e., nothing dim]. Where such a result comes from must, in our science of logic, be retained in mind. The result is not to be taken up without its derivation. It is a determinate nothing, but this negative determination has its own *content*, so that nothing at once contains an affirmation[, e.g., it is nothing dim, but is affirmatively something bright instead]. So we must not break off merely with nothing. From the infinitely many contradictions [of the diverse thought determinations of the understanding] we retain only nothing, but it is never the same nothing. This points to the *positive* result of whatever is dialectical. But how what is dialectical is distinguished from what is understandable [*verständig*], which is where we started out, we shall see in the sequel.

(§82) The third speculative side of the science of logic is a simple summation of what has already gone before. The contradiction has vanished. The contradictory determinations are the premises [or assumptions], and within them nothing retains determinate form. We must not stop simply with the nothing, since nothing [of a particular determination] is now itself something determinate, and this content now constitutes something affirmative. But what is newly affirmative is present in form as well as in content, since our determinate nothing stands in the relation of simple self-reference [in that it determinately is what it is]. The result of going beyond contradiction is concrete, since it is the oneness of different determinations. That is what is *positively rational*, in contrast to what is dialectical or *negatively* rational. The consciousness of contradiction, our consciousness that dialectical negation bears affirmation upon itself, is the resolution of the contradiction, which is what is concrete. This resolution is not the abstract oneness of something with itself, but is the reconciliation of the dialectical contradictories. Harmony is not just abstract oneness but the unity [of different determinations] which must be harmonious. The different notes must sound together in unison. Only harmony can be concrete: a single note by itself contains no contradiction, but it has no value either. Harmony is concrete unity. It is positively rational, and is alone in holding truth. God is God by containing within himself what is concrete. To be a speculative logician is to apprehend opposite determinations within their unity. This is what the understanding has such a tough time with, since it is always holding the determinations outside one another.

However, the truth is first the dialectical activity of showing contradiction, and hence of showing the different determinations as transitory. The process of the transitions is what holds truth. Both determinations in the transition are restless, raising themselves beyond themselves [into their unity], and yet they are both present in the course of the process. Here we reach the *speculative* moment of the process. It is not the oneness of a determination with itself alone, nor the opposition of the two determinations alone, but both together. It is what is affirmative as contained within the resolution of the contradiction. What is affirmative is affirmative by *negation of the negation*. Things in the world *are,* but we say they are finite. In saying they are finite we give expression to their self-negation. Negation of the negation is then the negation of this self-negation, which is what is affirmative as it is constantly bringing itself forth. The I is this simple negation of the negation. I behold an object, I hold to it in representation, but in doing so I no longer [remain merely] with myself but am one with an object that negated me. But what negates me, the object, is *my* thought object, my representation. So I negate what negates me, I make something out of it that is mine, and with that what has negated me has been negated [in its negation of me].

This process eventuating in negation of the negation is my spiritual life, but it is also my corporeal survival. Rest is death. What is living is this very process. I am hungry, and the lack of food is a negation [of me]. I satisfy this negation, and that is the self-affirmation arising by negation of the negation[, i.e., by the negation of my need]. What is speculative is to know objects as they are upon themselves, to apprehend them as a process. What is speculative cannot be expressed in simple judgments. The speculative process cannot be contained in a fixed proposition, for any such proposition is one-sided. What is true is the continuing process with its three moments given in advance. But we must first see and prove upon the showing of that logic itself that this is the nature of the science of logic. That is our course. The *method* of the logic is the absolute rhythm of all that is alive, the truth of everything in particular spheres as also in general, inclusive spheres. Spinoza said that we must apprehend things under the aspect of eternity [*in specie aeterni*]. But eternity for him is the rigid substance. True eternity is this true speculative process, once we quietly allow the content to come into its own fullness and contemplate it upon its own self-showing.

[I. Being]

We have before us the self-concept or, more determinately, the *idea*, and it is this in its various forms we must now consider [§83]. We cannot begin with the idea itself. We can only begin with completely simple, wholly immediate *being*. With whatever is *first* we have not yet proceeded to anything else. For mediation, two determinations are required, which are not yet present in what is only first, which is [only] immediate being. This beginning is not yet the self-concept, is not yet the idea in its full scope, but is the idea in its immediate form. The content of being posits itself additionally in the sequel to be only a particular determination, a form, the self-concept [still] merely in its immediacy. What is second [in relation to being], then, is the *essence* of being, mediation. We already have the determination that the essence of being is something *inner* in which we have abandoned what is *outer*. We have thus already gone beyond immediacy. The essence is the ground [of what is immediate]. (In bygone times, I have been what I have been. To have been is to be no more. Being in its essence has lost the immediacy of *being there*. The essence is the logical essence of being. The essence of my being, in one respect, is a determination of time, more precisely, the determination of times past.[29])

Being is what is straightaway simple and without difference. In the essence of being, its immediacy is interrupted. Its essence is, quite generally, reflected [in something else]. In its essence being is demoted to [mere] show, which itself comes to be something reflected in its essence. The essence of being has a being for itself, but in this being for itself it still bears reference to immediate being [as what is other than it]: the essence of being is not yet free. It is the realm of what is different, it is the sphere of *finitude* in general. Third comes the *self-concept at once upon and for itself*: it is the healing of the breach between immediate being and its essence, of reflection upon immediacy. What was showing forth is now mediation, being is immediate, but in the self-concept the two now find themselves united.

(§84) Being is the self-concept only as it [abstractly] at first is, [with its determinations arising] merely upon itself [and not for itself]. What is merely upon itself is still bottled up inside itself. It has not yet come out. What is still bottled up in this way is the driving force. It dispatches its determinations outside itself, into an element which is different from itself. The element of manifestation, in which the self-concept is [outwardly] realized, is only a one-sided determination of the self-concept. This element in which the self-concept thus unfolds is not yet the self-concept itself. The child is already rational, but only in

---

29. For example, a champion's essence includes what he or she *has* achieved, even if he or she no longer *immediately* displays the achievement. The achievement is still posited upon the individual as his or her non-immediate essence. The past achievement cannot be erased, but shows what the individual as a whole is capable of. (By extension, in essence a human being who has not yet died is already upon himself or herself dead. The individual is already as good as dead: being dead has already been calculated into the individual's essential potentiality. Because of all the human beings who have died in the past, death is already posited upon now living human beings as part of their non-immediate essence. The temporal determination of having died becomes the logical determination posited upon now living human beings. A human being's essence includes what past human beings in the end have turned out immediately to be. A temporal determination comes to be raised up beyond itself into part of the timeless logical essence of the individual.)

the sense that reason in the child is still merely [posited] upon the child. Reason comes to be posited [within itself, actually] only in the adult human being. What has being only as force is not yet present in its expression. Energy is then the process by which something brings itself to the point of self-manifestation. The determinations of the self-concept are first only determinations of being. In the logic of the essence the same determinations occur, but they recur as reflected, as [externally] bearing reference to one another.

The difference [between the logic of being and of essence] is this. Being and non-being are the simplest moments in the logic of being. The same moments can be expressed [in the logic of essence as explicitly referring to each other,] as *the positive and the negative*. There is already a difference between these two moments in the logic of essence and those of *being and non-being*. The negative is the negative of something, of the positive, while the positive [unlike being] is itself posited as having the determination of referring [to its opposite]. Whatever is positive has being over against its negative. What is positive is a being that is posited as reflected in something else, as bearing reference to something else. For it essentially belongs to the determination of whatever is positive *not* to be negative. That is the difference [between the distinction of positive and negative and that of being and non-being].

In the logic of the self-concept these determinations [of the positive and the negative] recur in their unity. In the sphere of mediation, which is the logic of essence, the other still appears with the determination of being other. In this sphere, reference to an *other* still has its place. In the logic of the self-concept, no opposition between the universal and the particular remains. The universal is all-encompassing, with the other particular determinations present within it. The particular is not the general. But the species[, e.g., rational animal] contains the genus [animal]: the particularization of what is general contains what is general. That is the unity of the moments of the self-concept.

The further determination in the logic of being [beyond determinate being] is the transition of something determinate into something else. Alteration in the logic of being consists in the fact that being, as something determinate, becomes something else. So what is other than something is likewise something. In the logic of the essence, reference to an other also occurs, but does so immediately[, without transition]. An other—for example, the effect—belongs to the very meaning of "cause," to the very concept of being a cause. By contrast, if we return to the logic of being and consider again something and its other, the other is also something [but is not a different thought determination in the way that an effect is a different thought determination from a cause]. Something as something is not affected by the fact that it is another something. Yet in all subordinate spheres [of the science of logic] we have the same basic development [appearing in distinct forms], and the sphere of this development is the totality.

In the logic of essence, reference to an other occurs [without transition into something else by the alteration of something given]. To the unaltered meaning of "cause," to its very concept, there belongs its other, the effect. Every sphere is a totality, a distinct development of the self-concept. We can also start out from the self-concept, the totality in which all its moments are posited. Being and essence are then the two distinct sides of the self-concept. The self-concept is the unity of these two determinations as posited. Every determination taken for itself on its own account[, posited without the immediate positing of its other,] is one-sided. The determinations each first attain to their truth only within the self-concept itself. If we take the self-concept and consider it from one side, we have the categories of being, and further on [when we take it from the other side] we have the categories of essence. But the self-concept [contrary to being] is not immediate, but is the mediation of itself with itself. The spheres of being and essence are but the mediation through which the self-concept emerges as the result. What comes to be proven thereby is that the self-concept is their truth.

The logic of the self-concept, in its self-determination in the logic of essence, clears the way for itself in two ways. First, self-concept posits itself upon the solid ground of being external to itself, and its further activity then consists in proceeding from outside itself back within itself. As it posits itself as the result of this activity of directing itself outside itself, it determines itself to be something that passes merely for an external element. The self-concept posits, onto this alleged external ground, figurations of itself. The logic of being likewise contains figurations of the self-concept. When being is no longer external [to the self-concept], it withdraws within itself. The self-concept thus explicates itself [in the logics of being and essence]. Being within the self-concept is no longer immediate being. It has ceased to be immediate to become a mere form within the self-concept. Being is no longer a ground [external to the self-concept] on which the logic of the self-concept inscribes its figurations. As soon as we elaborate further upon [the logic of] being, what arises is no longer mere being. Being raises itself beyond itself up into its essence, which in turn raises itself up into the self-concept. Yet being does not pass over into its essence immediately, but rather contains [as posited] upon itself its development into its totality. It is only by withdrawing back into itself that being raises itself into its essence. Just so does the essence of being also return back into itself, thus becoming the self-concept. This essence, posited outwardly before our gaze in the completion of its development, in the full show of itself, is the self-concept. The beginning of the whole development is at once its end. The development does not go off into the infinite. Its progress is rather a circle.[30]

(§85) The logical determinations can be applied to God. But God is then represented as the subject, while what we say of God is the predicate. In determining God metaphysically, God is present in pure thought, in the simple element of thinking. It can be said that, in the science of logic, the eternal essence of God is exposited as it still was before the creation of the sensory world.[31] In the creation of the world, the world as distinguished from the logic is externally present, posited as externalized thoughts. What emerges with the creation of the world is the fact that the distinctions [between thought determinations] are no longer posited within the ground of their unity[, i.e., within the self-concept]. Yet only the first determinations [in the logic of essence, e.g., cause], not the [correlative] second determinations[, e.g., effect], can be regarded as determinations of God. For the second determination is always a determination in differentiation [from the first determination or logical category by which God is identified]. The first determination is immediate, while the second one constitutes the sphere posited in its differentiation from the first. Within every simple first determination, [e.g., ground,] what is determinately different from it[, e.g, the consequence of the ground] is at once also present, but is at first present without yet being explicitly posited. In the second determination, finitude [and with it contradiction] again enters. The third determination is the unity of the first and the second, in which the contradiction is resolved. Thus only the first determination [in any pair of correlative determinations in the logic of essence] corresponds to what we first understand by "God." The progression is as follows. The beginning is simple, immediate. There the self-concept remains merely posited upon itself in its immediacy. The progression lies in the self-concept increasingly coming out into the open, while what came first[, the self-concept as being or the abstract essence of being] recedes back within itself[, i.e., within the total self-concept]. Every newly emerging concept is more concretely determinate than its predecessor. We are always carrying everything that went before along with ourselves into what is new, but everything prior is, within what is new, put in its

30. Hegel appears to mean, in saying that the science of logic is a circle that does not veer off into the infinite, that the system of logical categories is complete. Yet with each new, expanded edition of the *Encyclopaedia of the Philosophical Sciences* (1817, 1827, 1830), though the logic remains the same, the philosophies of nature and spirit which follow come to be stuffed with more empirical particularization of the logical concepts. Since the entire system is held within the circle of logical concepts, it does not veer off into the infinite either, but the circle of the system, unlike that of the logic, is empirically ever widening.

31. This statement has been used to sponsor a theistic interpretation of the science of logic.

determinate place. Whereas, in what preceded, each [momentarily im-immediate] determination [identifying God in its own time] passed as ulti-mate, it is now demoted into being only a moment of the self-concept.

We start with *being*, but matters at once proceed further. [1.] We first come upon *determinate* being, being as determinations, immediate [deter-minateness], i.e., *quality*. To be is to be a determination, but in the form of immediacy. [2.] Second come differences [between qualities], and with that the determination [of quality] is raised up beyond itself. The determi-nation of quality is no longer absolutely speaking what is, but now passes for itself into indifference [to a continuing qualitative determination], and so becomes *quantity*. An underlying state[, namely quality,] remains [through quantitative increase or decrease in the amount of units of that quality]. The size [of an aggregate] can be arbitrarily determined as such or such [without alternation of the common quality of its members]. 3. [Third] is *measure*, an external and indifferent [quantitative] determina-tion which has an enduring being[, e.g., as a ratio of a natural force or ele-ment that remains constant through proportionate quantitative changes in the terms of the ratio]. Measure is the unity of both determinations[, i.e., quality and quantity]. God, it has been said,[32] is measure, a fixed boundary [beyond which lies what is disproportionate or measureless]. Measure is [the highest concept of] God within the logic of mere being.[33]

II. [Essence]

Essence first appears to be as abstract as being. But essence is reflection. Being is raised up beyond itself into the mere show of its essence. Es-sence is a correlation [between itself and its show], but it is at once only by the mediation of being raising itself up into this show. Essence, first showing forth within itself, lies in the determination of *reflection*. But es-sence does not only show forth within itself [as essence]. It is also grounds of something further, the raising up of the mediation [within the abstract essence of being] beyond itself into immediacy, into *exis-tence*. Existence is being once again, but this time it is being as posited immediacy, immediacy posited by its ground. ("Being," "being there" [*Dasein*], and "existence" are usually used synonymously. But in the sci-ence of logic these expressions are employed differently, designating dif-ferent thought determinations.) The other of the essence of being is gen-erally *appearance*. That essence must appear, which is to say that existence is the essence of being showing forth [in what is immediate, not simply within itself]. What comes in the third place in the logic of essence is the unity of both essence and appearance, which is *actuality*. The sphere of

32. E.g., by the Pythagoreans, who viewed God as cosmic harmony.

33. The *Psalms* may express a view of God as the measureless, but such a view already falls within the logic of the transcendent essence of being.

mediation [within the abstract essence of being] comes to be posited in appearance. God is actual, and within actuality he explicates himself. Actuality is more than mere being. Explicated actuality is *necessity*, which is the totality and truth of essence. Necessity is essence [1.] determining itself completely within itself, [2.] showing forth and appearing, and [3.] posited in unity with its appearance.

III. The Self-Concept

Necessity is upon itself *freedom*. [1.] What is free is the self-concept enjoying being absolutely by itself. Absolute necessity posited as simple reference by oneself to oneself is freedom. The self-concept first shows forth precisely within itself. The development of the self-concept, insofar as that development is still held within itself, is the self-concept's division within itself. This development of the self-concept is [a.] *judgment* [*Urteil*], and [b.] the totality of the self-concept, the *syllogism*. [In the syllogism] the self-concept has raised the difference [of subject and predicate in judgment] up beyond itself, and has posited difference as having been so raised up. This closure of the self-concept with itself is the self-concept in its totality. 2. The further opposition, the difference, through which the self-concept loses itself in *objectivity*, is the freedom of the self-concept falling away from itself into objectivity. But objectivity includes the positing of oneself as the [subjective] self-concept, it bears a reference to subjectivity. With that come notions of the *utility* [of objects], wisdom, and providence [working its way through the objective world]. [3.] What comes in the third place is the *idea*, the absolute, the idea as the most concrete determination of the absolute [on the level of pure thought].[34] The idea is objectivity taken back into the self-concept, the unity of subjectivity and objectivity. The idea is first [determinate as] *life*, second as *knowledge*, but rather as finite knowledge, as the self-concept distinguishing itself [as object] from itself, with still no consciousness of what it is after. Third, absolute knowledge comes to be the consciousness of the idea, of which one form is science, another art, and still another religion. In absolute knowledge, the self-concept, the idea, brings itself forth as self-aware. The logic thus concludes with the self-concept of the logic itself.

That is the précis of our path, the development of which arises out of itself. The above breakdown of the path into its separate sections will be self-determining only in the exposition of the science of logic itself. Such divisions into sections must for the present be left, to some degree, as matter-of-fact demarcations without justification within themselves. Their justification will now rather fall within the science of logic itself.

34. "The idea," translating *die Idee*, is a common way of referring to Plato's form of forms. But by the end of this paragraph we are given an Aristotelian explanation of this pure divine form as self-conscious thought thinking itself.

BEING

1

Being

Being is the self-concept [*Begriff*] as it [exhibits its determinations] merely upon itself [taken abstractly]. It is the self-concept as it develops in the element of immediacy. All determinations of the self-concept take the form of immediacy. However, reference at once enters into this immediacy, showing forth in an other, but this reference itself has the character of an immediate transition into an other. Whatever passes into an other in this way is unfree, and comes to be annihilated. Being lies precisely in such an absence of freedom, in passage into an other, [i.e., into nothing,] into becoming, [and then] into determinate being.

Such determinate being is first given out to be the quale, *quality* [τὸ τί ἦν εἶναι], as Aristotle says. Something is constituted by such and such a nature, and if it loses that nature its very being falls by the wayside. Its [qualitative] determination is inwardly connected with its very being. In the second determination within the logic of being, [the determination of quantity,] that inner connection of being and quality is no longer present. In *quantity* being occurs with a determination that is indifferent.[1] The third determination [within the logic of being] is *measure,* which generally also falls under magnitude. Magnitude is indifferent [to quality due to the self-same quality of its units], but in measure [relative] magnitudes[, i.e., ratios] are themselves qualitative. If, within measure, the [relative] magnitude comes to be modified, its quality itself gets lost.

1. I.e., with a determination that does not contrast with another qualitative determination, that continues in qualitatively identical ones.

85

I.A. Quality

Something in being determinate is the negation of something else. Something is *determinate* [§86], and with that has a limit. Every being there [*Dasein*] is finite by the very fact of being determinate. Determinateness is limitation, and thereby is finitude. Whatever is finite is also the negation of the infinite.

What now follow are a. *Being*, b. *Being there*, finitude and infinity, c. *Being for itself*. The infinite is the finite negated, while the finite has as its quality the negation of the infinite. If I say "I have being for myself," I mean that I do not depend on any other being. I negate this being out there that would negate me. The finite is *being for an other*, the infinite is *being for itself*. That is the sphere of quality.

The categories and thought determinations [examined here, initial categories in the logic of being,] are most familiar to us since we are thinking beings and they penetrate all our representations and language. To that extent they are what is most pedestrian, most commonplace, the best known. They are without a doubt familiar to us, but what is in question is coming to know what their nature is. For we employ them unconsciously.

I.A.a. Being

What has been presented up to now is only in introduction to the science of logic. Only now do we enter into its content. The question is: with what are we to begin? In what does the determination of thought lie, whatever it might be, with which we are to begin? In the other sciences there is no difficulty concerning where to begin. Their presuppositions, the objects themselves, are simply there. But in this science we also have a presupposition, which is simply the consideration of thinking as well as of what is thought. Our presupposition is the contemplation of the simple activity of mind [*Geist*] —not willing or feeling, but the simple activity of thinking. In transposing ourselves into this standpoint we abstract from all particular, determinate representations. The beginning is to be made, therefore, in this pure, completely simple element. The sensory realm is something external, spatial and temporal, while thinking has the character of universality, simplicity. That we adopt this standpoint is, in this respect, an act of our own will.

So what now first arises to be thought, first in the sense of being nothing other than the most abstract and purest thought object? Only the subsequent progression will bring in determination. As we pass over from one determination to another, we still find ourselves with determinateness.[2] What is first must be simplicity, immediacy, with-

---

2. Determinateness is the common character of different determinations.

out [any posited] reference to whatever is other than it, and in this respect it is most abstract, i.e., immediate—it must be *being* [§86].

We could also call our abstract starting point *pure thinking*, the pure activity of contemplation. And yet pure thinking is already a more concrete activity of our own mind, an activity of our [rational human] nature, of mind [νοῦς]. But this activity already contains unrest, it is already mediated. If we call something "simple," it is simple already in the reflected light of something else, since it bears reference to what is composite. The beginning, then, is what is completely *immediate, being* rather than thinking. We have to make our start with a beginning that is totally and purely beginning, not with the beginning as space, as number, and the like, but rather a completely indeterminate or abstract beginning, the beginning and only the beginning.

Should we now ask "What is the beginning?" it is apparent that the beginning itself is already something, but it is also *only* the beginning. What only begins to be is not yet, and yet [as a beginning] it already is. This beginning thus already contains the determinations of both being and nothing [§87], and, beyond that, perhaps the third determination that matters should proceed still further. But with a purely immediate beginning this further determination still falls by the wayside. We thus might already lapse into beginning with "the beginning" itself as already pointing to something that is to follow.

Being is, out and out, the pure beginning. Much can still be said in its regard, but it is all quite unnecessary. *Fichte* began with the proposition that I = I. For him it was a matter of making an absolute beginning with something totally certain. For *Schelling* it was a question of making such a beginning with the *absolute indifference* beheld in intellectual intuition. Or it might also be said that we must start with *God*. But with regard to "I = I" as the beginning, there is no certainty in it. For the I already implies consciousness—I say I know something—self-consciousness has already entered, which is already a further movement beyond mere being. Moreover, what is certain here in Fichte's philosophy is the subject, not the object. Again, if I speak of "absolute indifference" or "intellectual intuition," it all already consists in further, more concrete determinations than that of mere being.

If it is said that we should start with God, that is quite correct, but the question then becomes "What is God?" The simplest representation of God is that of mere being. We may give logical determinations out to be the determinations of God. We can give them out to be definitions of God.[3] But then in the beginning we have, for the purpose of defining

3. To be God appears throughout to be the all-embracing (and hence non-relative) absolute, i.e., that beyond which there is nothing. Each logical determination or category "defines" God, not by analyzing the bare concept of being God

God, only the most immediate determination of thinking, which is *being*. There is absolutely no further difficulty in the matter—being is totally simple. Essence is just as simple as being except that it already contains reflection upon something else.

Among the Greeks, philosophy also in reality began with being. The Eleatic school said that God is being. What holds truth is being alone. To be sure, the Ionian principle chronologically preceded the Eleatic school. It asserted that the first principle [ἀρχή] is water, or fire, or the infinite, or the indeterminate, which would be matter. These thought forms of the Ionian school are natural formations, not pure thoughts, but something natural. The [Pythagorean] principle of number also [preceded the Eleatic School]. A number is a pure thought, but is the thought determination of what is sensory generally, namely, of [beings] *outside one another.* Number marks the transition from the representation of sensory beings outside one another [to the pure thought of beings outside one another]. But pure thought [by itself] was first apprehended by the Eleatic school.

In the science of logic we follow the trail of thought forms as they themselves develop. The history of philosophy is nothing but the external exposition of the mind's own activity. In our own thinking, in the science of logic, a sequence of before and after also exists. But the same sequence is followed in the sensory temporal order as is followed in pure thinking. With respect to this further progress of philosophy, the determinations of difference [as contrasted to those of identity] fall by the wayside [as we hit upon the starting point], for the differences themselves fall away. For we cannot make such differences into our principle, since they already bear limitation upon themselves. The

---

differently, but by proposing one way of identifying what God is under one or another particular determination or category in a logically developing sequence of such determinations. The science of logic seeks to show how each way of identifying God or the absolute, except the first and most abstract way, is made less abstract by adding still another particular determination also found in God. Each subsequent category, which in this sense is more nearly true, develops out of a contradiction discovered when the previous way was taken to be complete. Each prior category is successfully used by the reader to single out God and only God. But, since each prior way of identifying God falsely restricts God to falling under a determination which is exclusive of further determinations also found in God, it does so under a false determination. If we were to engage in linguistic ascent— which is always possible but which Hegel, living before Friedrich Ludwig Gottlob Frege (1848–1925), does not engage in—we might say that the reader of Hegel's texts on the science of logic is led to successfully refer to the referent of "God" under successive false descriptions each of which is subject to correction by redescription. On the possibility of linguistic ascent in connection with the science of logic, see Clark Butler, "Hegel's Science of Logic in an Analytic Mode," in *Hegel's Theory of the Subject,* ed. David Gray Carlson (New York: Palgrave Macmillan, 2006), chap. 13.

history of philosophy has meaning only insofar as we know the determinations of thinking within their own internal development.

The later philosophies contain the principles of earlier ones, but are more concrete over against them. So our own philosophy [absolute idealism] necessarily is also the richest, the most concrete, since it is the result of the work of millennia. Everything is contained in this result. The Eleatic, Platonic, Aristotelian, and other such philosophies cannot be the philosophy of our own time. Our principles are of necessity more concrete than theirs, which arose when spirit still stood at a lower level of development. Yet we begin from being, which was the principle of the Eleatic philosophy.

We could begin the progression by saying that we have analyzed the beginning. We would then say that *being* is contained in this beginning. But what is only beginning to be at once is not yet. We might cursorily say in such an analysis that we want to start with *becoming* [§88], and then proceed to see what it is. If we compare becoming as our beginning with *alteration,* the latter is already more concrete than becoming, since in alteration there is already *something* that becomes *something else.* Mere becoming does not yet contain *something.* Rather, being submerges within becoming and never emerges out of it, for within becoming non-being lies in wait to consume being. Being and non-being are both present within becoming, and yet are different. Becoming is totally simple in representation except that the determinations of being and non-being are also contained within it. If, not forgetting this, we at once know the determinations of being and non-being to be contained in becoming, what we have in becoming is something [relatively] simple within which those two determinations are contained, and what we have is thus a unity. Against this simple reflection on becoming, nothing is to be objected. We have the determinations of being and non-being within the single determination of becoming. Such is the fact of the matter, which cannot be gainsaid. It might be replied that becoming cannot be grasped conceptually, but becoming *is* the self-concept. There is really no difficulty here. But if it is said that becoming is the unity of being and nothing, it will be protested that we want to hear nothing of such a unity. For nothing is the negation of being, and being is the negation of nothing. Being and nothing are, to be sure, irreconcilable. We have here the sharpest of contradictions, and yet this contradiction is nothing beyond what has already been shown by our analysis. This contradiction is the fact of the matter. If I speak of "the unity of being and nothing," I have after all succeeded in bringing both determinations into my consciousness where they oppose themselves to each other, in giving expression to them in their complete contradiction to each other. But the fact of bringing this contradiction before my consciousness is off-putting. We will admit without a doubt that this is the most maddening of contradictions. But we will also say that the contradiction self-destructs. Becoming is precisely this unrest, this process of the destruction of mere being and nothing, for destruction is itself a further side of becoming, beyond coming to be. Becoming contains destruction within it. In becoming being fails to hold out, and just as little does nothing hold out within it. Becoming is this very [circular, alternating] movement. But becoming must still be laid out as the unification of being and non-being. It is the truth of being. Yet for the understanding, which remains fixed in its isolation of the one or the other, becoming is simply not to be grasped. But let us proceed, not from becoming, but from *being* as such.

(§87) Being is the most abstract of all. The abstraction of being is totally immediate and at once totally empty, but along with that it is at once abstractly negative. If we give expression to its merely abstract character, we will say that being is *nothing*. What is negative [in abstract being] is the non-being of anything at all. And yet, quite regardless of that, being is also blankly nothing in a completely immediate fashion. So, as the Chinese [Buddhists] say,[4] the absolute is nothing. It has been said that everything came out of nothing, and that it is into nothing that everything returns [Heraclitus]. Nothing is then both the beginning and the end. Nothing is, precisely, what is totally simple, immediate, and without distinction. It is thus the same as being, it arises from the very same abstraction. Being and nothing are abstractly opposed, and yet even in this abstract opposition to each other their identity is posited. If we fix on this [unity of opposites], we have becoming. Being and nothing each bears reference to itself in the same abstract manner. They are empty. But a host of reflections can be made about such an assertion.

In the understanding, being and nothing are distinguished and are held fast over against each other. Yet what determination belongs to the one that does not also belong to the other? We are incapable of indicating any determinate difference. If we call for a determinate difference, the very demand turns out to be contradictory. Something determinate, something in particular, is to be indicated in being that is not in non-being. But we have not yet reached any such determinate being, but still remain with pure being, with what in itself is empty of all determinations. The difference is unutterable, or, to put it otherwise, it is merely intended. We can state nothing, nothing determinate, that is found in being but not in nothing. But whatever is inexpressible is purely subjective. Whatever already contains some substance within itself can be stated.

So the difference [between being and nothing] is unutterable. We represent being to ourselves, for example, as pure *light*, and we then repre-

4. In the *Science of Logic* Hegel explicitly cites Buddhists in this context. See G. W. F. Hegel, *The Science of Logic*, trans. A. V. Miller (Atlantic Highlands, N.J.: Humanities Press, 1969), p. 83.

sent our relation to it as the pure intuition of light. But this intuiting is an activity that is as much rest as it is activity. As for nothing, it is represented as total *darkness*. But if now I ask what I see in pure blinding light, the answer is nothing at all, as little as is seen in total darkness. In the pure act of intuiting I must represent myself to myself as the purely mental eye, not the spatial corporeal eye. What is posited in being is complete indeterminateness. Totally formless, it is as much darkness as light.

But if I insist on saying that being and nothing are thoroughly different each from the other, what I say of the one is no different from what I say of the other. Any difference is merely intended, and so is no difference at all. Becoming [as coming to be] is this very unrest, this movement, and becoming as perishing is this same movement. The difficulty always lies in the attachment of the understanding to something one-sided. Furthermore, from the proposition "Being and nothing are the same" some will conclude that it is all the same whether I possess or do not possess something, whether the earth exists or does not exist, whether virtue reigns or does not reign. The immorality of this last proposition will be alleged as much as its absurdity. When such propositions are uttered, it is usually objected that one means something else than what the proposition itself says. The difference between the educated and the uneducated lies in the fact that the latter always go on to speak of something else than what has been brought up in what has actually been said. We have a good illustration here. If we allow the formula that being and nothing are the same to pass muster, it will be said that their identity is absurd. But the assertion of their identity gets twisted around because being and nothing are the same only within the process of each becoming the other, not in their respective resting points. But in asserting their identity we are only speaking of abstract being and abstract nothing. As soon as I bring up something determinate, e.g., a particular purpose, what I say falls in the province of what is particular. It is then a question of something determinate [whose being or non-being *does* make a difference].

In this connection definite purposes come to be presupposed, and only with this presupposition of something fixed does the difference between being and non-being enter. Philosophy and religion cast these particular purposes aside. In the case of limited, determinate purposes [based on fleeting interests rather than on the constancy of moral volition], it is a matter of indifference whether they are realized or not. [Philosophically as well as religiously,] a human being ought to remain tranquil with the loss or gain of such temporal things. There lies in this self-abstraction from such things a great truth. If we say it does not matter whether virtue or vice reigns, and the like, the statement is false because the determinate being that is present [in the contrast between virtue and non-virtue] presupposes a decision of the will. Such decisions of the will are concrete presuppositions in the realm of determinate being. But here we are speaking of abstract being and nothing. Yet when such abstractions are invoked, people will turn away and say they rather want to know what the good and true are, what God is, what the essence upon and for itself is. "Why do we even bother with abstract being or nothing?" it will be asked. A good question. We reply that we begin with these abstractions knowing full well that we want to get beyond this beginning, that these abstractions are what is worst of all, and that what is true is whatever is most concrete. Being and nothing are abstractions, and what we have is precisely insight into their nullity. We observe these abstractions as they develop out of their nullity, as they determine themselves further as such a concrete being, as God, what is most concrete.

If we say that pure being is nothing, that the truth is the concrete world, we can say to ourselves—if we leave behind what is concrete for what is totally abstract—that this abstract being is nothing at all, and that what is true is the state, the good, God. Being is indeed nothing at all. It is indeed what we ourselves say it is, and we say that it arises from the fact that we have abstracted from everything concrete. Its ground lies in the fact that we look away from everything else, and for that reason its being is completely empty. What belongs to mere being is total abstraction, the negating of everything, and that is at once why nothing belongs to being. Being cannot be without being nothing. Being and nothing are inseparable and in this sense are identical. Yet they are not one and the same if we may make reference to the one under the first determination [of blinding light] and then obliquely refer to the other under the second determination [of empty darkness]. What is true is the process [of becoming, passing back and forth between being and nothing], this unrest of movement.

The proposition that being and nothing are identical arises in the realm of total abstraction, as a totally elementary proposition. We can more or less readily be brought to believe that this proposition must first be solidly laid down. But this is the sort of foundational proposition that, no sooner than it is laid down, raises itself up into another proposition. Hence it shows itself to be no real foundation all. But if it should be regarded as such a solid foundation, we may come to believe ourselves obliged to pause in its regard for an unduly drawn-out length of time, and in whiling ourselves with the proposition we will always come to have particular bright ideas of our own in its regard. But any such ideas are further thought determinations that we do not and cannot yet assume here.

Precisely to progress further in the science of logic, we must first occupy ourselves with Eleatic thought. One might conclude that such thinking is not adequately grounded, and then settle on the aim of giving it a firmer foundation. But such a backward line of movement would get us no further. Philosophy does retreat into a foundation, but the foundation into which it retreats is [not abstract being, but] true in its determinateness. Through philosophy, the retreat into an abstract Eleatic foundation does come to be founded. It is founded in the result of the science of logic as the self-concept of this very science. This self-concept of the science of logic, the result, is the true foundation of this logic [in its beginning].

The *Phenomenology of Spirit* teaches us to contemplate the onward movement of consciousness. The last truth reached in the *Phenomenology* is pure knowing, pure thinking, conceptually comprehending knowing. It is this last truth in the *Phenomenology* that makes its start [as the first truth] within the *Logic* as being in general. The last truth in the *Phenomenology*, absolute knowing, thus grounds the beginning in the *Logic*. But this grounding of the beginning of the *Logic* is found once again in the subsequent progression of the *Logic* [in the philosophy of spirit]. This progression from abstract being is at once a retreat [from abstract being to the concrete whole from which it was originally abstracted]. But we must remember that, though it is always possible to tarry in the analysis as we arrive at the thought determination of difference, or of what is infinitely great and infinitely small, such dallying in our onward movement gets us no further.

Thus, pressing directly ahead, what becomes clear regarding the true beginning of the science of logic is that the abstract principles of being and nothing turn out all the more to result in becoming as their truth. In every concept that follows, the totally general concept of becoming again necessarily recurs. One gets used, in the progression, to holding onto fixated moments. The circle of becoming is the first [concrete] determination, and upon analysis it gives two [abstract] determinations, being and nothing. Being results from the fact that all determinate content has gone back into the simple oneness of being. This being is being by the fact that everything particular and determinate has negated itself. [Abstract] being is not, and cannot be, except by the negation of everything particular. Being taken abstractly for itself has no truth but this abstraction, this negation of what is determinate. We are not permitted to leave out of a result that from which it has resulted. [Abstract] being has resulted from negation, and this negation therefore belongs to it.

The [Eleatic, Parmenidean] proposition "From nothing comes only nothing" is an ancient one. The proposition that nothing [as empty] is only a transition into being [in its fullness], and that being is only a transition into nothing, is a further [Heraclitean] proposition set in opposition to that first Eleatic proposition, the ancient proposition of *pantheism*, the proposition of the *eternity of matter*. To matter belongs the predicate of being. To hold solely to being is the Eleatic principle, the principle of pantheism. We, on the contrary, say that God created the world, and that he created it out of nothing. But in saying this we turn aside from the proposition "From nothing comes only nothing," the very principle of *pantheism*, of the *eternity of matter*.

Regarding becoming, one more reflection can be made: if one says that nothing is nothing, nothing is posited as independent. But the truth of nothing is that it is being. We make a distinction within becoming so that we start from [mere indeterminate] being [viewed positively as total presence] and then pass over into nothing[, namely the same indeterminate being viewed negatively as total absence,] and then from nothing pass over into being again, so we have the two determinations of *coming into being* and *going out of being*. These categories greatly occupied the ancients. The pantheism of the Eleatics denies both coming into being and going out of being. Rather, being alone holds truth. Out of what, the Eleatics asked, is something to arise? From the nothing only nothing can come, they said. But if that which [determinately] is [*das Seiende*] were to arise out of being [*Sein*], nothing would come into being, since they are both [forms of] being.

Heraclitus said that the principle, the [ἀρχή], is becoming or process. He said that *everything flows* [πάντα], or that being *is* no more than nothing itself. This speculative opinion caused the reproach to be raised against Heraclitus of a certain obscurity [σκοτεινός], since his principle proves difficult for the understanding [even though reason can grasp it]. The process invoked by Heraclitus has won, through him, its place in the history of the philosophy. Heraclitus said, in a physicalistic mode, that his principle was fire, which is simply unrest, becoming, passing away. This unrest, like the pulsation of blood, is the very principle of everything that is *alive*. Heraclitus also says that *time* is the principle, that time is this same becoming, that in time we find only another way of intuiting becoming. In space everything is side by side, but what is now, even as I pronounce it, is no more. The present now is inseparable from the following now, is continuous with it.[5] The present now, insofar as it is, has vanished. Time is self-negating. Yet time presents us with but an abstract intuition of becoming. Being alive gives a higher intuition of becoming than time. Life is this very process of becoming, and this process, cast in relief as such, is the very *pulsating of blood* as it courses through a living being. Spirit is this same unrest, the pure process of

5. Note that the idea of "the following now" divides time into successive units, contrary to the supposition that between any two nows there is an infinity of them. Continuity does not here mean a mathematically continuous series, but a continuity of the quality of being now throughout a series of discrete nows. Note also that this Hegelian *thought determination* of continuity is incompatible with the Heraclitean *representation* of continuity at the start of the paragraph: "Everything flows."

being alive within itself. Alteration is also becoming, except that within it the more concrete content [of *something* that is altered] is present.

I.A.b. Determinate Being [*Dasein*]

(§89) What we now encounter is the transition from the disquiet of becoming to the quietude of simply being there [*Dasein*—i.e., being there rather than elsewhere]. The transition is located by contemplating becoming. Within becoming we have the particular disquietude consisting in the fact that being and nothing, as the negation of being, are one. Hence, within becoming, being is no longer simply being; and nothing, through its oneness with being, is no longer simply nothing. It is no longer the nothing that we supposed it to be. Both determinations are vanishing moments, with the result that becoming is now itself an absolute contradiction. As a contradiction, becoming absolutely collapses into itself. Becoming is becoming only through the distinction between these two vanishing moments. It may be said that, since becoming is a contradiction, in the end it is nothing.[6] But, if we say that becoming is nothing, we simply return to the former one-sidedness we already examined in nothing [as opposed to abstract being]. Yet becoming is not nothing, since being belongs to it as well.[7]

Becoming collapses within itself, within the simple *quiet* unity [of being and non-being]. Combustible material is consumed in fire. The quiet that now results out of becoming, the quiescent unity of being and non-being with itself, is still [pure] being, but it is such a being which at once contains non-being within it. Within becoming, the determination of non-being is also contained. But the quiet resulting from the disquiet of becoming is *being there*, determinate being, [pure] being burdened with a negation, [pure] being and nothing in quiet unity with each other.

So here is the result. Becoming collapses upon itself within simple self-reference, within a being that nonetheless necessarily also contains the determination of nothing [which is not pure being]. The two determinations, being and nothing, now lie within a unity. These determinations, starting with their prior isolation from each other, have raised themselves up beyond themselves into being simply there.

To raise up [*aufheben*] means to negate as well as to raise up, and it is at once to absorb and to preserve what has been negated. In becoming, being and nothing are raised up beyond themselves into each other. Precisely for this reason they do not vanish, but are contained

6. This nothingness of becoming may be understood by comparison with the nothingness of a brick wall constructed by forthwith removing with one hand the brick just put in place with the other hand.

7. The alternation of removing and replacing the brick yields nothing in the way of a wall, but it does have being as the very process of this alternation.

in becoming as lifted up beyond themselves, as moments that have validity, not for themselves, but only within the whole of becoming. Being there, unlike becoming, no longer contains *either* pure being *or* nothing merely for itself. Rather, the two together now make up with each other only *one* in which *both* are preserved, while the isolated being of each is negated, just as for all idealistic philosophy all determinations are only moments within a whole. Being there is simple self-reference, self-reference fully in the form of being. In being there, *becoming* is fully raised into the form of *being*. Being, as it was contained within becoming, is demoted into a merely [empty] form.

We must now analyze being there to see what comes of it by the above determinations. Being there is no longer the total emptiness that we encountered in [abstract] being. It is possible to give an analysis of something only if it is concrete. In being there we find [pure] being, but it is [pure] being only with a negation attached to it. This negation within being may be called *determinateness* within being itself [§90]. This nothing is the negative moment within being there[, e.g., the moment that distinguishes being there as being there and *not* here]. We can now say that we have reached, within the science of logic, determinateness [or being determinate], that we have arrived at the thought of it. There is no doubt that nothing as understood above occurs as embedded within being there, within quiescent being.

The question arises as to whether "determinateness" [as the negative moment within being there in the science of logic] is the same as what we call "determinateness" in ordinary language. [In ordinary German] we say "It is determinateness" [*Es ist Bestimmheit*[8] —it is definite]. That is a strong assertion. Maybe "determinateness" is falsely applied [in ordinary German, by the standard of the science of logic]. But that makes no difference to the result. When we say "nothing" [in ordinary language] we do not seem to be saying the same thing as is meant by "determinateness" [in the science of logic]. We have reached the point where determinateness is identical with being. Quite generally, in anything determinate we have a negation.[9] Spinoza said "All determination is negation" [*Omnis determinatio est negatio*]. That is an important principle, which was especially important to Spinoza. Relative to [Spinoza's] One, everything else is determinate, and everything determinate is a negation.

Being determinate is contained within being there. But nothing and being are now quietly identical, and so we say of a determinate being

8. This can no longer be considered an ordinary German expression.
9. This "negation" is ambiguous, since it may mean the negation of pure indeterminate being or the negation of another determination. To be is then to show determinateness.

that it is a *determinateness that has being*,[10] which is to say that it is a *quality*. Being determinate as found within any quality displays self-reference, and hence is a rigid, fixed, enduring reference point. Contained within any quality is the fact that the negation of [pure] being extends as far as the very quality itself. [Pure] being cannot escape being determinate. If I strip something of its quality, it is no longer anything at all. Thus being there is the unity of both determinations, both [pure] being and being determinate. Being there as the negating of both its differentiations [in their isolation] is *what is* [ostensibly] *there,* i.e., *something.* And with this thought of something we have the onset of subjectivity [in the science of logic], the onset of unity as negative[, i.e., as the subjective negation of mere being, which is itself negative]. Such are the determinations that lie within being there, determinations obtained merely by contemplating being there itself.

(§91) Quality, being determinate, has now been cast in relief. First we have being determinate insofar as it is. However, being, with its positive quality, is now not alone, but bears immediate reference to the quality that negates it [*das Negative*]. If we lay the accent on being determinate as it [positively] is, we have [positive] *reality* [§91]. A [positive] quality is reality, determinateness shown as being. Something negative is also contained within being there. Whatever is negative is also determinate, is itself a quality, but it is the positive quality under the opposite sign of its non-being [*Nichtssein*]. Being determinate thus contains nothing [*Nichts*] within itself. If the accent within something is placed on something else as nothing, we have negation[, i.e., a negative quality in the place of a positive quality]. It is being there[, not becoming,] that is the truth of being and nothing [*Nichts*].

The same determinations are present in [positive] reality as are present in being there. It is said of God that he is the most real of all beings [*Wesen*]. To say this is to explicate God metaphysically. In conceiving God in this way, we take up reality insofar as it is stripped of any limits, and yet being determinate lies in everything real. Divine power is not divine wisdom, God's justice is not his goodness, and so it goes. If God is taken to be the most real of beings, without any limits whatsoever, the fact of his being determinate falls by the wayside, and we are left with God only as [abstract] being.

Negation [in the form of something that is *not* something given] belongs to everything that we call "something" [§92]. Something posited with such negation attached to it is something else, which is again posited with its negation. Everything that is something contains negation. Negation is always one moment within anything that is something.

10. "Determinateness that has being" may be read as a determinateness that shows or exhibits itself.

Something insofar as it distinguishes itself from its negation is other than that negation. What is other than something here is itself something[, namely, something else]. What is other than something also has its being there. Everything that is something bears reference to something else. It bears reference to it insofar as it is differentiated from it as something that has its being there and not here. Thus to have a positive quality is to have *being for something else* that does not have that quality. What is ostensibly there bears *manifold* references to things other than itself. Its being is thus being for something else, indeed for a whole range of whatever beings other than it that are there. It is manifested through those other beings. God exists, but he manifests himself, posits himself, in his being for something else. We have, here and there, something and something else, and we at once have something in its being for something else. Something, in its being, comes to bear reference to itself in contradistinction to its being something else. Something posited [merely] in its self-reference, in contradistinction to this other, evinces *being upon itself.* (All prepositions introduced in the science of logic are apprehended according to the content of their thought determinations. It was Jacobi in particular who philosophized in prepositions.)

We have thus reached something both with being upon itself and with being for something else. But with that we have also reached [by abstraction] mere being upon itself [*das Ansich*], [what Kant called] the "thing in itself," something whose being for something else is negated. All determination falls under being for something else. In *mere* being "in" itself[, with Kant,] only indeterminateness remains. What is [merely] "in" itself in this way is nothing but what is left over upon total abstraction, a worthless residue [*caput mortuum*]. Being "in" or upon itself differs from being for something else. Being upon itself is thus expressed as what is *real*, as being only by having, over against it, being for something else.

What something is [ideally[11]] upon itself[, e.g., in the case of a human being,] is what we call a determination to which something is still only destined—a vocation or destiny. A human being has such a destiny, but at first has it only [ideally] "upon" him- or herself. When an individual's [ideal] being for another [thinking subject] comes to be what we call his or her *destiny,* the individual's negation by the other comes to be raised up beyond itself as that individual incorporates that other within that destiny itself.

Should we inquire into the determination to which a human being is

11. Hegel has just used the term "real" but does not explicitly use the term "ideal" [*ideel*] in this context. Yet the two bear reference to each other in the terminology of the logic. The present context shows that he is distinguishing between a human being's *ideal* or essential being as a thinking being *for* another thinking being, and that human being's *real* sensory nature which also has its being *for* the other thinking being.

destined, the question concerns the very concept of what being human upon itself is. The positive quality of a human being lies in his or her being determinate, but also lies in the particular determination to which he or she is destined. An individual's sensory nature and impulses fall under his or her [real] being for another. What he or she is upon him- or herself [ideally] is something different. Thinking is his or her positive quality [implicitly posited upon him- or herself by and for another]. It is his or her determination, but at once his or her destiny. This determination to which the individual is destined is now to be taken up with reference to his or her being for another. The individual's being upon itself in truth bears reference to the other. The determination to which one is destined is thus something that *ought to be,* but that still merely ought to be.

So we say a human being *ought to be* rational. This obligation, this striving, is the human being as he or she is [ideally] upon him- or herself. Over against a human being as he or she is upon him- or herself [as a rational being] stands the individual's other, all that negates the individual [in his or her sensory nature].[12] Reason ought to be, but it at first merely *ought to be,* and what merely ought to be is not. Being for another, like being upon oneself [whether really or ideally], is present in every human being. We blithely make whatever merely ought to be into something final, but what ought to be is then made to be quite deficient and impotent. We then represent reason to ourselves as impotent. The vocation of being a human being ought to be fulfilled. Such fulfillment arises from a human being in the determination to which he or she is destined, i.e., from his or her [ideal] being for another. For in one's [real] being for another one ought to conform to the determination to which one is destined.

If we have something with a determination merely *in* itself, [as in Kant,] being other than it is at first excluded, and yet the thing contains both moments. Negation generally, something's being for something else which it is not, is just as essential a moment of something as what it is upon itself. Being for something else belongs to being upon itself. Something is something only through the moment of this negation, which belongs to it in its very being upon itself. Something positive extends as far, but only as far as, whatever borders upon it—and thus is limited. Its *border* is its limit, and what something ought to be

12. A human being's sensory nature depends on its accidental relations to an accidental environment as that nature exists *both* for things as some kind of other in its environment *and* for other persons who observe its being for other things. A human being's destiny as written upon itself depends on what it essentially is for other persons who have realized themselves as rational, thinking beings. A thing's ideal non-sensory being upon itself for another, for a thinking subject, is an incidental anticipation, within the logic of being, of its "essence" (*Wesen*) as it will be thematized in the subsequent logic of essence.

runs up against this limit. Being upon itself bears reference to this limit, and is itself its limit. Something has a limit, and so will be taken as being ostensibly there, as real [within its limit]. So there is a border, a limit, which, as it were, only lies on something's surface. The border doubtless belongs to something. But the border contains the contradiction that it both belongs to something as its border and at once belongs to something else taken affirmatively in its own right.

In negation two things come together. They are alike. At first something has negation upon it as a limit which encircles it. In negation something borders on something else that, reciprocally, also borders on something as first given. The border itself thus falls between something and something else, and yet one thing's border also belongs to the other in its very being upon itself.

If we say "one hundred," the hundredth unit is the border of the hundred units. But the hundredth unit is itself merely one of the hundred. If I take this unit away, I no longer have a hundred. What is more, every unit within the one hundred units is, just like the last unit, a border unit for the whole hundred. A border first falls outside something it contains, and yet it also belongs to it. Something is what it is only through its border, and therefore is not outside that border. The something goes within its quality only as far as its border reaches. Indeed, that quality lies precisely within this border.

We say that a point is the border of a line, and that the line is the border of the surface, which is the border of the body in its volume. We imagine that the point as the border of the line lies outside the line. But something is what it is only through its border, and to this extent the border comes to be characterized as the line in its very element. It is often said that a line arises from a moving point, as if the motion were accidental to the point. But it is rather the case that the origination of the line is a necessary result of the point. For, put affirmatively, the point lies in its passage into the line. This results from the fact that the point is the negation [of itself as a solitary point and is the positing of further points], and hence is a pure border in a space [of other points]. By the fact that the point passes into being such a pure border in space, it is itself spatial. As for the line, it is the purely spatial border, and stands in relation to the further space [of the surface]. The line is a border of yet another space: it proceeds out of itself into another space, the surface. The procession of the point out of itself is the line, and so on. [In the procession from the point through the line and surface to the volume] we have an inner necessity which is dialectically constructive. The border is not outside what is [qualitatively] affirmative. Rather, it reaches as far as something's affirmative being itself reaches. Or rather, the border is the very element of the line, its very essence.

A [contained] border is identical with something of which it is the border. Suppose one represents to oneself two spaces next to each other. A field has its size only through its border. Now if something's border belongs to it, it lies entirely within its border. Any other adjacent space lies equally within its border. Something has something other than itself lying upon its border, and with that the first something is posited as being in contradiction with itself[, i.e., as being other than itself]. It is posited as self-annihilating, as putting an end [*ein End*] to itself [as a single something]—it posits itself, in other words, as *finite* [*endlich*]. *Something* is an everyday category for us, as likewise is the category of *something* else. From these categories the further determinations result, namely, that something is not merely such and such upon itself but is also for something else.

Something's [real] being for something else we call its "nature," which we distinguish from its "destiny," from the [ideal] determination to which it is destined. The nature of something [though not its destiny] can be what it is accidentally, but something cannot be what it is without its being such upon itself. Such is the course of the dialectic. Anything that is something contains negation in the very fact of its being there [and not elsewhere]. Simply by being there, it already evinces subjectivity as negative unity. Something lies merely in its one-sided determination upon itself, but it is also to be posited negatively, as something else [and hence as in contradiction].

Something's negation is distinct from its being, and is to be posited in distinction from it. But if something's negation were entirely different from it, that something would be merely nothing. But instead of being nothing, something is present and determinate as being [ostensibly] there. It is posited as having that very sort of being—being there as nothing at all of some initially given something. This nothing is thus in reality something else than something given. The first something is repelled from itself into something else.

We distinguish in our mind between something and something else, and it seems that neither has anything to do with the other. But the inner connection by which something else is a moment of the first something's own being has now acquired being for us [in the science of logic]. Both moments have being. But it is now to be brought out that both moments, beyond their being for us, bear mutual reference to each other: that the determination of its negation is present within everything that is something. Being other than itself thus belongs to something itself. Something thus contains being other within itself, but it also contains reference to itself [as well as to its other]. In referring to itself something differs from its being other [than something else]. First, it is there. Secondly, however, it has being for something else, it bears reference to another. Something else at first simply differs from any first given something, but the first something bears reference to the other something through its own being for that other. Such is the development of the logic of being. The noted determinations lie in the very self-concept of something itself.

Such metaphysics is totally abstract, and is dry as dust. The other is at first independent and purely self-referential. Plato calls it τὸ ἕτερον, that which is different. In the *Timaeus* he says that God first made what refers to itself. He then created what is, upon and for itself, other than that self-referential being—matter, nature, whose being consists in being [side by side] outside itself. The ancients in particular took up such simple determinations as the objects of their philosophizing. What something is [at first] merely upon itself[, e.g., as something merely bright by direct inspection] is itself a negation [of what is other than it, e.g., being dim], so that what it is [positively] merely upon itself is to be extracted from its being for its other. And, with that, something [with a positive determination] upon itself has a negative determination lying [positively] upon something else [so that to be dim is not to exhibit the brightness of something else]. The [German] language itself makes this distinction between what something is [positively] "upon itself" ["*an sich*"] and what it is [negatively through a quality that lies positively] "upon an other" ["*an ihm*"]. For something's being upon itself to lie [in *not* being what positively lies] upon an other makes up the first thing's being for something else. What is [negatively] upon itself also lies [positively] on its other. For a determination to be upon something else is for something initially given to have being for the other. What something is upon itself at once [negatively] includes a determination which lies [positively] upon the other.

We have also designated what something is "upon itself" as having a [negative] determination to which the thing is [positively] destined [so that, e.g., what is bright is destined to be dim and vice versa]. What something is upon itself is [at first] positive over against its being for something else. [The category of] reality is subsumed under [that of] being for something else. What is real is also immediate being, it is qualitative, but it now exhibits a quality that [as a negative quality] stands over against what it [positively] is upon itself. Thinking ought really to [observably] lie upon a human being, thinking ought not merely lie [bottled up] upon itself. Something's being for something else has been called its "reality." It has also been called its "nature" as determined by its external mode and manner of being.

In something's [real] being for something else the other from without sets itself in play within the first thing. The fact that something else can impinge on something initially given, that it can work itself upon the first thing from without, [requires that this change] must already lie [as a possibility] upon the first thing itself. That possibility must lie out there upon whatever is acted upon. For example, suppose one man is killed by another. What is first posited only as coming from the other man already lies [as a possibility] upon the man who is killed. The possibility is already there.

Thus we have the [immediate] *determination* of the thing, what it is *upon itself,* and its *nature,* i.e., its being for something else. A contradiction emerges within something taken merely in itself[, e.g., the thing in itself]. Something's being as it occurs merely in itself is its fixed being, its substance. But this being of something in itself is also [and quite inconsistently] being for something else. Something else holds sway within the first something, there is something else that also belongs to it. Here we have the contradiction inherent in something. The contradiction arises precisely at the point where what something is not determines itself as its border.

What something is not, we have said, belongs to its very being. Something's negation lies upon it itself. Something already implies in general a *border* or *limit* over against its being upon itself. Its [ideal] being upon itself is what it ought to be, over against the [real] limit [which prevents it from being what it ought to be]. Its [ideal] being upon itself transcends the limit.

We speak, for example, of limitations of the mind, of the limitations of human reason. These limitations pass for being something ultimate, which ordinary human representation cannot get beyond. But the limit of something is its limit only over against something else which upon itself limits it, [in the case of a human being] over against what the individual upon itself [ideally] ought to be. But as human beings we know of this limit only because we have upon ourselves (i.e., in thought) already crossed the border that would limit us. Natural things only have borders, though their borders fail to be the sort of limits that have any being *for them* [i.e., within their own self-knowledge].

Leibniz said of beings that each has its nature, whose unfolding is the very expression of its freedom. A human being takes him- or herself to be free. Since he knows the laws of his being, they are his own laws. This is what, taken formally rather than naturally, freedom is. A magnet directs itself toward the north. If the magnet were conscious of this northward direction of its motion, Leibniz says, it would be conscious of it as its own action, and that consciousness would formally define its freedom. But we view its action merely according to its qualitative character, according to its law [and not according to any knowledge it has of that law]. In being fixedly determinate, this law would constitute, for the magnet, its formal freedom [if it were conscious of it]. This is no doubt formally correct, and the content of the law would also have to be the freedom of such a magnet. Here the content is nothing other than that of being directed to the north, and being directed to the north is what we call the limit of being a magnet.

If the magnet were conscious, it would be a thinking being. It would then know its universal law, and its exclusive direction toward the north would be something totally particular and limiting for it. But *for the magnet* as it in fact is, this direction is no limit or negation at all. But such a limit within the magnet does have being *for us* as thinking beings, if not for the magnet itself. A limit is a limit only *for* those for whom it is at once posited [in thought] as a negation [of what is limited], i.e., in reference to what is limited upon itself for those individuals, or in reference to the universality of whatever is limited.

So we say that reason is limited. But our very statement that reason has a limit is proof that reason has transcended this limit, that it is not limited. For it is only by comparison with [an allegedly unknown] being *in* itself[, e.g., the Kantian thing in itself,] that there is any limit to reason. In the case of reason, to want to set any limits to it is the greatest of follies. For all such limits have already been overcome. What we have called the "negation" and "other" lies squarely upon something itself. It belongs to its determination. The negation lying upon something itself is first its border. If the negation of something [real] refers to what it nonetheless is [ideally] upon itself, that negation is for example that of a [real] person and what he or she ought to be.[13]

Something's being upon itself is already beyond all limits. Within its border the contradiction within something determines itself according to its negative side. A border divides something off from something else which it is not. The border lies on the far side of whatever something is, and yet it also lies within the thing's own being. Whoever wills to accomplish something great, Goethe tells us, must place limits upon himself. He must lay hold of something determinate, and then shape it further. In that something's border is determinate as its negation, it is through its border that something is what it is. Yet that is a perfect contradiction. Something is first taken up as a thing in itself in its pure self-reference, without negation. But the thing's other[, its negation,] also belongs to this being *in* itself [which is thus in truth negated *upon* itself]. This contradiction is now posited as such. We see the contradiction, but the contradiction also lies objectively within the very determination of being something with an [unrealized] destiny.

Something, when posited with such a contradiction, is *finite*. Finitude is negation. What is roughly understood by something being "finite" [*endlich*] is that a time will come for it to come to an end. Finitude belongs

13. Thus something's being for a thinking being, which may be either immediate being for another thinking being or mediated being for a non-thinking being through being for a thinking being, is also ambiguous in a second way: it is either something's real being for a thinking being, or it is its ideal being or destiny for a thinking being.

to something. Something, we say, *is* finite. It is not accidental for it to come to an end. Doing so rather belongs to its very nature. The hour of its birth is the hour of its death. Every finite being enters into the world fatally wounded at birth. Negation belongs to such beings as written upon them themselves. To say that something is "finite" is to say it is *alterable* [§92]. The suffix "-able" seems to allude to possibility, but [real] alteration also belongs to something finite in its very being upon itself. This follows from what it is to be something. To be something ought to consist in being that thing affirmatively, but in the end it surrenders its affirmative being [to something else that negates it], it is finite. When we say that things are finite, our statement seems the result of accidental observation. But the finitude of things belongs to their necessary nature.

For something to be finite is for it to raise itself up beyond itself into the infinite—and with that we reach the opposition of finitude and infinitude. Something's alterability is, as it were, its superficial finitude. Finitude lies upon something insofar as the thing is contradictory through the self-negation which constitutes the very determination to which it is destined. Something, posited negatively, is something else. It thus lies within the very determination of something to alter itself into something else. The negation of something's being upon itself lies upon something else. The negation of something is something different from it, it is something else. With this development posited upon something, it is alterable. Something becomes something else— and still something else again, ever onward. But now, way off in the distance, we see the *infinite* [§93] beginning to emerge into view. (Thus, the infinite also appears in cause and effect, where the cause is also effect of a prior cause, on and on endlessly.)

(§94) This first infinity is the *bad* infinity. To put it otherwise, it is infinity posited merely negatively[, as not finite]. Let us imagine that we have an infinite series. Everything in this series is something, something finite which comes to be negated. This negation will then again be negated, and will again be posited as something else. Two things are going on here. First, something gets beyond itself. We first merely have the negation of something, but this negation becomes something else, which is thus something positive in its own right. The negation of something comes to be negated, something positive again enters, and the negation is thus given up as negation, and so it goes. Such a series is the bad infinity, which is only an infinity that merely ought to be but never is. Something is raised up beyond itself, but something new arises again. Thus matters do not come to merely negating the other, which is what they really should come to. Rather, something positive again arises. In the infinite series there is thus always a determinate number which ought to bring the series [were it truly infinite] to an end. But what follows is once again only another such number, which is again something finite, and so on. All we have is an ought, the infinite series is never finished, it is never simply there. The infinite is out there, and is represented as a beyond. Something alters itself and becomes something else. This is merely the contradiction contained, as noted, within something. Something is finite, and thus is its own negation. But something else comes to be, positing is once again present, and something else again is posited. Yet this endless emergence of something else should not be. Again we have negation, and once again something else is posited. This infinite is a perennial exchange of something for something else again. This is how we first find the infinite before us. Thus in space or time we proceed away from the place from which we first begin to another place which also has a border, and so off we go in the direction of the starry heavens and the like, off in the direction of the infinite.

This infinite series expresses the thought that we will never reach the end of it. This thought is equally true of an infinite series in time as in space. And in time as in space, a hundred years are a borderline, a benchmark, but so are a thousand years. Reaching any such a benchmark in time is no sooner accomplished than it fails to satisfy us. The same is true of the infinite divisibility of matter. As I proceed outward in space, so I can also proceed inward into space, into time, or into a material object. Space, time, material objects bear upon themselves the characteristic of the mutual externality of parts. As a consequence they are divisible. They can all be posited as each containing parts outside one another. What I identify as parts of a space, of a time segment, or of matter are once again space, time, matter, and so it goes. Passing off into the infinite is considered sublime. To be sure, it is a case of passing beyond any borderline. But a new borderline marker always reproduces itself after passing beyond the former one.

Kant says that dreaming is like ambling further and further into the far reaches of some lengthy space. Suddenly one awakens, unable to bear the immeasurable expanse. We succumb, in the very thought of such a space, to our representation of the immeasurable. But succumbing to such an expanse is really only boredom. It is forever a question of the same thing over and over again, and repetition of the same thing always makes for boredom. Our sense perception contains nothing other than the perennial exchange of one finite thing for another. Thought always passes beyond abstract negation, but what it gets anew is the same abstract negation, it continually runs up against that same border marker.

But all of this is, quite generally, the doing of the understanding. The bad infinite is through and through a beyond, never anything present. The fact of the matter is that something positive comes to be recognized as equally something negative, its negation comes to be negated [by something positive again], and this makes for the second negation. The infinite beyond itself is negated, since something finite emerges anew out of it. Thus *negation of the negation* is now at hand. But negation of the negation is *affirmation*. What is negated is also itself a negation. Negation of the negation bears reference to another negation [which it negates]. Thus we have negation referring to itself [in referring to its object], and this self-reference is affirmation. This sort of affirmation is our first example of the *true infinite* [§95]. What lies within our consciousness is that both the finite and the false infinite represented as beyond it have been negated.

Nothing stands over against the understanding so fixedly as the finite standing over against the [false] infinite. They are supposed to be as clearly opposed as being is opposed to nothing, and they are just as clearly irreconcilable. Knowledge is finite, so it cannot reach the infinite. But if we take a closer look at knowledge, we already find ourselves beyond this extreme opposition [between the limitations of knowledge and an unknowable infinite]. A first something becomes something else, which is other than the first. Thus something else stands still again over against something else. From something negative we proceed to something else again, to something equally negative. Hence, something present, itself something else, is always self-referential [in referring to something else].

When we say that something else comes to be something else again, what appears before our eyes is nothing but negation and diversity. But the fact is that the other comes to be on top of another other that comes before, that each is truly said to be something else, so the two are equally other, so that the first other comes to itself in the second. The determination to which something is destined is no longer one of exchange between something and something else. This point emerges from a reflection that is as simple as can be, and yet is fundamental. The self-reference we find here is in fact the true infinite. All that we have that is new is [the self-concept of] *the other of the other,* which turns out to be affirmative. Being is positive rather than negative, this affirmation has being. Anything that is something is the other of another, and so in referring to its other it returns to itself. It contains the other in itself. It is the other of itself, and it thus negates itself as other. What is negative comes to be negated, which yields affirmation. That is true infinity.

With the true infinite the stupendous question of the opposition of the finite and the infinite is resolved. *Dualism* holds fast to the opposition of the finite and the infinite, and the understanding is on the whole dualistic, as in the ancient Persian representation of light and darkness, and as in Manichaeism. God and the devil, good and evil—good as the infinite and evil as thoroughly finite. The resolution [of all such dualisms] lies in an examination of the determinations already at hand. We have on the one side the finite, the entire finite world, and to the other side the infinite. So there are two sides, with the infinite merely off to one side. As long as that is how matters stand, the finite stands outside the infinite. The infinite is thus not what it ought to be, since the finite is outside it, and with that the infinite is itself finite and limited. Because the infinite stands yonder beyond the finite, it is not a perfect infinite. Being one of two, it is itself finite.

The false infinite generally expresses the negative moment: it is the one-sided negation of the other finite side. But the negative infinite is at once identical with itself in its finite [and hence negative] other. Its other, the finite, coincides with the negative infinite, and that is the affirmative moment of the infinite. But this makes matters, as it were, too easy. We have an other and then still another other, and with that a sort of coincidence between the two others which is all too easy. But now posit, in the place of the self-same determination of the other and of its still further other, the determinations "finite" and "infinite." These two new determinations admittedly do not seem to be the same as the determinations of something and something else again. The transition from the finite to the infinite seems to imply that the finite is to have nothing in common with the infinite, and vice versa. On the one side, we have the infinite in such a manner as to be only one of two. This false infinite runs up against its border with the finite, which holds it within that border. We have said that the finite bears the determination of being something that is there. We have said that negation belongs to something as it is upon itself. This is what has already resulted from the development of the self-concept of something. But we at once have this further result: since what is negative belongs to something as it is upon itself, we have in what is finite a contradiction which then raises itself up beyond itself as finite. What is finite is upon itself contradictory, and it thus raises itself up into what lies beyond itself.

Whatever is finite must come to an end. It is thus something negative as well as affirmative. This is the truth of the finite: it raises itself up into what is beyond itself. At first it is therefore in truth only nothing at all of anything else. We have long since gone beyond abstract nothing [in the science of logic]. The result of something, something finite, is no mere abstract nothing. We have here a nothing that is at once something upon itself, a nothing that is self-referential [under the determinations of being something and being something else again]. The true result of something as nothing of anything else is the infinite. But this infinite is not merely negative, not merely non-finite, for it contains affirmation as well as negation.

Insofar as it is something, a being is what it is by the mediation of its negation. The infinite is not the finite. The finite is a negation [of the infinite], and the [true] infinite is a negation of this negation. Since the infinite is a second negation, it is affirmative. The finite contains upon itself the infinite. The infinite, as it is for itself, is a self-referential negation. Such self-reference is negation of the negation—is what is identical with itself [within its other]. Mere being upon itself, [i.e., Kantian being in itself,] within such negation of the negation, is merely negative, and hence is an incomplete moment. It is only abstractly affirmative, and with that it is itself also negative. The true infinite is concretely affirmative, not the abstractly affirmative being of mere being upon itself [or being in itself], but rather the concrete affirmative that arises through negation of the negation. Within the false infinite we at first have only negation of the finite. But the finite is itself a negation, so negation within the true infinite arises as negation of the negation, negation as self-reference.

One must distinguish here the first negation—it is the other which is not something given. The second negation is the negation of what is negative, [of the thing itself,] the other of its other. Infinity, insofar as it is merely the beyond, is the bad infinity. The main point is the return [of the infinite] into itself, which is the reflection of the beyond [in the present]. We have already shown that this return transpires within the infinite itself. Infinity is thus something affirmative, something assuredly present. In the bad infinity we have a mere negation of something[, and not yet negation of the negation]. But we have seen something itself to be something finite, hence to be something negative. Yet there is nothing so very excellent about a true infinity that is now present, since such an infinity is found in every self-concept. Becoming is already such an infinity.[14]

As Spinoza defined infinity, it is what is affirmative in any matter. Infinity for him is the *infinitum intellectus*, the infinity of reason. The other infinity[, which Spinoza rejected,] is that of the imagination, the bad infinity which is only an endless alternation of determinations. Zeno already said that it is all the same whether we say something a thousand times or only once. This is what Spinoza calls the infinity of the imagination. What has been left behind [in an infinite series] is always retrieved in something new.

The Spinozistic determination of infinity, by which infinity is the unlimited affirmation of any matter, is one-sided, since it does not include infinity as negation of the negation. The true infinite is that which remains identical with itself through mediation. But infinity is also the raising up of mediation into something beyond itself, into something else, or rather mediation by itself is the raising up of itself. One other becomes another other. That both sides are identical is what raises the mediation beyond itself into self-mediation. This is an affirmation, but one that has passed through negation.

14. This should be understood to mean that a "true infinite" may be true only to a limited degree. Only at the end of the dialectic could it be completely true.

Examples of the true infinite are life, the self, and whatever has being for itself. I am for myself, since I am at once there and am something other than myself. But in that I am for myself, I negate the other [for whom I am] as other and posit the other as something ideal [*ideel*], I raise up its independence beyond itself. Because I am infinite, I negate the other within me. As a subject I am *finite*, and in consciousness I run up against the *object* of consciousness as the border that contains me. But already by the fact that I represent the object to myself, the content of the object is mine, it belongs to me, and so its independence of me is negated, and any behavior toward it is behavior toward myself. I am myself an example of true infinity, but a true infinity that is still abstract.

Life is a true infinite. I breathe in oxygen, and with the air around me I reach the borderline of my being. In negating the air I negate it insofar as it is other than myself, I cause the other to be mine. I transform food, equally negating it as other than myself, and in so doing I produce [and reproduce] myself.

Spirit is a true infinite. In its higher form the true infinite is reconciliation. One makes the other over into oneself. Love and friendship are examples of the infinite. As a single person I have being for myself in total rigidity. The other person is also rigid and hostile. But [in reconciliation] I make the other over into myself.

Our knowledge of nature also illustrates the infinite. I leave aside here any claim that reason belongs merely to me. I transfer reason over into nature, while nature leaves to the side its own show of being something merely external or irrational. The other of nature[, i.e., the self,] knows in nature its other, knows that it is the same as the other. Spirit lies in the capacity for accommodation with the other, and the ability to assimilate it. In no way is the other hostile to spirit. A free man can bear up in the face of an other, can remain at rest with himself even in being with it.

Something as found in the physical world fails to maintain its presence in the face of its other. When I bring two objects together in the mechanical sphere, they collide into each other. In the chemical sphere acids and bases neutralize one another. But this neutralization is not infinity, since neither acid nor base maintains itself in the process.

So that is what the true infinite is. It is the foundation. What lies further is knowledge of this infinity in its more concrete forms. The understanding holds finitude and infinity apart from each other, and is persuaded that it holds the infinite entirely clear of the finite. The finite is thereby itself made into an absolute. The great self-deception of the understanding is to claim that we cannot reach the infinite. The understanding would make the finite into what lasts, where in fact the finite is but a transition to the truth of itself, to the infinite.

The infinite, then, and the finite. Whatever the one is the other ought not to be. But each is thereby the opposite of what it is [as posited] upon the other [*an ihm*]. For the finite has the infinite [posited] upon the infinite itself [*an ihm*]. The finite is the negative of itself as it raises itself up into something beyond itself, and it thereby becomes non-finite, which is what it in truth is. Infinity is at first the non-finite, and only afterwards is it the affirmative reference of itself to itself [in the finite]. If we say that that the infinite is the non-finite, we thereby say that the infinite contains the finite [posited] on the finite itself [*an ihm*]. Within the infinite there are two negations: a first negation and the negation of that negation. The true infinite, as negation throughout, already contains the finite within itself. But the finite is contained within the true infinite only insofar as it is as negated, only as raising itself up beyond its finitude into the true infinite.

This inclusion of the finite in the infinite is twisted around into something altogether different should we come to say that the infinite is "finitized" and thus made into something finite. This would be to say that we no longer have anything but what is finite. But to make such a statement would be to forget the other side of the matter, namely, that we really have nothing merely finite. For within what we have now seen develop, within the unity of the finite and the infinite, the finite has directly disappeared into the infinite. We have nothing merely finite, since the finite is precisely the negation of itself and is thus at once the infinite. We grant that the infinite has become the finite, but the determination of being finite consists in precisely negating itself. Finitization [correctly understood] is this process of the finite negating itself. If one speaks merely of the "unity of the finite *and* the infinite," the expression is, as indicated, twisted out of context insofar as what has [dialectically] preceded it is not expressly posited within it. Precisely because the finite is one with the infinite, the finite cannot hold out in relation to it.

There are two kinds of infinity to be distinguished, much as one distinguishes the universality that stands over against particularity from the universality that contains both universality and particularity within itself. [Within this second infinity] the finite is no longer to be apprehended as *something*. The finite is what straightaway disappears. But the "oneness of the finite and the infinite" as an expression is twisted out of shape because it places the accent on *oneness* while *opposition* between the finite and the infinite also belongs to their oneness. Finitude and infinitude are inseparable. The finite is this transition, this self-transposition into infinity, and infinity at once consists in having the finite within it. Neither apart from the other holds truth. But when I say "finitude *and* infinitude," I represent the finite off to the one side as the absolute—like some pillar of Hercules. But nothing, when thus taken thus in isolation, holds any truth.

Plato also treated the thought determination of finitude, the limited, πέρας, and the unlimited, ἄπειρον, the indeterminate and thereby the infinite. The finite [*peras*] was for Plato much higher than the infinite [*apeiron*]. Every determination falls within the sphere of form. Plato does battle with the barren desert of all that is indeterminate or infinite. The πέρας is not only the finite, but is also the border and, at once, the [activity of] determining. Determining is the activity of distinguishing. Thus the finite [*peras*], understood as the border in its totality, as pure form, appears much higher than the infinite [*apeiron*]. By "form" we understand limitation, but the activity of limiting is self-determining activity. Plato holds that we must break out of the barren desert of the infinite.

The second negation is negation of the first negation—so to speak the square root, the first negation being the root. The true infinity is an infinity that is present[, not beyond]: it *is* and at once it is present. If we now look about in the German vernacular for an expression with which to designate the infinite as present, this purely determinate infinite, such an expression is close at hand. For the logical determination in question is the most familiar of all. The expression for which we are looking is "being for itself" [§96], which is completely ordinary German. If we ask how the unity of the two determinations of the finite and the infinite arises in all its simplicity, this unity is being for itself, which represents the [logical] self-concept in its genesis. Being for itself: first it is being there, second it is reference to its other, but third it is at once the negation of the other [as merely other]. As I negate the connection that I have with the other [merely as other], I remain by myself [even with the other]. I posit myself in simple self-reference [even in my reference to the other], and it is precisely in such self-reference that the affirmative infinite lies.

Being for self arises in the logic of being in the third place[, following *being* and *being there*]. Being came first, while being there—being for other, being with a negation of itself—was second. So in third place is being for itself, self-reference through negation of the other [as merely other], the negation of any being there [that would in turn negate it]. In being for itself we have the *ideality* of the other, while in being there we have its *reality*. The ideality of anything finite consists in the fact that it is posited only as raised up beyond itself [into true infinity, into being for self]. Ideality lies in nothing beyond the fact that nothing finite has true being. Its being is raised up beyond itself and is something negated. Its being is only one moment of the truth.[15]

---

15. To be "ideal" is first to be a passing moment in an accomplished dialectical process. To have a determination posited ideally *upon* itself is for the ideal determination to have the dynamic potential for passing into its realization. The ideal maturity of a child is a passing moment in the still incomplete process of its realization. Thus Hegel distinguishes between ideality as an actual moment in the process and as the potential for its full realization.

[At first] we take "ideality" in the sense it has in [Fichte's] *subjective idealism,* according to which everything is merely *my* representation. Within my representation things in their own independence of one another are raised up beyond themselves. In that I know them, they are raised up beyond themselves [into beings of my subjective representation]. But such ideality is purely formal. Subjective idealism is but a trivial abstraction, since the question is how the content itself of things is constituted. I myself am, within this content, ever so finite a being—so there is no true reality to any mere representation of mine. In my activity of grasping anything conceptually, my own subjectivity is itself overcome. For whenever I grasp something my being is contained within the matter at hand, that matter itself. But there is an idealism [beyond subjective idealism] that is present in all true philosophy—an idealism based on the ideality of whatever is finite.

In *everyday life* we ascribe truth to the things [*Ding*], but already in *religious consciousness* we deny any [enduring] being, any eternity, to the [finite] thing. The question will still be asked: how, beginning from what is finite, is it possible to reach infinity? We are also struck with a wish to clearly see how, beginning with the infinite, we may reach the finite. This second question is with good reason asked of Spinozism. For Spinoza, everything goes back into the one substance, but how anything finite ever comes out of that substance is not apprehended. How does the finite have any being in the infinite? The answer is that when we first have hold of the infinite we have it alone, much as God before the creation of the world is alone. Yet when we have the infinite alone it is the bad infinite—just as God is not the true God if he does not manifest himself outwardly. For God is God only in the act of creating the world.

The infinite that we first represent to ourselves is the bad infinite, and as such it is only a finite infinite. By virtue of this very fact we already have the finite [as apparently reached from the infinite]! Here there is no need to see how the finite emerges. But we may still reply that the question is not yet answered—this question concerned the movement from the true infinite to the finite.

The infinite, we see, must be so apprehended as *dividing* into the true and false infinite. The false infinite consists in falling outside itself, which is precisely what the finite also does. That the infinite must be apprehended as so dividing in this way we have already seen. The infinite is mediation, and lying within it is its own positing of itself as determinate. One must bear in mind the presupposition [that lies behind this question of how the finite comes from the true infinite]. To ask how this is possible is a quite empty interrogative form[, for to pose the question is to already know the answer]. For the matter at hand is the infinite with this dynamic of the finite emerging from the infinite already contained within it. Every presupposition[, including the presup-

position that there is a question as to how the finite comes from the infinite,] is to be abandoned. Being for itself, affirmation as negation of
the negation, has already passed through the mediation [of being with
its other]. Being for itself is now being, being that refers to itself, and
that does so precisely through the ideality of its other. Being for self is
thus the being there [of the other] taken back into itself.

    What now follows we shall take up more briefly, for the method has
now on the whole been exhibited.

I.A.c. Being for Itself

Being for itself is being, but as being for itself is immediately more than
being [§96]. The subject within being for self is a being, but in such a
manner that it is the negation of what is other than it. This subject is a
oneness that within itself is mediated through the negation of this very
mediation. What has being for itself has being merely by referring to
itself.

    Being for self in immediate form is the *one*, the negation of every dif-
ference, something absolutely determinate within itself, but at once
without differentiation from anything else. I can also view the one as
having within itself a hundred ones or more, but that is not yet how it
is to be considered here. Here the one will rather be viewed as brittle,
merely as an arid point [and not as proliferating into a continuity of
ones]. The one here is exclusive and immediate. Inasmuch as the one
has being it bears reference to an other, though it immediately negates
this other. The one excludes the other, and is within that very other [*in
ihm*] the very negating of it.

    (§97) In German we literally have the everyday expression "What is
that for one [such and such]?" In using this expression we inquire into
the matter itself, into that for [the sake of] which something has its being,
which is the very matter itself. This expression is unique to the German
language, which thus assigns to the associated logical determination of
being for itself a place of privilege. "What manner of such and such is
that?"—or in German "What is that for one [such and such]?" The meaning is that something else than what is first cited is now supposed to come
along, but that what comes along [as that for the sake of which the first
thing has being] is still precisely the very same object of inquiry.

    Negative reference in something's being for itself means its self-dif-
ferentiation. The one bears negative reference to itself, to the one. The
one bears reference to itself, to the one, but the reference is negation.
The one is itself the act of making reference negatively to itself, and it
is thus the *repulsion* of further ones from itself, the positing of *many*
ones [§97]. The many as such is indeterminate, but as the number
two the indeterminate many becomes determinate. The many themselves are beings. The one is a being, and the many contains ones,

each of them a being. If we say "one," we at once say many ones. "Where do the many ones come from?" we ask. By its very concept the one is itself many ones. The one is the transition into many ones in making negative reference to itself. But insofar as it has being, the one is its negative self-reference as a being.

Plato exhibited this dialectic of the one and the many, and Proclus and the Pythagoreans followed suit. The one, and then the atom, the individual, is in its determinateness undivided simplicity. The atom necessarily comes forth in the development of thought. In the history of philosophy, the thought of the atom marks an essential standpoint. But a principle such as the atom then becomes the ultimate, passing for the very essence of things. The one is at once dispersion [into the many]. But if the one is this reversal into many ones, the many ones are also the reversal into the one, the negation of the many.

(§98) The truth of the many is the one. This observation could not be simpler. What is the many? The first, the second, and the third are each a many. But, alternatively, the first one in the many is a one, the second one is likewise a one, and so on. Thus the first, second, and third are each and all the same, they are each the one. Nothing could be simpler. The repulsion of the one from itself is the being of the many. Exclusion is a form of reference, it is reference in the affirmative determination [of positing another one]. The many in negating the one each negate what each of them is, and so they negate themselves. Or rather that to which they refer is the one, and they all refer to it. In its repulsion of *another* one from itself, the one bears reference to *itself.* Repulsion is thus *attraction,* the reversal of the many into the one one.

In contemplating the oneness of God we constantly go off in the direction of these categories [of the one and the many]. But what reigns in the *atomistic philosophy* is accident. The atoms are all alike. Absolutely no determination of a concrete manifold lies within any of them. The existence of an atomic manifold is thus mere accident, entirely devoid of thought, purely external [to any given atom]. The atomists asserted the many and the void, and held that the atoms bear reference to one another by way of mutual exclusion. An atomism of more recent vintage speaks of "molecules." Atomism is driven into minute particles—into a oneness empty [of internal qualitative differentiation].

[The opposite forces of] repulsion and attraction are inseparable. If one represents to oneself the flow of the many ones [by their mutual attraction] into a single one, ever new ones enter the representation. Precisely this is what is meant by saying that attraction is at once repulsion, at once the production of new ones. One imagines that something new comes out of attraction. Or, seeing that there are after all many ones, it is asked how attraction emerges between them. Attraction is present in the many ones like the weight of *gravity,* since the accursed manyness of ones never reaches its truth in a single one.[16] These blighted ones only seek their center of gravity but never reach it. Many material ones seek the one one. There are many ones, but their manyness is an untruth. So long as matter is of this accursed sort, it remains stuck at the level of merely searching for the one one.

Atomism comes forth in the political sphere as well. A people consists in many individual wills, which make up a general will. The singular is here, too, the principle. The attractive [force bringing individuals together] lies in the individual's needs, inclinations, and social action for the sake of utility. Beyond such atomism, substance, reason, the will upon itself, right [or law—*Recht*], and justice are the foundation in the political sphere—all of these [non-atomistic] categories being categories of being for itself.

In attraction [between qualitatively identical ones], the raising up of being many beyond itself into something else[, i.e., into the one] is posited. In attraction the one refers to what is qualitatively *itself*, and with that the logic of quality is raised up beyond itself [into the logic of quantity]. Being for itself is quality in its developed totality, the [full] determination of a being that endures [without further qualitative alteration]. The raising up of what is qualitative into what is quantitative raises it up into a new, non-qualitative determination. It is the determination of a qualitative indifference of ones [in increasing or decreasing quantity]. If we now look about to see how this new determination presents itself in representation, we find it present in representations of *quantity* [§99].

The logic of quality at first consisted in a simple transition within the nature of the quality, a transition from something into something else that was qualitatively different. From this transition we now have to distinguish what comes to be posited as a different sort of transition. This new quantitative transition at first lies [recessively] only upon the surface [of qualitative being] even in its being for us. What happens in the second place is for the new transition to be posited by us. What comes last is always our positing of what already lies upon the surface of being as contained within the self-concept. The negative determination[, the determination of the one referring to itself as *not* being itself, as another one] which unobtrusively lay upon being within the self-concept, in showing itself, now comes to the fore. Repulsion posits a quantitative one [which is expelled by an initial one negating itself], while attraction is its negation [of that negation].

---

16. The manyness of ones is accursed because intrinsically they are qualitatively the same. They are distinguished only externally or accidentally by spatial location. The manyness of ones which is essential to atomism contradicts the intrinsic discernibility of non-identicals.

I.B. Quantity

Quantity, put generally, is magnitude [§99]. But the term "magnitude" is not quite right. For it means a [particular] determinate quantity, whereas quantity is [1.] general. After [indeterminate] quantity comes [2.] the quantum [§101], which is quantity insofar as its being is determinate, with a border posited upon it. [Extensive] quantum, taken back into its simplicity, is [3.] intensive [quantum] or degree.

The question is whether by the ordinary term "quantity" we understand the present conceptual determination [of quantity in the science of logic]. It is said in mathematics that what has magnitude is susceptible of increase or decrease. In other words, any magnitude can be added to or subtracted from any other magnitude. But such a statement really clarifies nothing, though it carries with it the implication that magnitude is quite generally variable. Variability is contained within it.

Quality is already variable, but variability comes to be posited [in quantity]. As quantitative variability comes to be posited in the foreground, the [qualitative] determination of being retreats to the background. Consider, for example, an intense red. If I alter its degree of intensity, if I remove a dim redness, redness as a quality still remains in the background. But if I alter the quality as a whole rather than merely its [quantitative] degree of intensity, we have in the foreground a color that is no longer red at all. If I alter something's quantitative determination, what results is nothing [qualitatively new]. Its quantitative determination is understood to be *posited* in the foreground as alterable, rather than being alterable like something qualitative merely upon itself [*an sich*] in the background.

Space in all directions is capable of being held within borders, but these borders never interrupt the continuity of its extension. For space is continuous, as also is time [§99].

(§100) *Continuous* and *discrete* magnitude. Quality contains both [indeterminate] being and its negation [through one or another determination]. It contains both only insofar as they occur within being there [*Dasein*], only in their unity. What we have there is nothing if we remove from it its being determinately there. In quantity, as well, we have the posited form of unity, in which the border [as containing something] is raised up beyond itself and yet still exists [as containing something further]. Both the repulsion of a new one from a first one and the subsequent attraction between the two—so that through their attraction the separateness of repelled ones is lifted—come to be contained within quantity. They are distinguished, but are both held within quantity. They are distinguished but are no longer external to each other [like atoms in physical space].

We must now contemplate this repulsion and attraction of ones as they are held within quantity. If we take the one as it occurs in quantity we first have *discrete magnitude,* and this is the whole of quantity as posited in one of it forms. The discrete one exhausts quantity in its entirety, but it provides only one of the determinations under which quantity exists. The other determination under which it exists is *continuous magnitude,* which [like discrete magnitude] also contains borders, but borders posited under the determination of [qualitative] equality between the ones lying within them, and thus under the determination of the negation [of ones as mutually repulsive or discrete]. Using the self-concept of discrete magnitude, we say, for example, "a hundred men"— which is a discrete quantity, every man, everything, counts on its own as one. But continuity is also necessarily present when we say "one hundred": everything contained in one hundred is itself a one, and that by which all ones share something in common we call "oneness," which is their continuity. Only by virtue of this [continuous] oneness is it possible for discrete magnitudes to be posited. In discrete magnitude we do not have merely [mutually repulsive] ones that would differ from one another. Rather, the ones are also [qualitatively] equal, and in that lies their continuity. Space also contains borders [between line segments, surfaces, volumes], as indeed it must since [the thought determination of] the border is contained within the very determination of space as space. Discrete and continuous magnitude each bear imprinted upon itself the determination of the other.

But an antinomy arises here. It is said, on the one hand, that *space* is not divided by any borders, that it does not contain [discrete] atoms or points, since these come to be raised up beyond themselves [into their continuity, into their oneness with another]. On the other hand, mathematicians do speak of space and time as consisting in [discrete] points, and in this they are quite right. It will be asked whether *matter* is infinitely divisible, whether it consists in atoms, or whether it is the composition [of atoms] that is the first principle—whether what we come upon is always composite.

Atoms are indivisible. From this indivisibility arises the contradiction according to which both the discreteness and the continuity of matter can be equally well demonstrated. But this equal demonstrability only means that we have exhibited the two discrete and continuous sides of what it means to be a border. True, the [discrete] one is an essential principle. But the assertion of continuity and of composition is equally essential. One can go on dividing forever, but what one comes up with always contains further borders—it is one, but is also a continuity. Here we find the simple solution to our antinomy. Only the inseparable identity [of discrete and continuous quantity] holds truth.

The second [stage in the logic of quantity, the stage beyond indeterminate quantity] is quantity in its determinate being here or there—as we find this quantity in contrast to that quantity. Here we find that a quantity with a border, discreteness rather than continuity, intervenes. But such a quantity, a *quantum* [§101], within itself immediately passes for a continuity [of ones]. The one is the principle of the quantum, of the border in its being for itself, but within a quantum this one passes over into a manyness of discrete ones. One hundred is a quantum which [as one] at first excludes manyness, but which is already within itself this very manifold of one hundred.

[§102] A quantum is perfectly determined as a *number* [*Zahl*]. *Geometry,* by contrast to *arithmetic,* is the science of continuous magnitude. But, in order to determine a space, we must make use of number. Number is perfectly determinate because its principle is the one. The principle of number is the totality, which is the one. If we begin with one [as our unit], we may view it as consisting of a thousand parts. Our one has many ones within it, and it is thus designated as an *amount* [*Anzahl*] of the one viewed as the unit—it is an amount of some unit. An amount is a contained manyness of ones—all contained by a border. These many ones have a common *oneness*. A number contains both discreteness and continuity: many ones and their oneness.

There are three *arithmetic operations*. Regulating them throughout is the distinction between the amount of a unit and the [continuous] oneness of the unit itself. Performing arithmetic operations comes down to *counting*. It is only a matter of seeing how such calculations come to be differentiated from one another. The combining of numbers yields the identity of each as external to the other. Each unit neither loses nor gains [anything in its internal qualitative identity] by being combined or not combined with another one, regardless of how many ones it is combined with.

Reason [*Vernunft*] is absent from the determinate character of number. A number is thought under the form of a being completely external to itself [in any further number]. To express philosophical thoughts by means of numbers is the worst conceivable way of proceeding. *Pythagoras* never advanced far enough to be able to abstract thought simply as thought itself. The first to do so was the Eleatic School. Number, admittedly, is also an object of thought, but it is thought only in the form of externality.

Number helps make the sensory realm determinate. For sensory beings to be is to be [determinate as] external to one another, outside one another. What is sensory is at once raised up beyond itself into the abstract determination [of quantity]. The general nature of number is thus to stand in an intermediary position between pure thought and whatever is sensory. This is why number is not suitable for expressing the self-concept, which essentially is merely one.

Counting is our first arithmetic operation. But what is at issue is how we count. To number units in an amount is, quite generally, to *make* numbers, to construct them. An initial one, a unit, is not yet an amount. If I divide one into four parts [or units], an amount thereby comes to be posited. I say "1, and, then, 1 again," and the result is what I call "2," and similarly with "3," and so on. This is how we construct numbers: we take many ones together as a single one. But the other types of arithmetic operation are likewise only a matter of counting—except for the fact that what is brought together by counting is diverse in nature.

[1.] First comes the combining of numbers which are not ones as such, but which are already amounts. We can add such amounts, but we can also subtract them. If we assume any given number and any other given number, their combination we know as "addition." The numbers available for combining by *addition* are already constructed ones. To a number such as 7 I add 5, i.e., I add five counts and then stop counting. Adding is thus nothing more than numbering, while *subtraction* is the dissolution of some number that has already been added up. [By subtracting 7 from 12] I so dissolve 12 that the remaining number is 5. But 5 is not required as the result, since I can break up 12 in a number of different ways.

[2.] Second, among arithmetic operations, comes a form of addition in which the numbers added together are equal. Two numbers are capable of such identity or equality. So I can add 4 and 4. These two numbers come together to form a sum that is itself a new unit, beyond each of the two 4's that was already a unit in its own right.

But now the question arises as to how many times such a unit [e.g., 4 or 8 as unit], which is itself also a many and not just a unit, is to be taken. Taking it three times illustrates the arithmetic operation of *multiplication*. Here the distinction again arises between unit and amount. Yet the distinction is indifferent. For each of the numbers multiplied by the other can indifferently be designated "unit" or "amount." We learn multiplication tables by heart.

Dividing is once again[, like subtraction,] a negative operation of dissolution. I ought to dissolve a number so that the different numbers into which I set the dissolved number apart from each other are equal. Multiplication is distinguished from addition only by the way in which numbers are brought together[, whether by the combination of any two numbers in addition or by the combination of the same number with itself two or more times in multiplication].

[3.] In multiplication, amount and unit need not be equal. Yet they can [as with the case of a number squared] be equal, so that I can have 3 as my unit and 3 at once as my amount. That is what occurs when we rise to the *second power* of 3, which is the arithmetic operation of the third type [beyond addition-subtraction and multiplication-division]. In this third type of arithmetic operation, the negation of the operation is the extraction of the *square root* of the number raised to the second power[, i.e., of the original number squared]. Suppose I identify a number squared, a unit equal to the amount of that very unit. We may then proceed into still higher powers, but at that point matters become purely formal. Finding the square root is the basic [third] operation. The reason for making resolution into the square root basic is that only the square root can be extracted. The higher roots[, e.g., 9 as the square root of 81,] cannot be irreducibly extracted, but must be reduced to extraction of the square root [as 3 is the square root of 9]. Similarly, surfaces in geometry have to be reduced to the right-angle triangle. This is the thought determination that provides us with the guiding thread.

(§103) The quantum is indeterminately any quantum. The unit within a quantum that borders on another quantum is identical with the entire first quantum. One hundred runs up against its border. But it is not merely the hundredth one that is the border within one hundred ones. Equally each and every one [within the quantum] is such a border. And every border unit is identical with the whole quantum.

The border unit within a quantum can primarily assume the form of either manyness or simplicity, or more particularly of either *extensive* or *intensive* magnitude. This latter opposition, we shall see, differs from the opposition of *discrete* and *continuous* magnitude that determines quantity in general. Extensive and intensive magnitudes pertain to the particular way in which a quantum becomes determinate. Discreteness and continuity are inseparable within quantity in general. But each limited quantum likewise assumes the form of manyness every bit as much as that of [intensive] oneness.

When a quantum [of some material] weighs down more or less heavily on something else, that quantum shows intensive magnitude. But it likewise has extensive magnitude. Wherever there is weight, there are just so many [extensive] points of contact that exert [intensive] pressure, just so much leaden weight, just so many pounds. If a light shines brightly, its brightness is an intensive magnitude, but the same light manifests itself extensively in space. If I am given a color of a particular intensity [within a limited surface area], I can color a larger surface, but ever more faintly as the size of the surface increases; or I can color the surface more vividly the smaller the surface becomes. The more intensive a characteristic is, the more extensive it is—it expresses itself in a greater number of planes. The more intense characteristic, expressing itself outwardly, is all the more universal and effective. As expressed, it at once acquires extensiveness—without which it must remain contained within itself as a rigid and abstract point.

A degree is quite simple in its reference [§104]: the warmth I feel is an intensive degree of warmth that is quite simple as this determinate degree. But it is also determinate as an extensive magnitude. As an extensive quantum the warmth I feel is a determination indifferently external to the intensive warmth I feel. Yet if my body temperature is 20° centigrade, all the degrees below that degree belong [internally] to the determination of the twentieth degree. The attained degree has its determination only thanks to all the others, to their aggregate. The intensity of a degree of warmth is thus also extensive. The extensive quantum assumes the form of simple self-reference, but in such a way that the determinate warmth [as a felt intensive magnitude] still falls outside the extensive quantum.

In a circle degrees are determined by the circle's division into 360°. The more exact determination of a given circle is then the determination of the size of its periphery. If many ones essentially share a single oneness, their oneness still bears manyness upon itself. When the quantum is laid out as one, yet in such a way that it bears upon itself reference to an external one, it is a *ratio* [§105]. Such a ratio is at first simple. Thus 3/4, 2/1, or 3/1 is not merely an amount [in the numerator] and a unit [in the denominator], but is also a ratio; 6/2 is 3, but 3 is expressly given as something divided, as a quantum that bears upon itself external reference to another quantum. Thus 6 and 2 no longer pass, within the ratio, as immediate quanta, but rather 2 is taken as determined through 6, while 6 is similarly what it is only in reference to 2. Hence each is only a relative quantum. But what happens is then that, in the place of these two numbers, all possible numbers can enter. Instead of 1/3, I can just as well posit 10/30, 3/9, and so on. Here 10 counts for neither more nor less than 1, so 10/30 passes for the same as 1/3. Normally, if I substitute 10 for 1, the result is a completely different quantum, but here [in the quantitative ratio] the new quantum is posited as indifferently the same as the original quantum. The determinate character of being a quantum already means that it is upon itself something indifferent, but [in the quantitative ratio] this indifference now comes to be expressly posited.

But we not only have ratios, we also have *different ratios* that bear reference to one another. A quantum in a ratio bears reference selectively to something else and only to it, and such reference is itself a qualitative determination. An infinite quantitative progression [of ratios] enters here [§104]. An exponent is a quantum. If I say 6/2, I have the exponent 3, which is equally expressed as 90/30, and so on. I can posit ratios to infinity, but what I posit is always a distinction of equivalent ratios all contained within the exponent itself. The two finite numbers 2 and 6 are [each taken absolutely by itself] negated. Their value within the ratio lies solely in their reference to each other, and thus they are variable magnitudes that vary with each other [but only within the invariable ratio]. The determination contained in the exponent remains constant, while the expressions "2" and "6" no longer have any value as distinct determinate quanta.

The relation of the infinitely great to the infinitesimal is the same as the relation of other quanta in a ratio. To be *infinitesimal* is to be smaller than any given quantum, but the implication is that the infinitesimal is no longer a quantum at all. What is infinitely small is no quantum at all, and yet it is somehow to be retained as a quantitative thought determination. Mathematicians must face up to the difficulty here. [Following *Leibniz*] they speak of this quantum as the increase *dx* where the difference *d* [on which the value of the variable *x* depends] is infinitesimal. The ratio of *dx* to *dy* is to be exhibited. It comes to be said that every resulting increase in *x* and in *y* is, as [infinitesimal] quanta, simply zero, i.e., no quanta at all. And yet the ratio between these infinitesimal values is still to be given.

What matters come down to is that this ratio is to be determined. We have the ratio of zero to zero. But that is no ratio at all, since both terms are said to be infinitely small, which is to say that they are no longer quanta at all. The solution to the difficulty invokes the concept of determinations of quantity which are infinitely small, and which therefore are no longer quanta at all. Such determinations of quantity lack all sense [*Sinn*] outside their relation to each other [as extrapolated by mathematicians from relations between really existing quanta]. The terms have meaning [*Bedeutung*] only for one another [as posited terms having no existence in themselves independently of the ratio].

Newton clarified the matter in a different manner from Leibniz. Newton says that we are always to take the magnitudes within a ratio as existing. He held that vanishingly small magnitudes, before they actually vanish, remain finite magnitudes and have coefficients, while after they vanish, their coefficients become zero. He wants to say that, even when finite magnitudes vanish, their ratio still exists. He means [contrary to Leibniz] that the different terms within the ratio exist but are no longer quanta or finite magnitudes.

The infinity at which we have now arrived through our consideration of quantitative ratios is the *true quantitative infinity*. In mathematics we have a diversity of infinite series. We seek to capture each such series in summary fashion, to find a suitable finite expression for designating each series. Thus 2/7 is the *simple* finite expression for a true infinite series. But the infinite series [of *complex* expressions for 2/7] is itself an imperfect, finite or false infinite, since [in reaching no matter how great a finite member in the series] I never exhaust all [complex] expressions of the number 2/7 itself. But 2/7 is perfectly complete, and corresponds to all that can be expected of it.

I.C. Measure

(§107) Within a quantitative ratio every quantum becomes determinate only through the other quantum within the same ratio. The self-reference [of each quantum to itself through its reference to the other] is thus posited, a determinate oneness of different quanta with each other in which every quantum has its sense only insofar as it is inseparable from the other term. This absence of separation between quanta, their determinate oneness, their self-reference through reference to each other, is precisely what is qualitative within the quantitative ratio itself. In this way, within measure, quantity and quality are already united [§106, §107].

A quantum is posited amid the externality of ones as qualitatively bearing reference to itself alone. It has being for itself lying on its very surface, and is the negation of different alternative quanta. This unity of a sensory qualitative determination and a quantitative determination constitutes a measure.[17] A quantum within a particular ratio can be altered, but such quantitative alteration within a ratio is not by itself a qualitative alteration of the ratio. Yet when the measure changes, the quality of the ratio contained in that measure also changes [§108]. The externality of quantity attains to its truth only in the quantitative ratio, in something qualitative. A measure is a quantum with quality already exhibited on the very face of it. The absolute is a measure. Everything is a measure.

"Nothing too much!" the ancients said. The quantum shows itself as something to which a measure is attached. Whatever oversteps its measure, the measure to which its quality is attached, is cast down by the Furies. A measure is a quantum with the determination of being not merely quantum but also a quality. The transition [to something qualitatively different by gradual alteration of the quantity] was particularly striking to the ancients, as shown by certain paradoxes to which they gave popular currency.

An example is the paradox of the baldhead. If one takes away one strand from a whole head of hair, the quantum taken away makes no difference to the head of hair as such. This will be readily admitted.

---

17. The term "quality" within the logic of measure has two possible referents. First it refers, as in the previous paragraph, to the quality of a ratio—e.g. $2x$ is qualitatively different from $3x$, which is how it was already understood in the logic of quantity. But second it refers to the sensory quality with which some quantitative ratio of materials, forces, and spatiotemporal magnitudes is correlated, as for example the sense quality of water is correlated with H_2O or felt force is correlated with the ratio of mass times acceleration. Water is conventionally measured in gallons, but it naturally measures itself off in a number of units of H_2O.

But by doing nothing more than pulling out one strand of hair again and again, ultimately not a single strand is left. This will appear to be a joke, but contained in it is the concept of the transformation of quantitative into qualitative change. Out of a hundred thalers one can easily give away one thaler, but after doing so repeatedly ultimately nothing is left, and one's savings thus come to be qualitatively altered.

The development of the logic of measure leads into many categories, and it would require an immense [natural] science to develop this whole logic out of the very concept of it. The principal matter is the relation of powers. A measure [as a ratio] is on the very face of it qualitatively determinate, but on top of that its determinate qualitative character [in the sensory world] must be discovered. In the case of the free fall of bodies, the space traversed bears reference to the duration of the fall. We might imagine the slow mechanical speed of that space remaining constant. But the particular velocity of a body in free fall which is *discovered* in nature itself falls within another ratio: in a free fall of bodies the space or distance through which a body falls stands in a ratio determining it as the square of the motion's duration. If the body has fallen five seconds, it has passed through twenty-five units of space, and so the power relation enters.

Intervention of the power relation is even clearer in the case of the free movements of the heavenly bodies. The square root of the duration required for the orbit is the cube of the distance traveled. That is Kepler's third law. The system of measures is immense in its content. This system consists in all possible goings, hither and thither, as contained in the logic of quantum and measure. And yet there is always a border. Quantity and quality always pass into a different [measured] quantity and quality, and beyond all determinate measures is the *measureless* [§109].

The same passage happens in the social sphere. The constitution of the city of Hamburg would probably be very good for a small state, but, if we transferred it over to a large state, such a state would fall to the ground. As the Roman state became larger after the Second Punic War, freedom was brought down by quantitative change. The destruction of measure entered—the measureless. It was but a relative change in quantity, but with that change the quality of the whole fell to the ground. Water is liquid, and as the temperature rises it remains liquid. At 80° in Reamur's temperature scale the point arrives where quantitative change comes to be overstepped in favor of change into another quality. First we have liquid fluidity, then the [ambivalence of the] measureless intervenes, and then another quality enters, water's state of being steam. The warmth of water will be also be reduced to another quality in the opposite direction. At one degree of temperature water is still perfectly liquid. It does not pass into another state [gradually], but rather [after the intervention of the measureless] becomes all at once ice, solid ice.[18] This is a qualitative leap. Qualitative change is precisely this alternation between a determinate measure and the measureless. But what we have reached here is measure raising itself up into what lies beyond it. It first raises itself up into something measureless. But a new measure once again emerges out of the measureless, and thus one measure reaches closure with itself in another [§110].

18. It has just been said that the measureless intervenes apparently in momentary hesitation and ambiguity between two stable measures. Assertion of the intermediary moment of the measureless must qualify the statement that liquid water becomes *all at once* ice.

ESSENCE

2

Essence

[§112] The three subsections of the logic of the essence of being are essence as the ground of existence, as appearance, and as actuality along with necessity. Only in this third subsection does the essence come to be perfectly explicated. Essence, we may say, is self-explicating. All being, and all [empirical being in the form of] being there, serves only to lift itself beyond itself, and to show its essence. Yet this inner essence of immediate being is itself replete with a content all its own. Being now comes to be known through the explication of its essence, and this now becomes necessary. What is explicated is this essence, which itself appears.[1]

Being is the self-concept merely reduced to its immediacy. Now, in the logic of the essence, the self-concept comes to be posited [by us as speculative logicians], but it is not yet posited upon and for itself [as happens in the third and final branch of the logic, the logic of the self-concept].

Thought determinations in the logic of the essence are purely relative. Ground has meaning only by reference to existence, cause only by reference to effect, and so on. No such category is any longer purely independent of the other, but each is marked by its reflection within the other, by its reference to the other. They all bear the mark of reference to each other, and with that everything comes to be something posited or mediated by another, so that it has its being solely through something else. Here the form of mediation becomes the universal thought determination.

---

1. It may seem that logic, pure imageless thought, should have nothing to do with "appearance" taken as sensory. But the logical concept of sensory appearance, though abstracted from what is sensory, should not be taken as itself sensory.

Essence and Being. "The essence" has the same referent [*Bedeutung*] as "being." In going from being to its essence, we pass grammatically from "is" to "have." A thing in the logic of the essence has its properties—it no longer is its determinations but rather has them [§125, Note]. The verb "to have" and the participle "have been" are used in expressing the past perfect tense. "I have seen something" in the past perfect expresses possession of it. Seeing something [in the present tense] is the immediate intuition of it. But only when immediately intuited being is lifted up beyond itself do I come into possession of it, do I come to have it. Yet in thus taking it into my possession, I do not relegate it to past time. For the possessed content is contained within me ideally [*ideel*] even now, it is purely relative to me.

What has immediate being has now passed over into its essence, and in its immediacy is no more. The essence of being expresses being as it comes to be reflected within something else. What I have seen is present—οἶδα [I have seen, I know]. What I *have seen* I now know, and so it is present. This logical essence of being is thus higher than any determination of [past] time. The essence of being arises by the fact that immediacy raises itself up into its essence by the mediation of itself with itself. Being is now demoted to [the thought determination of being a mere sensory] *show*. Within its essence being is only this show. But whatever has being is lifted up into its essence, and so being in no way stands way outside its essence. So if we represent something to ourselves as inessential, as lying outside what is essential, its show still belongs to its essence, and the essence is the showing forth of itself within what is inessential. But the essence of being also shows itself forth, beyond this external show of being, as the ground of that being. Ground is a further, broader determination [to be taken up shortly]. But the essence of being first shows forth within itself even prior to its determination as ground. We have here, in the logic of essence, a new definition of the absolute:[2] the absolute is the essence, it is what is inner.

(§113) The essence of being is simple self-reference understood as the abstract *identity* between what does the referring and what is referred to, as the referent's own *self-reflection within itself*. Abstract identity is mediated by the negation of all mediation [§114]. The negation of mediation by something else returns thought back to simple self-reference. In abstract identity, the form of mediation by something else is suspended.

Sensory awareness lies in taking what is empty of thought, what is finite, to have being. The understanding gives validity to every man-

2. If definitions in a theory remain constant, if "the absolute" remains that outside which there is nothing, "a definition of the absolute" is rather an identifying description.

ner of being limited, each being abstractly identical with itself. The essence of being is abstract. For [unlike the self-concept] it comes to be apprehended in the form of [mere] identity. Force *has being,* and the expression of force also *has being.* Each is thus abstractly identical with itself. [Falsely] holding the two apart from each other is the work of the understanding.

From the abstract essence we first distinguish what is inessential, which is generally whatever has being. Secondly, the understanding holds that essence fixedly in mind, while what is inessential is shunted off to the other side. But what is inessential also enjoys self-reference and so also has being, and to be sure there is something inessential. Yet logic is concerned with being in its truth, not with a being so pathetic as to be inessential. The essence of immediate being is being within itself [*Insichsein*], being that quite generally has its self-identity through negation of the negation[, i.e., negation of what is finite, which is itself negative]. This essence, like immediate being, is internally a movement, a process, a showing forth within itself.

The sensory show in its diversity is what [in the logic of being] first has being. But that being is then reduced [in the logic of the essence] to something ideal [*ideel*]. The whole, what we call the essence of being, is the negation of [immediate] being. It is being as it now first and foremost is, being that has passed within itself, being as explicated, but which has not yet explicated itself. It has not yet explicated itself in its true [concrete] identity [as will be done in the logic of the self-concept]. It is not yet self-explicated[, in the logic of the essence,] that the whole cannot in truth be this one-sided form of the essence showing forth merely within itself. Mediation is already contained within the essence of being, but is not yet posited by it.

Because of the one-sidedness of this determination of the abstract essence of being as showing forth within itself, the other inessential determination[, that of the sensory show,] still remains to be posited within itself. The determinations of the essence of being are determinations of self-reference by whatever is self-identical. But the showing forth of this abstract essence within itself bears reference to something else. In other words, its showing forth bears reference to the fact that something other than it also shows forth within itself. These references[—self-reference and reference to an other—]are not yet posited as identical [as in the logic of the self-concept]. The sphere of the essence of being is therefore the sphere of contradiction. A *cause* is abstractly self-identical merely with itself, but it is also a showing forth of itself within something else, within the *effect.* It is not yet posited as identical with its effect. What is merely inner is in truth at once merely external. To be merely inner [as in the abstract essence of the logic of the essence] is one-sided.

II.A. Essence as the Ground of Existence

The essence of being must necessarily appear. But this essence is also a *showing forth* merely within itself. We therefore must first consider this show as wholly and merely abstract. What is second is, then, that the determination to which the essence of being is finally destined is that of the sensory show, but this show must fall to the ground, and so its essence is determined as its *ground*. The ground is precisely this show falling to the ground, where this falling to the ground is then the *existence* of the ground: the ground of the show raises itself beyond itself into what exists. But existence is immediately posited being, being as totality. This totality is the *thing*, the unity of essence and existence. What we have then is the thing, the totality of both essence (along with self-reference) and existence.

II.A.a. The Show of the Essence of Being

Show [as abstractly contained within the essence of being] is a wholly simple overall determination which at once has successive moments to be considered: [1.] the determination of *being self-identical,* which is simple identity; 2. the determination of *difference,* a showing forth that includes mediation, *diversity,* and *opposition,* the reflected being of being other than oneself; and 3. the determination of *ground,* which marks the totality of this showing forth.

II.A.a.α. Identity

The Showing Forth of the [Abstract] Essence Within Itself. With this self-identity one finds oneself driven about in manifold directions. Self-identity first has being for itself. The understanding holds fixedly to such identity. It finds self-identity in a limited content, to which it clings fast. A *cause* [in abstraction from its *effect*] is something incoherently fixed upon by the understanding. The absolute is something self-identical [*Identität*]. The very expression "the absolute" is an expression of the understanding, an abstract expression.

Regarding identity and the determinations that follow, it is to be remarked that expression has been given to them as the laws of thought.[3]

---

3. The reader is misled when Hegel gives the impression that he rejects the three traditional "laws of thought" of formal logic, since the three laws of thought which he actually examines and rejects are quite different. In the following paragraphs he rejects an uncustomary law of *abstract* identity ("A is merely A") because, for example, magnetism is not merely magnetism but is indentifiable under a different description. He rejects a novel law of non-contradiction—"–(A = +A. A = –A)," "–(A generally is both A in particular and non-A in particular)"—because, for example, the state of satisfied need (+A) alternates within the general life of

Identity is the first [thought] determination within the logic of the essence, and thus is itself an essential determination [§115]. Everything has an essence, it is said. But that is poorly put, since we have already seen a progression parade by with its beginning in the logic of being, and only then proceed to the logic of things having an essence. We should rather say that all being in its determinateness acquires an essence, and that this is how everything is self-identical. According to a fundamental law of the understanding [in the logic of the essence], every being is determinate in its essence, and as a consequence everything is self-identical.

[True] philosophy is no [Schellingian] system of mere self-identity. For [beyond affirming that everything is self-identical] we also affirm that everything is diverse, that everything is an opposite, and that everything has a ground. This legislation by the understanding [in the laws of thought] is self-contradictory, since each law, as we shall see, cancels the preceding [absolutized] law in favor of the next law.

Everything is [abstractly] identical with itself. A = A. A cannot be both +A and −A. This is the law of non-contradiction. The law of opposition[, i.e., of the excluded middle] states that A is either +A or −A. It is said that this law cannot be proven, for everyone grants it as a primary fact without proof. The law holds sway with all. Should the appeal to be made to experience, according to the law of abstract identity we are always left with a tautology. Yet identity must not be taken so abstractly. Rather, self-identity is self-mediated through a manifold of determinations.[4] If we say "Magnetism is . . ." we do not afterward expect the same thing, magnetism, to be repeated all over again. We rather expect [in the predicate] a development [of the subject of the judgment], which development in its totality nonetheless becomes the equal of what was first given [in the original subject, which is now grasped concretely]. Experience thus shows that we are wrong to make abstract identity into the law of all truth.

The same false law [of abstract identity] also comes to be expressed in the form of [the false law of non-]contradiction. It is said that we cannot think a contradiction. But in giving expression to a contradiction[, i.e., "both +A and −A"], we most surely do immediately think it. [Contrary to the abstract law of non-contradiction,] we cannot say that nothing contains within itself a contradiction. For many, many things

---

an organism (A) with a state of unsatisfied need (−A). This in turn leads to the rejection of an uncustomary law of the excluded middle—"A generally is either merely +A in particular or merely −A in particular," "A is either A in particular or non-A in particular"—because a living being alternates between the fulfillment of satisfied need and the unfulfillment of unsatisfied need.

4. "What is merely A taken abstractly = what is merely A taken abstractly" is a tautology, but "A taken concretely is merely A" is not tautological, since it is false. A human being taken concretely is not merely a human being, but is also particularized by nationality, sex, religion, etc.

are within themselves self-contradictory. Everything that is bad is self-contradictory [since its existence is in contradiction with its own concept]. Whenever I am in a state of need, the very negative of my feeling of being present to myself[, of the satisfaction my need,] is also posited within me and at that point I am myself a contradiction.[5] Every activity is a contradiction.

II.A.a.β. Difference

The essence of being is [thus contradictory] self-negation, negation directed in its reference upon itself. This essence essentially contains the determination of difference as well as identity. [Abstract] identity is the oneness of something with itself. But it is also the negation of what is diverse. Suppose that two beings are identical. With their identity I at once have their *difference* in that they are [referred to under different descriptions as] two [§ 116]. It will indeed be demanded [by the understanding] that we think their identity alone [without difference]. Yet the fact is that two and not one are present. Negation directed in its reference to itself is identity with itself [within what is not itself]. Such [concrete] self-identity thus contains difference within itself. Without difference self-identity cannot in truth be. Thus, according to the logic of the self-concept [but not according to that of the abstract essence of being], difference is also present. Therefore, [abstract] identity is a false, untrue thought determination, since it is merely one-sided, mere self-reference.

What comes next is the consideration of difference for itself, that is to say, difference as merely identical to itself. Whatever is different is self-identically different: what is different, in bearing reference to itself precisely as different [from something else], is thereby lifted beyond itself as merely different back into self-identity as different. Whenever we take difference as it is for itself on its own account, what we have is at once its self-identity as such. What is different is at first immediately different. Everything distinguished, whether as [immediate] being or as self-referential [under different determinations], is diverse in relation to all other things. Yet their *diversity* from one another is a matter of indifference [insofar as they are all identically diverse—§117].

The difference between two beings acquires its being through *comparison* [§118]. Their diversity falls solely within a third term, within

---

5. The contradiction in the living being is between its immediate state (e.g., need) and that state (e.g., satisfaction, absence of need) posited upon its immediate state by reflection on the cyclical life process. Thus need, within the circle of need and its satisfaction, is need and then at once the negation of need. But need and its contradictory negation posited within the concept of the life process are not simultaneous as in a logical contradiction, but are successive moments of that process.

the activity of *comparing*. Difference through this third term is externally posited, and similarity and dissimilarity are the two forms which difference assumes. Similarity is the identity of different things when compared, while dissimilarity is their non-identity [when compared]. But the two moments of similarity and dissimilarity bear reference to each other in an external manner [through a third term, the activity of comparing]. Difference here is external difference.

Diversity, difference, is a category of the understanding. Everything within any diverse assortment of things has being for itself. Viewed in one respect, everything is identical upon comparison to everything else. Yet viewed in a different respect, it is not identical upon comparison to anything else, but is ever different as seen in that respect. Just so is diversity to be apprehended. But even if it should now be demonstrated to the understanding that the two sides of the matter are inseparable, the understanding will still always separate them into identity and diversity. The understanding makes its appeal empirically. The claim is then that we directly see the matter at hand, that we run our fingers over it, and that we accordingly pronounce it to be merely diverse. But this empiricist pronouncement by the understanding is simply false. Gold has its specific weight *and is* yellow *and is* glittering, and so forth. Gold thus comes to be falsely separated [into its self-identity and diversity].

So the further law of thought, beyond the law of abstract identity, is: "Everything is diverse [or discernible from everything else]." This is a famous law of Leibniz's. Yet it is a matter of complete indifference whether [by comparison] we ever find a second sense object exactly like a first or not. An object's [*Gegenstand*] indiscernibility from some other object is a determination completely external to the object itself. It makes no difference to an object whether it is exactly like some other object or not. The matter is wholly without interest. It may be wondered how this law could have awakened the interest of a Leibniz. Yet for Leibniz the law did not have this sense of mere externality [based on empirical comparison and contrast]. The intended sense for him was rather the thing's [intrinsic] character of being different from any other thing [*Ding*]. The thing's determinateness belongs to the thing itself. The difference between things does not, according to Leibniz, lie merely in external comparison, but lies in each thing's own determinateness, the determinate difference lying within the thing itself.

(§118) If one now speaks of similarity [*Gleichheit*], one means the identity [*Identität*] of two things [in some respect]. Yet what I have immediately before me [empirically] are various things that are not identical in any essential respect. The determination of dissimilarity [in some respect] is inseparable from that of similarity [in some other respect]. (The triangle as such is completely determined [in its essence] as soon as its three points are determined.) Similarity [in one respect] is such that it is at once entails dissimilarity [in another respect]. Just so does dissimilarity between things lie in a similar reference of dissimilar things to one another. Such common reference of things to one another is quite generally their identity, the fact of their being one. Thus similarity [in some respect] lights up dissimilarity [in other respects], and reciprocally dissimilarity lights up similarity. The two do not fall outside each other. That is upon itself the essential difference between similarity and dissimilarity. It is the essential difference consisting in the fact that the similarity and dissimilarity in question are inseparable. So there we have similarity in some respect and dissimilarity in other respects, both belonging to the essential difference between the two.

So we have upon itself the difference to which similarity and dissimilarity both belong. If we take this difference as it is upon itself, it is posited with the determination that similarity in one respect has being only with reference to dissimilarity in another respect. Here we designate similarity in one respect as *the positive,* and dissimilarity in another respect as *the negative* [§119].[6] The positive and negative carry the sense that the one has being merely with the determination of not being what the other is. By this opposition the negative is not what it is without the positive. The one is not what the other is. We thus arrive at *opposition* [between things inseparably positive and negative, essential and inessential].

Previously we set up the [Leibnizian] law of thought: "Everything is essentially different [from everything else]." We now assert "Everything is *something opposite* [to something else]," which is yet another law of thought. These two laws contradict each other. The first [Schellingian] law of thought with which we began was that everything is merely identical with itself. The second [Leibnizian] law says that everything is diverse [or self-differentiating]. The third law is now "Everything is the opposite [of something else]." The first law is "Everything is merely identical with itself." But, as an opposite, everything bears reference to something else, and so [by the third law] is *not* identical with itself. It refers to something else.[7]

This law [of "opposition"] is known as the law of the excluded middle: A is to be either positive or negative, either +A or −A. It is said that there is no third possibility. But insofar as we say this and yet wish to make any assertion at all, we have already stated the opposite of what we intended. If A is either +A or −A, a third [middle term] arises which

---

6. Thus the three-sidedness of a triangle belongs to its positive abstract essence while the length of the lines is opposed to its three-sidedness as a negative, inessential aspect of the triangle's positive essence.

7. Thus a triangle is not merely a three-sided, closed, plane two-dimensional figure, but is such only in opposition to the inessential property of having lines of a certain length.

is the indifferent A, which is neither merely positive (+A) nor merely negative (−A), which is as much +A as −A. This third [middle term] is A taken generally, A that is neither merely +A nor merely −A. I express this middle term in the law [of opposition] by positing A generally, but then by positing it alternately both as + and as −. It must be said that nothing can be found that is not [at bottom] a third [or middle term]. Truth lies only in the third term: + and − are differences, but neither is fixed. They each have being only in their reference to the other. This is the third [or middle term]: what is neither/nor as much as it is both/and. What we have here is indifferently the one as much as the other. Yet it has been said in Schelling's philosophy that the absolute is marked by mere indifference, without any such alternation.

But even for Schelling it surely makes a difference whether I have six thalers in assets or six thalers of debt. If I owe them they are a minus with respect to my assets, but those same thalers are in the plus column as the assets of others. Yet that in no way affects the six thalers for themselves. We bring forward "contradictory concepts" such as being both blue and not blue. Blue and yellow, on the other hand, are contraries, not contradictories. The contradictory is merely non-blue, mere negation, no matter what color the other thing has. The universal, color, lies at the foundation of [different opposed colors]. The law according to which "Everything has one of any two predicates opposed [as contradictories]" passes as the greatest wisdom. Yet, to take another example, if we take spirit [as subject] and white [as one of two contradictory predicates], such a law totally fails us. For spirit is neither white nor non-white.

Opposite predicates become *contradictory* predicates when they are thought of as belonging to one and the same thing; we then end up saying of something that it is both round and non-round. If one says that something is round, it is [not] non-round. That is what correctly follows if we suppose that it is round. Yet geometricians suppose a circle to be a straight-lined polygon, [so that] its *curve* is viewed as *straight* [i.e., quite inconsistently as *not curved*].[8] But being a circle is [a thought determination of the understanding,] not a concept. The line [of a circle, despite its representation by geometricians,] is indeed merely curved, not straight. That is the one fixed determination [of a circle].

8. Hegel is saying that being curved and straight are opposites, that opposites are mutually exclusive, and that mutually exclusive predicates attributed to the same thing yield a contradiction. Being curved is not being straight, being straight is not being curved, so that something that is both curved and straight is inconsistently both curved and not curved. He may be taken to mean that the possibility of self-contradiction can be derived from opposites because it is always at least possible to attribute opposites to the same thing. Note that this is not to derive the truth of any contradictory assertion, but only the possibility of such a false assertion.

Within the self-concept matters proceed differently [from the logic of the essence of being]. God is as much the middle point as the periphery, but we say this of God [with seeming contradiction] when we base ourselves solely on the sensory image[9] which God calls to mind. In the sensory realm things as contradictory opposites fall outside one another in different things. But God is everywhere, present in all life, and yet is at once the middle point. Here, in the logic of the essence of being, this determination of being a middle point remains finite and goes its separate way from the way followed in the logic of the self-concept.

(§120) Something is this insofar as it is not that. As long as we retain its opposition in mind, the one expressly excludes the other. It is not what the other is. It is not supposed to be taken as the one along with being at once the other. To be sure what is in fact expressed is the unity of both opposites. But we shall have to inquire [in the logic of the self-concept] as to whether this form of the unity of contradictories is what such unity should in fact be. Something is what it is only insofar as it is not something else. The other thing thus in fact belongs to the first. For, again, the first is what it is insofar as it is not the other. Saying this, we directly need the other [if we are to have the first].

Polarity, magnetic polarity, is currently a widespread representation in physics that has now been carried over into chemism. It amounts to an important advance insofar as what lies therein is opposition and not mere diversity. One does not merely say that things are diverse, but also that each is what it is only insofar as it is not the other. That is what opposition means: the North Pole is the opposite of the South Pole. As mere regions of the heavens they are not opposed to each other. But as soon as we say "polarity" we represent to ourselves the fact that the one is what it is insofar as it is not what the other is. To have the quality of the one I need the opposed quality of the other. We have here nothing but the identity of both.

If we think away the North Pole, north and south poles still exist on our magnet, and there they are to be sure still opposed. The acid is what it is insofar as it is not bound [neutralized] with the base. And yet the North Pole does not exist without the South Pole. The two are inseparable. The one is what it is only insofar as it is not the other. The acid is acid only insofar as it is not alkaline. If I have hold of what acid is for itself, it to be sure harbors an impulse toward its base. An acid that is not bound with the base, that is totally waterless, is but a pure opposite, a smoking acid full of unrest until it neutralizes itself. It eats away at its other. An opposite is what it is insofar as it is not that other, which is also to say in-

9. Representation pictures opposite contradictory predicates, attributing them to spatially separate things. Conceptually God is the middle point through being the periphery, not to its exclusion.

sofar as it is its other. The North Pole has its other in the South Pole, and that leads to a true view of what, upon itself, its other is.

A human being differs from a tree, or from the air. Yet air is also an opposite. Indeed, from one side of our nature as living beings, air is even our very own other. A human being cannot be without air, and so we are always struggling to get our next breath. Such, generally, is the life process. In hunger a human being is also directed to his or her other, to food. Food is not merely something else in general, but is a human being's opposite. A human being can posit the other only as identical with him- or herself. Such is the inseparability of opposites. Their inseparability is nothing other than their reference to their others, which is nothing else than their identity. If we take opposition between two things merely by itself it is not true opposition, since unity also belongs to them. To say what one opposite is I need its other. In opposition I have both the thing and its other.

Now let us determine both opposites more closely. Each is similar to the other, since each is similarly in opposition to its other. In this they are in no way different, but this similarity belongs to [the realm of] comparison. Yet if I am to give the opposites different determinations, the one is *positive*, the affirmative [term] that bears reference to itself, while the other is *negative* and with that opposes what is positive, lies in opposition to its other which is positive. If we consider each opposite merely for itself, it is positive. Yet what is positive is not supposed to be negative, and in this lies its reference to its other. Taking now the negative, it is the negative *of* something, *of* the positive, and with that we have an expression of its reference to its other. With that we have the negative itself and its other.

If we take the negative in its being for itself, in its being within itself, it is the very negative of itself; it refers negatively to itself—which means that it raises itself up beyond itself into something else. The negative as it refers to itself is nothing other than unity, nothing other than the affirmative. The negative raises itself up beyond itself, it refers to itself, and with that we have identity. Putting it otherwise, if we say of opposites that one is positive and the other negative, both fall under what is opposite. The positive is the affirmative, what is self-identical. One of the two opposites is thus identity. We can in no way escape this fact, however we take the matter. The essential difference is the self-reference of difference, and, with that, this difference itself contains identity, even while one of its two members is also identity.

Such is the dialectic of essential difference [as contrasted to inessential diversity]. The positive and the negative are each the same activity of each raising itself up beyond itself. The positive is posited as not being the negative, but therein at once lies its reference to something other than itself. With that the positive is the contrary of itself, since [by the law of mere abstract identity] it ought to be merely self-referential[, merely positive]. The negative is self-referential as negative, and with that there is identity in what is negative. Yet both the negative and the positive fall to the ground, and are themselves the very unrest of this fall. An acid and alkali consist in negating each other, thus becoming neutral. But the North Pole and South Pole remain opposed, which is their imperfection as opposites. The chemical process shows this to be true of the opposition of the two poles. The opposites in their very being for themselves each fall to the ground. In chemical processes the negative side is the first to be cast in relief. But the *ground* [into which the negative side falls] is affirmative [§120]. To this ground we must hold fast—the ground into which the opposition of the negative and the affirmative returns, with opposition raised up beyond itself. Opposites collapse in upon themselves, as [did being and nothing] in becoming.

II.A.a.γ. Ground

(§121) The ground is the [abstract] essence of being as that essence comes to be posited in its totality. We talk of getting to the bottom [*Grund*] of matters, i.e., going into their very essence. Yet this ground is no dry essence, nor is it essence as [mere self-]identity. Rather, the essence of matters is a self-identity that at once includes something still different from this very self-identity. The ground [of a matter] is different from the matter itself. What is essential [as ground], insofar as it has been repelled from itself as essence, is what is *existent*. Ground is self-identical but is also different from itself. The ground, so-to-speak the ground floor, is first self-identical. The ground of a house is something firm and fixed. It is no mere abstraction; it is not something that is not. On the contrary, the ground floor at once holds up the whole house. The house arises from this ground, in differentiation from it and in opposition to it.

This thought determination of the ground is contained in our usual representations. The house is *something* insofar as it is not its ground. It is the other of its ground. In the thought-determination of a ground all the determinations of essence are present, the totality of [abstract] essence. Identity and difference, identity and non-identity, positive and negative—having all been posited they all now raise themselves up beyond themselves. The difference between the two terms in each of these pairs comes to be lost, and with that the totality of the determination of *identity* is posited, but this identity is within itself at once repulsion. The ground is the totality of the [abstract] essence of being as that essence now shows forth. This essence as it shows forth is self-identical, while at once giving a show of having its opposite within itself.

The law of thought according to which "Everything has its [sufficient] ground" has been put forth like the others we have considered. This law again contradicts the prior law [of abstract identity] by which "Something is what it is, A is merely identical to A." If one thing has a ground, this thing bears reference to still something else as its ground, to something which, over against what is grounded, is the essence [of whatever is grounded]. Leibniz placed great importance on the law of the sufficient ground. The term "sufficient" at first appears superfluous, since a ground that is not sufficient simply cannot ground anything. Yet the distinction has been made between final causes and efficient causes. Final causes are purposes. If, in apprehending life, I say that certain means of nutrition, digestion, and so on, belong to it—these means are the efficient causes of life, which are in reality its external causes. Yet to consider a living being as it is for itself is to consider it as [embodying] purpose, and when life is considered in this manner purpose is its sufficient ground. Air and the means of nutrition are necessary, but life is still something else than these things. Life comes to be determinate and active as purpose. Its own purposive activity is the sufficient ground of itself.[10]

The ground [as the abstract essence of what is grounded] is essentially identical with whatever is grounded by it. Yet what is grounded is repelled [from its own ground], which is essential over against what is grounded. The ground [as distinct from something existent which it grounds] is thus something formal[, i.e., a formal cause]. The ground is what is essential insofar as it is form. The ground is not yet the self-concept, which is the whole totality and is not merely [like the ground] a single moment of it. The ground [as the formal cause] is the good. It will be said that the ground, taken in this way is totally indeterminate. Everything is good, which only means that everything bears reference to itself, has being for self. We can point out a good ground for everything, no matter how bad it is.

If someone is a thief, the theft can have the very good ground of feeding the family. [Under one determination] the action is that of taking property into one's possession. This action surely has this aspect of keeping body and soul together, and it must be admitted that the content of this motive is essential [and good]. The intention, the ground, is good, and so it is said that the action is perfectly justified. The good ground takes from a multi-faceted action a single facet and makes it essential, but that facet is then taken [merely] for itself. The action is reduced to this single simple determination, which is precisely its essentiality. But the action taken according to its self-concept

---

10. If the category of ground is expressed as the deterministic principle that every occurrence has a sufficient external explanatory ground for it being thus and not otherwise, the principle fails because each individual occurrence exists beyond its general grounding conditions unless the occurrence's existence itself is included in its sufficient ground.

is something else again. When we grasp the action conceptually, we do not abstract and isolate merely one side of the matter. The self-concept determines what the action by its very nature is, and over against this nature of the action whatever is other than it does not come in for consideration. Some things have [beyond their internal conceptual nature] an external nature. They accordingly have different external sides to them, and each such side is susceptible to being made into the main side, the thing's ground. The ground can thus always mean something good. A ground can either have or not have a given consequence [*Folge*]. But for a ground to be effective [and thus to be the sufficient ground of an outer action that follows as its consequence,] my own [free act of] will [directed at this consequence] is necessary. What has being not only upon itself but at once for itself gives validity to itself in the world [by being carried out by an act of will].

(§122) The essence first shows forth within itself. It is mediation within itself. As ground it is the totality of all mediation. This totality first has being for itself, but it repels something away from it—it grounds something. What is grounded is simply there, it has immediacy [beyond its mediation by the ground]. A ground thus betokens at once the return of being. The ground is the collapse of all mediation merely within itself [*in sich*]. What is posited by the ground is something immediate. The ground is still what is reflected within itself. It is at once the simple reference of itself to itself, but only insofar as it mediates [what is grounded]. What is mediated by the ground[, i.e., what is grounded,] is mediation raised up beyond itself into immediacy. The determination of immediacy is thus posited along with that of ground.

What is posited [beyond its ground] is the *existence* of the consequence of the ground. It is generally asserted that, in doing one's duty, one must not think of the consequences of doing so. Duty for duty's sake is thus formally or universally good, but only formally. An action posits something in existence. Existence itself is inner inasmuch as it comes from an inner [ground]. What the action itself is develops and reveals itself in its external existence. The correctness of every action, of every intention, is manifested in its [external] existence. The action gives itself out to be known in its consequences. Insofar as I act, I posit my purpose in its [external] immediacy, in its being simply there. Yet contained within it is a reference of my purpose to something [unintended, something] which is other than itself. Something else comes into play here that has not been posited by me. These further consequences do not lie within my action. The action finds its development in the consequences, and then something else comes on top of the intended consequences that does not lie within my action. It is a question of the very content of the action, and what follows otherwise does not belong to it. The next category is existence.

II.A.b. Existence

Here the nature of the ground is given. If I inquire into the ground of something, I want to see within this ground the very matter at issue, I want to see imprinted upon this matter what is essential to it, what is present there in the form of its own self-identity. Existence also contains within itself a determination of identity with itself. But it at once contains a determination of difference from itself, of showing up something other than itself—both reflection within itself and within something else.

As existing everything is being, is immediacy, but is such by raising the mediation of the ground up into immediacy. What exists has being, but something other than it at once shines forth within it. Here is a *world of reciprocal dependence* [§123]. Everything is ground and everything is at once grounded. The other imposes its rights. Existents are grounds, but are at once also grounded. Such, in general, is the world of relations.

(§124) Anything that is something has being, but at once shines forth within something else. Its reference to something else belongs to it itself. Taken as a ground, something is reflected within itself. Anything that is something is itself the totality of these two determinations of being reflected within itself and of shining forth within something else. The two determinations both belong to whatever exists. Such an existent is, through its reflection within something else, at once reflected within itself. And with that they make up a whole which now is itself posited as ground.

II.A.c. The Thing

Whatever exists is called a *thing* [§ 124]. A thing is something existent, hence something with immediate being. But it is more than immediate being, since it is also abstract in being interconnected with thought. An existent thing, beyond its immediacy, has being as something that is thought. Imprinted upon the thing is thought, thought in the form of reflection within itself. That a *thing* is abstract is seen even from children, who give the name of "thing" to everything they cannot specifically determine. Moreover, no one can point out a thing to anyone [as distinct from pointing out its immediate being or properties]—and this argues for the abstractness of things.

An existing thing is first taken up as reflected within itself, not yet as exhibiting its external reflection within another thing. For its reflection within another thing, indeed within other things, would make it a manifold rather than a single thing. A thing subsists with being for itself, and upon every thing lies the show of the whole essence of being. For every thing is *self-identical,* and lying upon it are all the determinations of reflection. A thing bears imprinted upon itself *difference,* its reflection within something else. There are at once many diverse things. But their diversity is not only their diversity over against one another.

Each thing also itself exhibits a diversity upon itself. The diversity of a thing within itself diverse, we call the diversity of the *properties of the thing* [§125]. Diversity lies upon the thing, but this diversity of its properties is the thing as reflected within something else, within other things. This reflection of a thing within something else at first differs from its reflection within itself. To reflections of something within something else [in the logic of being] belong certain diverse ways of being determinate which are now [in the logic of essence] called *properties* of a thing, insofar as we have now distinguished the thing within itself from its properties. For we distinguish between the thing within itself and its [immediate] qualities. The properties of a thing are reflections of diverse things as they lie upon the initial thing taken as something other than them, upon the thing as the ground that bears these very properties.

Within something [in the logic of being,] being and being determinate are not separated. Being determinate ranges as widely as being itself ranges. But in the logic of the essence, being a thing as reflected within itself is to be set apart from its determinations or properties. The properties things have imply a relation of things *having* their properties. Being and having are both essential categories. [Grammatically] they are temporal participles, but [logically] they are determinations of the category of ground, [a category of essence]. Compare "I am sick" and "I have a sickness." If I say "I am sick," I assert an identity between myself and sickness. But if I say "I have a sickness," the property sickness is differentiated from me, separated out. In "I am sick" my being lies in "[being] sick." But if I say "I have a sickness" the persisting subsistence of the property sickness has entered externally into the thing, into me.

A thing in its development lays out on all sides a contradiction for us to see. It is the development of show, but this show is no longer held within essence [as it is abstractly within itself]. The thing is existent, it is immediate. But in a thing the determinations of the show gain subsistence in their differentiation from one another. The field in which these determinations have their being is that of the thing. The determinations give forth contradictions on all sides. A thing has properties that are different from it. These properties make up the thing's reflection within other things. Yet the thing and its properties are not separated. The thing's reflection within something else is equally reflection within itself, since the thing refers to itself in its reference to what is different from it.

The thing's properties themselves characterize grounds or rather "matters" [*Materien*] in the plural [§126].[11] A thing has properties, and

---

11. "To have" may mean either to exemplify or to contain. The noun *Eigenschaften* is translated as "properties" understood as universal determinations

these properties themselves mark such material beings. A thing consists of [portions of] different matters. For example, a thing has color. That a thing has a scent can also be extracted from it. The property subsists for itself on its own as a matter with a scent, or as a magnetic or electrical matter. Thus we take a thing as consisting of [portions of] different matters.[12] If we bring the different matters together [in a single primary matter], to be sure we no longer have a thing, which will now be totally compressed in that matter. The thing is the bearer of its properties. But these properties themselves subsist [independently of any thing]. The thing is the external connection of the matters [received into it as properties], and hence something superficial. It is the matter that subsists.

(§ 127) [Primary] matter makes up what truly subsists in the thing. But no one can point out this matter to anyone else [any more than one can point out a thing]. This matter as such is indeterminate, while there are many [determinate] matters. We do not call these matters "things," for a thing is a unity reflected within itself which at once has a manifold of properties. A matter is, by contrast, simple, not a synthetic unity of many determinations [*Bestimmtheiten*]. Still, a matter may be generally described as a thing insofar as it is somewhere out there. By a [determinate] matter one understands being, immediacy, reflection within another—but so that such reflection within another is taken up in a completely abstract fashion. There are various [determinate] matters, but [primary] matter as the immediate unity of existence is indifferent over against the diversity of determinate properties. Such matter is merely, self-referentially subsistent or existent.

(§128) Reflection as set identically in reference to itself, lying upon itself without diversity, is the one matter. Diversity altogether falls outside this matter, and the great swarm of determinations lying outside of this matter are called "form." The thing converts into the independent subsistence of its properties, and the properties as themselves subsisting are the determinate matters. These matters are at first diverse, but [primary] matter is the One of existence reflected within itself. It is indifferent towards the thing's determinations. Difference is also present, but it lies outside such matter.

A thing falls apart into matter and form. Materialism asserts that ev-

which the thing is thought "to have" in the sense of exemplifying them. But to refer to the universal determination of being water as a thing's property is then also to refer to the element or matter which more directly exemplifies that property. A living organism exemplifies the property of being watery, but another way of saying this is to say that, since the organism "has" water in the second sense of containing it, the organism has (contains) a portion of a material element which has (exemplifies) the property of being water.

12. Thus a soup may have vegetable matter in it.

erything is merely matter. Primary matter in its being for itself is said [by Aristotle] to be eternal. Self-identical subsistence is without differentiation. Alteration [or change] has thus been withdrawn from such matter. Yet this matter has a capacity for form, and is molded into its form. But form also has being for itself. Generally, it has determinateness, the totality of all determinateness, the whole of difference in its being for itself, difference in its reference to [primary] matter. Form we allow [with Aristotle] to be externally added to matter. God is the process of giving things their form, the demiurge or fashioner of worlds.

But matter and form [for Aristotle] are not what they ought to be. Indeed they are here, upon themselves, the very opposite of what they ought to be. Matter merely for itself ought to be indeterminate existence, though with that it indeed does contain existence. Yet matter [in its existence] ought to be out there before our gaze. It ought to be present before our very eyes. If matter were completely simple [as primary matter], it would be mere self-identity. It would contain nothing but what is also contained in the I. But matter is not completely simple, but ought to be an existing matter which is yet identical with itself. For matter to have a potentiality to be something or other, a capability, means that it is *itself* a determinate potentiality, that it has being as such and such a potentiality. The fact that matter upon itself *exists* implies that it bears upon itself the imprint of being for something other that itself. Form thus appears upon matter: as existence, matter has this relation [*Relation*] to its other, i.e., to form. Form in its being for itself is the totality of form, infinity, infinite activity. Form at rest is one among forms, but all forms ought to lie outside of [primary] matter. So, as the totality, form for itself bears reference to itself. Yet this self-reference of form is the same self-reference as is found in primary matter. From whence does the creativity of form derive? It derives from itself. So form has, imprinted upon itself, the very same moment [of mere self-reference] that is said to make up the distinctive character of primary matter. In themselves matter and form are identical, unseparated and inseparable. Such is the thing in the upshot of its logical development.

(§130) Each thing ought to have its form, which is responsible for what the thing determinately is through its properties. But the thing also has matter in it. Matter ought to be nothing more than having properties; it ought not subsist merely for itself. Through its mere form, matter comes to be reduced to having properties. But [determinate] matters are what subsist, while the thing does not subsist. A thing [as self-subsistent] is self-contradictory.[13] It is said in physics that things

---

13. A thing is contradictory because it is *referred to* under the contradictory determinations of *both* subsisting walled off in itself as singular *and* being a composite of matters receiving various properties from other things. Thus the glimmering of the

consist in diverse matters. Metals have warmth, shininess, clang—we may call metal matter with a ring to it. Metal also contains within itself magnetic and electric matter.

If I take up the thing in this way and cut it into tiny parts, all the parts that I find in it are [portions of] determinate matters. But how is this to be understood? It is said that materials subsist independently in given places. But the precise place where one material subsists is not the exact place where the other subsists. The non-subsistence of a material thus comes to be called "pores," holes where that matter is not. Every material is scattered, each being stuck inside others. There we have our explanation. Without a doubt pores do occur in skin and in plants. But in stone and metal pores are a mere invention of the understanding. What is in fact present here is the moment of the negation of independent matters by one another. Within a thing different matters cease to be self-subsistent.

The thing in itself is now the unity of matter and form. Being in itself is now no longer at hand. Matter is now itself only one moment of form. But this unity of the thing as both matter and form is at once its falling apart into subsistent [matters], and these matters are at once distinguished from one another, but again lack subsistence for themselves. Thinghood[, succumbing to the circle of its contradictions,] thus now converts itself into *appearance* [§131].

II.B. Appearance

The abstract essence [of being] must necessarily outwardly *appear*. The very identity of this abstract essence passes over into an existence external to it, into immediacy. *Existence* [in contrast to being] consists precisely in having its *essence* [concretely] within itself. But existence falls apart into many existents, which, however, bear reference to one another, and which again pass over into the moment of [their distinguishing] forms. This is the process of appearance. Diverse existents have being, but they are catapulted into being mere forms, with their [essential] being contained merely within themselves. The essence [of what exists] does not now lie way over on the other side of what appears. That essence lies within what exists, in that its existence is the appearance of its own essence. Appearance is a matter of the essence itself, and the es-

---

lake is a property received from the light of the moon. It is consistent with what Hegel says about the *thing* to suppose that it does not really *exist* under contradictory determinations. But our reference to a thing under such determinations may be *intersubjectively* shared in everyday thought, and at least in this sense the thing might be an *objective* contradiction.

sence must appear. There is an important principle here. For what has being [as essence] is now only inwardly a one-sided abstraction. The essence outwardly has its being in its appearance, and brings existence to the point of the appearance of what is essential. In appearance three stages now arise: 1. the world of appearance, 2. form and content, and 3. correlation.

[II.B.a.] The World of Appearance

In existing, what exists subsists only as one of the moments of form [§132]. A human being has his or her own purposes, is independent, but he or she is equally but one formal moment within [the world of] his or her overall purposeful activity. The world of appearance is the explication of appearance itself. But, within this world of appearance, a difference is cast in relief between "form" in a further sense and "content." We have already beheld in the above the difference between form and *matter,* but now we come upon a distinction of form and *content.* The world of appearance is one of mutual externality between appearances, since their forms are diverse. The world contains existent appearances. These mutually external existents make up a totality, and are contained within their mutual reference in the world of appearance. Whatever appears within this determination of self-reference between appearances will now still prove to be the entire explication of any limited appearance.

[II.B.b. Form and Content]

In the first place[, in taking up the distinction between form and content,] consider form as content [§133]. Consider the content of a book. Such a content is a developed material that bears, imprinted upon itself, its own form. But the content of a book is also something quite simple. Any content that lacked form would thereby lack content. Thus an [essential] form is lodged within any [essential] content, within its determination as the whole. Within the content, its form is the whole content as taken up in its simplicity, and the whole content quite simply resides within that form.

We distinguish from the just-mentioned *essential* form that is one with the content of the book, a still further form that lies outside this content, outside what is essential to the book. This second form is the *inessential* form—in the case of a book, the print, the paper.[14] But the essential content of the book is given out as the whole law governing its [limited] appearance. The two determinations of essential content and its [limited]

---

14. Essential form and content have previously been identified. Now inessential forms—print, paper, cover, binding—are identified with essential content. Such inessential forms are demoted to mere appearance. The essence is in the accidents.

appearance belong in their inseparable unity to each law governing such appearance. To cite another example [of a law that governs appearance], punishment is inseparable from crime, an action whose content is in itself null and void. The punishment is only the exposition of the very nullity of the criminal action—the punishment annuls the action.

We attain determinate knowledge of the world by bringing it under the system of law. These laws do not linger in the background as if the appearances themselves were lawless, but rather the law is right out there in those appearances themselves. The form of law contains self-reference, but it also contains reference to what is other than it. Form is therefore twice present, [once essentially and once inessentially]. In finite things, external [or empirical] form is diverse. But every inessential externality in the orbits of the planets is identical with the inner law of such orbits. To know the world of appearances as the system of its laws is important, even though to know that system is not yet to grasp the world conceptually [as in the third branch of the science of logic]. One and the same whole is both content and form.

[II.B.c. Correlation]

Our distinction between inner [or essential] and external [or inessential] form construes content as inner form. It encompasses the content, not within external existences, but within true existents. The content comes to be posited as the developed, essential form. Each of these two determinations, the content and developed form, embraces the same One. The content of both[, first as undeveloped and then as developed,] is the same, so that the distinction between them is only superficial, and such a superficial distinction we shall call a "correlation" [§134].[15] The undeveloped content and its formal development each pass as independent of each other, but they are likewise posited as both being mere determinations of form itself. The three particular correlations are those of the whole and its parts, force and its expression, and the inner and the outer.

[1.] The whole and its parts

[§135] The whole has a certain content. The parts are the same as the whole. The whole is spoken of as referring to itself, while the parts are referred to as broken up outside of one another. If I take away one

---

15. Self-identity first appeared *without* difference, and *upon reflection* we were then led to think difference. The correlation of identity and difference was thus uncovered, but not immediately posited in positing identity. What Hegel calls a *correlation* is a correlation in which the two terms, e.g., the whole and the part, come pair-wise, so that to think the one is immediately to think the other. The relation of the whole to the part is co-posited simultaneously with the relation of the part to the whole.

part, the whole remains. But when the parts pass as independent in this way, they lose the determination of being parts, since parts are parts only as parts of the whole. But again, the parts and the whole are thus one and the same. So at first the whole is independent. Yet if I have no parts, I have no whole. And if I take the whole away I have no parts. Such is the contradiction in the correlations of whole and part [taken as both independent and at once dependent]. The whole ought to be independent [of its parts], but without parts it is nothing.

Moreover, the parts are parts only in their reference to one another, and only in their reference to all the parts taken together, which is [the good category of] the whole. The bad category of the whole and parts occurs where the parts lie in merely external, mechanical[, non-organic] connection. What is defective in this correlation is that everything is represented as having an [independent] being for itself, even while the whole has no sense without the parts. Each side essentially contains reference to the other. The parts, being outside of one another, essentially bear reference to what [as the whole] is self-identical [as they also bear reference to one another].

[2. Force and its expression]

When[, as in the correlation of whole and parts,] everything is so posited as to have the determination to which it is destined only within something else, we arrive at the correlation of *force* and its *expression* [§136]. Force is the entire content, which comes to the fore in appearance, in the expression of the force. The content [or essential form] is the *law* of the force, and the law appears only in being reflected within the force [taken along with its apparent expressions]. No matter how the force is determined, we behold its determination within its expression. Both the force and its expression have the same content, but force falls within the form of self-reference, simple reference of self to self. Force is simple—it is what is inner. Hence, force has the same determination as the whole, and its expressions, which lie outside one another as external parts, likewise have the same determination. Force, we say, consists in positing itself outwardly as its expression. The parts come forward as each having a being for itself. But we have seen that they do not in fact have being for themselves. The whole consists in positing itself as being under the determination of parts outside of one another. Thus the force, in its self-reference [merely as force and not as expression], is something one-sided that must necessarily express itself. But the expression of the inner force is itself only one side of the total form of the force.

The expression passes merely for what is posited, while the force passes for what is independent. Yet this is by no means the case. Rather, the force has being only insofar as it expresses itself. The inner force passes for what subsists, and the expression at once appears as what is merely posited, as what essentially bears reference to the inner force as its other. But this inner force consists precisely in raising its one-sidedness up beyond itself. Force as a whole is force only through the fact of expressing itself. Each side is itself the whole. A force itself is the expressing of itself, and the expression is already posited as mediated by its reference to the inner force as its other. Thus only one and the same content is present within the different determinations of force and expression, just as is the case within the [determinations of the] whole and the parts.

We must show experimentally what a force is. The content of the force is the same as the content of [sensory] appearance. Conversely, we feign to derive appearances from the inner force. What this means is that we have in fact so arranged the content of the inner force as to conform to its appearances. We make matters easy for ourselves by introducing into the inner force what we already have in the appearances. But to truly grasp something conceptually is to lift it up out of any false opposition [of a force and its expression]. What is true in the apprehension [*Erfassen*] of force [in the physical sciences] is that we have lifted out of the appearances what is essential, what remains self-identical in those very appearances. The opposition of force and its expression is a pure fiction of the understanding. When we intuit electricity in the particular circumstances belonging to its expression, we strip away what is accidental [to electricity in those circumstances] and hold onto what is essential, to electricity in its very simplicity. I reduce electricity to the simple determination of what it is. It was, in particular, Newton who introduced the reflective determination of force [withdrawn into itself, e.g., gravity,] into natural scientific research. Yet the sensory appearances themselves are, in their determinateness, the sole content of any such force.

(§136, Note) Force is finite. It is Herder in his text *God*, an edifice of Spinozistic representations, who principally speaks of "force."[16] Force is finite, and so is at once finite in its content. Force within itself is the essential content in one-sided form, but so that this one-sidedness comes to be negated through the expression of force. But the force comes to be laid out as if it were independent, with a being for itself. A force expresses itself, but this expression transpires as if it were something accidental to the force itself, as if the force could sleep without ever gaining expression. The determination of expression is not yet immediate in the inner force; the force must be solicited [by something else, by another force] in order to express itself, and without such solicitation its expression is not yet immanent in it. This is what makes a force finite. It is dependent on an other.

16. Johann Gottfried Herder, *God. Some Conversations* (Indianapolis: Bobbs-Merrill, 2002).

It comes to be solicited by an other. But the soliciting other must itself be solicited to do its soliciting, and so on [to infinity].

Mathematicians [in contrast to Newton] protest that the *metaphysics of force* does not concern them. They want only to observe the expression of force. But if they do only that, they do not make use of [the determination of] force [withdrawn within itself] at all, since for them the entire content of the force is present solely in its expression. For them, the force is thus completely known by its apparent content. The *form of force* is left alone by itself, and this form is that very *content of the force* posited merely in reference to itself. What resides within the force in this its form is something entirely known. This form is that of the force's reflection solely within itself. To be sure, the content of any given force is finite. And since the content of a given force is finite, it contains intimations of its dependence on something beyond that force[, i.e., on another force within itself soliciting the expression of the first force]. We have intimations of a force such as magnetism or electricity as coming in its content from something beyond it that remains still unknown to us. What remains of scientific interest is the systematization of this finite content with its reference to something else.

It is important to see that isolated forces lack independent being for themselves. The greatest of incongruities occurs when one takes the mental forces [or faculties]—fantasy, sensation, etc.—to each have being for itself. To proceed in this way is, conceptually, completely empty and barren of thought. For spirit is absolutely one.

[§137] A force is a force only in its expression. It is the negation of its one-sidedness. The expression of the force is the mediation by which the force as force acquires its being. In fact the force returns to itself in its expression. In its expression the force is all it is ever to be. In the expression of force any distinction between the force and its expression, which have both passed as independent, raises itself up beyond itself. And with that the correlation between force and its expression is reduced to the correlation of the *inner* and *outer,* where the identity of both is now simultaneously posited. Force and its expression are not independent, but each is only a formally distinct determination of the other.

Force and expression are one in content. The [inner] form of force is purely external and meaningless. The expression of a force is a clarification of the form of force, of its unclarified being merely for itself; it is a clarification of the form of force as something initially meaningless, something purely null and void. Thus the identity [of the unclarified form of force and its expressed clarification] is [implicitly] present within that very form. But that inner form of force also comes to be differentiated into [external] formal determinations which[, being due to other soliciting forces as mentioned above,] are not themselves essential to that inner form. The force's [outer sensory] determinations of form are thus posited as a merely defective expression of it. The inner form is the *ground,* but in such a manner that this ground is posited in the merely empty form of reflection within itself [§138]. Just so is its external reflection within whatever is other than it reduced to another empty determination. But the content of what is merely inner lies, so to speak, in its drive to become non-defective external expression of itself. For this content posits the form of reflection within itself at once as its reflection within what is other than itself, as befits the content of whatever is merely inner.[17]

[3. The inner and the outer]

(§139) What is external[, crowning the success of the inner force in its drive to become outer and thus abolish itself as force,] now has the same content as what is inner.[18] There is now nothing within the abstract essence of immediate being that is not outwardly manifest. There is great truth in this perfect oneness of the inner and the outer. A human being, what he or she is, his or her character, how he or she has worked him- or herself out to be what he or she now is—all that is inner, but all that is now perfectly external. A human being thus lays him- or herself out in an external exposition of him- or herself. All the actions of a human being make up the totality of his or her acts—and that totality is what that human being is. That this is so is noticed should a human being ever wish to hide him- or herself in his or her totality. The few cases in which one can [seemingly] succeed in hiding oneself, do not in the end turn out to be real cases of concealing the totality of what one is.[19] What God [is, as the inner,] is now revealed in the outer world.[20] What a people is comes to be revealed in its existence, in its customs, in its acts, in its constitution. In pragmatic, psychological history writing it will be said that a human being who has accomplished great deeds has

17. This is to say that force as merely inner, solicited to imperfectly express itself by another soliciting force, is driven to attain perfect expression in an inner content which is no longer merely inner, but which is an inner content fully and perfectly expressed in what is outer.

18. Thus the complete set of causal laws of nature is the inner stable intelligible image of the entire range of unstable external appearances. The same content is compressed inwardly in the laws of nature and expressed outwardly in the sensory phenomena.

19. A possible interpretation of this is that, in choosing to conceal part of oneself, one still reveals all of oneself precisely in trying to reveal only part of oneself.

20. If we may assume that God as the inner is alone perfectly revealed in the external world, a person or nation is perfectly revealed in the external world only if that person or nation partakes of God and is thus taken to be fully revealed only in the entire external world including all other persons and nations.

such and such [hidden] weaknesses and passions. It is a common saying that no one is a hero for his valet. Nothing could be truer. The service of revealing such weaknesses is the one often rendered by pragmatic writers of history. But this service has its source in the envy expressed when such an historian proceeds to bring another person down to a plane of equality with him- or herself.

It is said that large effects can follow from the slightest of causes. Yet what is not already present within minute causes can never emerge out of them. True, a great event has an inner dimension. But nothing inner exists within nature comparable to what is inner within spirit. Within nature, everything is directly out there in the open—it is all directly given. To grasp something conceptually is, to be sure, not to grasp it stuck in the externality of its forms. Such externality is separated off by the [abstracting] understanding. Nature itself exhibits no such separation of externals by the understanding. As human beings we are capable [by the understanding] of abstracting [external forms] and of remaining stuck in a one-sided manner of proceeding.

The inner and the outer are, to be sure, opposites as formal determinations. The inner merely as such is only inner, and the outer is at once only outer. Whoever holds fast to abstraction merely of the inner at once already falls into externality. These are the two categories now in question. They are to be sure formally separated from each other, differentiated, except that each within itself has the same content as the other [§140]. A human being has reason as his natural impetus [*Anlage*], but at first reason is only something inner, while reason as it unfolds in customs and laws is still, at that early point in his or her development, something external to him or her. Thus the rationality [of custom] still assumes the form of externality for such an individual. Nature has the *idea* imprinted upon itself. But if we do not yet know the idea, it is first present only as a purely inner concept within nature. A human being is endowed with an impetus to give him- or herself form. For a child, its parents are reason itself. But such understandability perceived in its parents is, for the child, still something external to it. Further on, customary lawful regulations become rather something inner for the growing child. Rationality is something inner only for the person for whom it is also still something outer. Children strive to grow up, and so have, already imprinted by themselves upon their own selves, intimations of being grown up. They come to be in fact grown up when adulthood is not only upon themselves but also within themselves. What is [still] inner, imprinted upon the child, possesses an impulse to become outer or external. The determination to which whatever is inner is destined is a determination to pass over into what is external. It is this [activity of] making oneself external that makes possible the eventual positing of the oneness of the outer and the inner.

Empty abstractions come to raise themselves concretely up beyond themselves into one another. What is inner[, e.g., the system of causal laws,] is translucently only outer [as the totality of phenomena], and what is outer is only inner. Or, to put it otherwise, these very abstractions of the inner and the outer from each other disappear. The instinct of reason is precisely for such abstractions to disappear. This identity of these formal abstractions of inner and outer is actuality [§141]. Actuality is the identity of [outer] existence with [inner] content. The difference between the inner and the outer is absolutely raised up beyond itself into actuality—the inner is raised up into the outer, and the outer into the inner. In the correlation of the whole and the parts we have seen that the whole becomes determinate only in the parts. The whole bears necessary reference to the parts, and equally the parts to the whole. In the inner and the outer we have opposites that are emptied of any opposition, and the impetus toward the disappearance of opposites is an impetus toward the disappearance of each opposite. This impetus is already certain of realizing itself. It has only to work itself out. The form of mere inwardness is imperfect, defective. The certainty of this impetus regarding its self-realization is the total determination by which both the determination of the inner and that of the outer coincide in the same content.

II.C. Actuality

What is essential now fully lies within its appearance. Appearance is no longer burdened [as *mere* appearance] with the opposition of existence and essence. Rather, existence itself is immediately the essence. We have here the third position within the logic of the essence of immediate being as a whole [following the ground of existence as the first position and the concrete appearance of essence as the second position]. We have now beheld the logic of the abstract essence of being within its own development. The abstract essence of immediate being must appear. The essence lies upon appearance itself once the opposition within essence between the [abstract] essence and existence ceases. What we then have is actuality [or efficacy, *Wirklichkeit*—the efficacious process of real possibility actualizing itself— §142].[21] The entire [outer] content of the essence is identical with its

21. Note that actuality is the universal process of the essence of being, of its essential potentiality actualizing itself throughout the diversity of all existents. For Aristotle an Olympic prize winner actualizes a single human being's physical po-

[inner] form. The opposition between essence and external existence has raised itself up into a purely empty distinction of mere form. Actuality is the oneness of essence and existence.[22] It contains the determinations of essence and existence within itself, and is their content. But actuality when developed is, as we shall see, *necessity* [i.e., the process of necessitation].[23]

(§143) Actuality contains the determinations of inner and outer, both the form of reflection within itself and the form of reflection within the other. Actuality is immediate only by raising any oppositions [of essence and existence, force and its expression, whole and parts, or inner and outer] up beyond themselves. These opposed terms, lying within this difference of inner and outer, are thus posited upon actuality itself [where they are *raised up beyond* themselves] into the process of efficacy. This difference will still be posited within actuality, but the moments of this difference are each the same whole of actuality [as an efficacious process]. Actuality, efficacy, at first lies within merely one of two formally distinct determinations, namely, merely within the form of being an essence, i.e., the form of self-reference, reflection within itself. Thus it is first of all possibility that comes to be inscribed upon whatever is actual.

So we first say that whatever is actual must be possible. It will also be said that what is [logically] possible is whatever does not contradict itself. The form of being an essence is thus reduced to something logically possible or non-contradictory. What is merely inner is only logi-

---

tential. For Hegel all existence appears to actualize the entire essence of immediate being. "Actuality" as a universal process singles out (Hegel says "defines") the absolute. It seems to follow that, since there is nothing outside the absolute comparable to other substances that actualize the potential of a given Aristotelian substance, the absolute is self-actualizing. It gives itself actualization; its actualization is so to speak freely self-creative or rather spontaneously emergent in "activity."

22. In an Aristotelian vein, actuality is outer existence as the actualization of an essential inner potentiality. The identity of the inner and the outer which preceded actuality in Hegel's exposition was a tranquil identity in which the inner (the law) and the outer (the phenomena) were each transparent in the other. Actuality is, by contrast, their dynamic identity. It is the process of actualizing the inner in the outer. The inner translates itself into the outer realm, and the outer realm then translates itself into a new real inner possibility or potentiality for the actualization. The process of actuality is the alternation between a momentarily stable outer actualization of one real possibility and the crumbling of that actualization, which withdraws into its potentiality for some further actuality.

23. Since actuality is a universal process, necessity as actuality is also such a process: the process of necessitation. This necessity is not logical necessity, since it can be the surprising actualization of real possibilities that are not logically necessitated by prior conditions. This seems to be because, beyond *prior* conditions, the actualization of a possibility is itself one of the actualization's necessary conditions.

cally possible. Yet such possibility is a one-sided form of the inner. Such possibility is indeed one general category [within the efficacious process of actuality]. It is especially in philosophy and history that we must do away with such mere logical possibility, which is only the abstraction of self-reference. Whatever is concrete is upon itself set in opposition to itself, so that everything is contradictory, everything is impossible. But everything remains logically possible if I merely consider its simple reflection on itself [and not its concrete reflection within anything else].

Yet all such talk of mere logical possibility is quite trivial. Everything must be taken in interconnection with something else. What has validity in *philosophy* is not what simply can be, but what must necessarily be. In *historiography* we must grant validity to whatever is simply there as reported [without its being necessary]. As soon as we say of something actual that it is only logically possible, we at once recognize that we are dealing with a one-sided, defective form of the thing. Within whatever is actual, non-contradictory identity with itself is present, but it is present only as a single aspect [of an actual whole process], and is thus considered to be by itself something untrue.

[Moments of Actuality as an Efficacious Process: Contingency and Mere Possibility versus the Real Possibility, Pre-Conditions, and Necessity of a Matter at Hand]

In §144 of the *Encyclopaedia* we find that the other of what is reflected merely within itself is logically possible. We find reflection of oneself within what is other than oneself, within mere external actuality. Thus the determination of whatever immediately is, we say, is *inessential actuality*.[24] This inessential, accidental actuality, standing over against essential actuality, we call *contingency*. What is [abstractly] essential, understood only as logically possible, is in truth inessential. Such an [abstract] essence is as inessential as can be. But whatever is actual but only contingent is also only logically possible. Contingency here is actuality that merely has the value of logical possibility attached to it. But what is contingent, merely as such, is something that either can be or cannot be.[25]

---

24. Thus what is reflected within something external to itself is reflected within an actual entity (or "actuality," as Hegel says, privileging reference to universals) that is not essential to it.

25. Hegel has just said that what is contingent is something merely possible. He now admits that what is contingent (non-necessary) either can or cannot be actual, is either possible or impossible. A married bachelor, being contradictory or impossible, is not necessary, and so is contingent. So, when he said that what is contingent is something merely possible, he may be taken to mean that what is referred to as *merely* contingent without being further designated as either actually existent or impossible is merely possible for us.

We have here the thought determinations that together make up actuality [as the efficacious identity of essence and existence, inner and outer: contingency, mere logical possibility, impossibility; and real possibility, necessity as necessitation]. Whether something is logically possible or not depends on its content [§145]. Possibility and contingency both depend on the content in question. But it may further be said, in view of its content, that something harbors a *real possibility*, where a real possibility is understood as its *necessity* [i.e., its necessitation by prior conditions]. Whatever is really possible is both actual and necessary. If we explicate the point at which we have now arrived [through the determination of real possibility], we have arrived at the category of being a *condition* [of what is necessitated—§146]. Whatever is [abstractly or logically] possible or contingent is merely posited. When we view things as external to one another, what is external to something else is [inessentially] actual. It is merely something posited. In other words, it is posited, but because it also is, it is at once something immediately given [and thus not something merely posited]. Its being merely posited by us is thus raised up beyond itself into its immediacy: its being merely posited bears reference to what is other than being merely posited, i.e., to the mediation of what is posited by the immediacy of its being. In that I take what is contingent as something purely posited but at once say "It is," I raise its being merely posited, i.e., its being merely presupposed [or pre-posited], up beyond itself. It is and yet is something posited. It has existence; its existence is out there, even while it is only something posited. It is, but its being is also that of being posited. Insofar as its contingent being is merely posited, its existence is only a possibility and has the determination of being raised up beyond itself [as a mere possibility into something that is not only posited but is an actual efficacious condition of something else, of a consequence]. In possibility as actual and efficacious there lies an other[, a posited consequent]. [Antecedent] possibility is thus the possibility and thus a condition of something else. But conditions are specific existents that have validity for themselves. The existent conditions of a house include stones, beams, funds, which are all necessary conditions of the house. These conditions first exist out there with a being for themselves, without any regard to the house. They are also conditions of many other outcomes than the house. And since they also bear reference to something other than the house, as conditions merely of this house they are contradictory.[26]

(§147) So necessity contains contradiction[, i.e., contradictory outcomes of prior conditions each with a being for itself]. It is only as con-

---

26. This seems to say that conditions at first contain alternative possible outcomes, although as matters develop the possible outcomes are narrowed until there is but one necessary outcome.

taining such contradiction that this [hard] necessity [in contrast to logical necessity] is to be apprehended. The earlier determinations, those that have gone before, thus contain an alternation of contradictions[, i. e., contradictory outcomes]. What is [really] possible must be separated [by the future] out from these prior conditions understood as what is immediately actual. What is immediately actual differs from what is possible. The possibility [that becomes real] generally contains something other than what the immediate actuality has been. Within the contingency of immediate actuality there is still something else than that actuality, and with such immediate actuality we thus have a *condition* [of something else]. If something else is to be [really] possible, its [necessary] conditions must all be present. But its conditions are existents that, in their immediate existence, do not bother themselves with anything else to come. Yet something is *really possible* only by virtue of having such conditions. Further, to any real possibility there also belongs, beyond its necessary prior conditions, its own content, the matter at hand [*die Sache*] which is not only upon itself but at once for itself determinate. What has been immediately actual is broken up. It has its own being, but it contains within itself something different, the [real future] possibility. Immediate actuality within itself is thus broken up.

Consider, for example, political revolution. The [pre-revolutionary] present is what is immediately actual. In order for some other state of affairs to become present, the conditions of that new state of affairs must be present. Thus first the [pre-revolutionary] present is broken up. It bears within itself something else. Yet these two determinations—the initial conditions and the outcome they contain—are not merely likewise broken apart, but rather come together in a unity. The are not only upon themselves but for themselves the very fact of the matter, [the revolution itself,] the very content for which the initial existents enter as mere conditions. Contingency [in the initial conditions] is destined to fall away, and the [real] possibility of something else is itself a condition of itself. This is the mediation in question—the [real] possibility of something else. Such is the course of externality in its development, and this externality is the real possibility as it runs the course of these its own determinations. The course of the mediation as such is the totality. But the course of these diverse determinations is simple in form, reflected within itself. Thus reflected within itself, this whole is the content which is equal to itself.

[II.C.a. The Matter at Hand]

This content, then, is the *matter at hand*. The course [that has been externally run through is] reflected within itself [in its inner intelligibility]. The same [tranquil inner] course recast in its [external] form, as the totality of that form, is then disquiet and activity. In its closer determination, the matter at hand is the translation of the inner into the outer, and of the outer into the inner. In translating the matter at hand as inner into the form of the outer, it is activated, and to this extent the matter as inner is the ground [of the same matter as outer]. The real ground, the matter at hand [as inner], is raised up beyond itself into actuality. Conversely, what is outward, immediate actuality comes to be reduced to mere possibility, and to be used up in the matter [as the unity of the inner and the outer]. The conditions, which are external, come to be used up in the matter at hand. This is the complete course, a course that is a circle of courses grasped conceptually through and through [as leading] into one another.

The course of the matter at hand takes its start from what is external [*Ausserlichkeit*]. When all [necessary] conditions are present, that matter must become actual. Given those conditions, the matter is a real possibility. The complex of conditions, the totality as the completeness of conditions, the whole—this is real possibility. Insofar as these conditions are present, the matter at hand must become actual, and the actualization of this fact raises the difference [between inner and outer] beyond itself, whereupon the matter comes to be posited in its existence, gaining the moment of externality which thus far had been missing within it. This course, in which the outer course is overturned and hurled into the inner one, in which the outer receives a counterblow projecting it back into the inner, is what is meant by "activity." This alternation between the inner and outer courses we now call "necessity," the actuality lying within what it has posited upon itself, within what actuality upon itself is. This we have now seen. Necessity is defined as the unity of actuality and possibility. On the whole, this is correct—necessity is the third [term], but it is not well expressed. Necessity is this very course. What is difficult here is coming to know transition. The transition is a manifold one, but these manifold transitions then constitute a single course.

Just one example. If we represent to ourselves the great revolution that occurred with the passage of the Roman Republic over to rule by a single individual, that revolution was a necessity. To have insight into this necessity means to see what has run its course in that revolution. The course of events starts out with the existence of the state of the Republic within all its innocence. The Roman Senate held sway over the entire civilized world. The Roman Republic thus had its constitution, its immense splendor, its power, its wealth, its culture—the whole stood there as a glorious empire. That was the immediate state of affairs. But this state of affairs came to be reduced to being a mere condition, a state of affairs broken up within itself, which contained within itself a totally different spirit and called within itself for still another formation. No longer did that state of affairs have a hold on actuality. This other, the inner spirit [contained by the established state of affairs in itself] now became the matter at hand. The break with the past then comes to be seen more closely in the fact that the spirit of the empire was ill-suited to the constitution of a republic. Along with that incongruency came a disappearance of [republican] patriotism. The general matter at hand [in the empire] becomes too large for the actual interest of all individuals in the Republic to be excited, and with that self-seeking originates within the Republic. These circumstances of the Republic are broken up [internally only insofar] as they are destined to be the mere condition of another state of affairs. That [other state of affairs] is [a real] possibility. The whole is the [external] matter at hand reflected within itself. The [new] matter at hand could only step forward, it could not be withstood, it was now the absolute power. The rich unity of purpose found within individuals [in the Roman Republic] could not withstand the rupture. Power no longer resides within the single individual.

The greatest of statesmen contain this rupture within themselves. What is powerful and active is rather the whole, the matter at hand. Yet within the matter at hand there lives an activating subject. There must be an [individual] subject who has an intimation of the coming rupture. Individuals like Caesar have felt this rupture coming and have gained definite knowledge of it. One who knows the outer conditions to be null and void, something destined to fall by the wayside (like the German Empire with its determination frozen in time), becomes the executive agent of the matter at hand. Individuals within whom there is consciousness of the matter, who know what the times call for, are agents of the matter at hand. They place themselves at the forefront because they know and feel the matter itself, and the nullity of the formation in which that matter is still enveloped. Heroes are those who make the new matter at hand their own personal matter. The preceding existence falls, and is reduced to being mere material used in the new formation. What previously was only a condition for a new formation is now material serving that very formation. Here is the course, the condition, the possibility of something else, of the new matter at hand, this very matter in the form of its activation. Particular individuals are always required to translate what is outer into what is inner, and to posit what is inner in its being externally out there. If we want to come to know this translation of the inner into the outer, such knowledge is called the contemplation of something in its necessity, and to such contemplation the very course of the matter belongs.

[II.C.b. The Moments of Necessity]

(§148) The moments [of necessity] are now to be set apart from one another more exactly. These moments are the three moments of condition, the matter itself, and activity.

[1.] Conditions

At its outset, a condition enjoys immediate being for itself. It is a merely accidental, external state of affairs destined to fall by the wayside. As something purely posited, a condition is a condition only relative to the matter at hand [of which it is posited to be a condition]. In this state of affairs, the matter at hand exists [implicitly] as the contrary of what it will be [explicitly]. When the totality of conditions is present, the matter at hand must come to be. To apprehend the [present] state of affairs correctly means to apprehend all that is presently at hand, [all] the conditions. These conditions come to be utilized as material, and so they enter into the content of the [new] matter at hand. The content of the matter at hand is already present in its conditions.

[2.] The matter at hand

The matter at hand [such as a political revolution] is at first something merely inner and purely possible. Yet such a matter has an independent content with a being for itself. It is this content that holds truth. It is by its utilization of its conditions that the matter at hand receives external existence. There are states of affairs in the world where all is [apparently] in order, but where something else suddenly breaks out, and the entire state of affairs is overturned. Yet that state of affairs will never be overturned if nothing smolders underneath it, if the state of affairs does not already contain within itself some quite other matter at hand. But there is a certain illusion of heedless insouciance that consists in limiting one's attention to only the immediate present. The matter at hand then strides forth from out of its conditions.

3. The activity [of a matter at hand actualizing itself]

Activity has being for itself. A man, a character, [e.g., Napoleon,] places himself at the head, existing for himself. The content which makes him a power to be reckoned with lies in the conditions that are present, along with the fact that he himself makes the matter at hand into the very content of his activity. The matter gathers unto itself its own individuals. They will not be lacking. No individual is capable of doing anything against the matter at hand. The individual is capable of something only by placing him- or herself on the side of the [ascendant] matter at hand. The activity finds its content only in that matter.

The activity is thus the movement of translating the conditions of the matter at hand into that matter itself, into the affirmation of the matter insofar as it enjoys a being that is simply out there as present. By this movement, the [sufficient conditions of the] matter at hand lend necessity to the matter itself. What comes out of the movement is the matter itself. Whatever emerges with necessity attached to it has a certain *hardness* to it due to the fact that one form of existence, with

the form of being something actual, comes to be raised up beyond itself into the form of being something else that comes onto the scene as
equally actual. Something befalls the first actuality that is alien to it,
and this show of an alien second actuality befalling the first is a relation of violence [*Gewalt*] done to the first. Necessity appears as violence, a loss of freedom. Through something alien to it, the immediate
actuality is annihilated. Freedom, by contrast, consists in the fact that
what seems to happen to us from outside is really identical with us.

For example, in crime and punishment, the punishment appears to
the criminal to be an alien essence, to be the will of men quite other
than himself. The law first comes down on the individual, and does violence to him. Yet in the end it comes to be experienced by the criminal
as something to which he has a right. The law becomes a determination
of the criminal's own reason. In being punished the criminal is set free.
Insofar as the law comes down upon us from the outside, we suffer violence and so lack freedom in our relation to the law. Yet if, by contrast,
they have the laws as their very own, they stand in a relation of freedom
with regard to the law. In the first case a human being behaves as inwardly compelled against his will. He owns up to the matter at hand
only ruefully. Yet if he is conscious of [his oneness with] the matter at
hand, the law, he behaves within it freely.

If we consider more closely this transformation in one's relation to
the law, it is the matter itself that here brings itself to completion. Formations that are actual existents over against one another topple one
another down. But the matter at hand only brings itself forth through
this transformation in one's relation to the law [so that it is no longer a
relation of the criminal and the law in opposition to each other]. Necessity upon itself thus contains *freedom* within itself. This freedom, whatever is free, is the self-concept [as examined in the third part of these
lectures]. The correlations that we are now about to consider explicate
necessity and raise up the determination of actualities as posited over
against one another [into the freedom of the self-concept].

What the ancients took to be fate may be recalled here, especially
as it arises in the tragedies belonging the highest level of Greek consciousness. Tragedy lies in the fact that the hero goes under. The cho-
rus always preaches that one must recognize fate and go along with
the times. But the Greek heroes who go under refuse to surrender
anything of their character, and rather show themselves to be free in
the face of their very fate. The freedom of the tragic hero comes down
to saying "It is so, and because it is so we accept it" [§149]. In Sopho-
cles' *Heracles* it comes to pass that Heracles says to his son that even
ungratifying work is gratifying. Freedom, the maintenance of one's
independence, lies in the fact that one exhibits steadfast serenity. Such
equanimity refuses to succumb, it allows nothing alien to pass muster

within itself, but rather solely allows the expression "It is so" to pass. Such equanimity is the simple reference which one bears to oneself. It is the mediation that raises itself up into the simple being of the matter at hand. Spirit takes itself back into this simplicity. It has raised everything up and is unbroken in its being for itself.

The dissatisfaction of a human being, his unhappiness, lies in the contradiction of suffering a loss because of something done to him [by hard necessity]. My greatest unhappiness is due to the contradiction between my consciousness of the [current] state of affairs and that to which I have my highest right. I have the highest right to something, but suffer the highest grievance. This contradiction is quite generally unhappiness. To be thus unhappy is to remain sunken in this contradiction. But when a human being says "It is so," he has withdrawn into simple equality with himself, and into imperturbable freedom. So long as I harbor claims of any sort, so long as I hold fixedly to some end, I remain sunken in such a contradiction. But if I give up all determinate interests, all ends, all bonds, the contradiction is lifted and I ensconce myself in the simple expression "It is so." The ancients had no use for consolation. Such strength as theirs needs no consolation. The need for consolation is a need for something lost, something that one ought have back. Consolation is an expression for substitution, the fact that something else is to fall my way [in compensation]. Lying at the basis of consolation, then, is the supposition that I have lost what I ought by right to have. [Receiving back the equivalent of what is lost—]this for consolation is the highest freedom. But the freedom [of the Greek tragic hero] is abstract. Merely succumbing to necessity is lower [than the freedom contained in consolation]. Yet we are attracted to a human being who maintains his strength of character [in the manner of a Greek tragic hero, accepting what is without needing consolation]. The ancients had no need of consolation for losses. Yet succumbing unperturbed to necessity is not higher [than consolation], but is deficient, since within the ancient world we have the surrender of all ends, [the acquiescence in] indeterminate necessary being. Yet this state of being bereft of all ends in antiquity still remains within the logic of necessity. For to be subject to necessity is to have hold of the self-concept only insofar as the self-concept is merely upon itself. The end here is still the self-concept only as it is upon itself. Only when freedom has passed over into [its particular] determinations do ends [cease to be merely upon themselves and] come to be posited. The alternation of necessity is difficult, but is of the greatest interest. All the relations of [the logic of] being and [the logic] of essence are recapitulated in it.

[II.C.c. The Forms of Necessity]

Three forms of necessity are: 1. the correlation of substantiality, 2. the correlation of causality, and 3. that of reciprocal interaction.

[1. The correlation of substantiality]

(§150) *The correlation of substantiality* we have already explained: it is necessity within its immediacy. The *substance* is what we have already been calling "the matter at hand." This matter explicates itself through the course which it runs. It explicates itself within the sphere of accidentality, within accidental actual existents. This is what is first posited: the substance is immediately actual. What is accidental, what is internally ruptured, then comes to be translated into another actual existent which as such is equally necessary. Yet this other is, and with that it is an immediate actual existent. Thus the exchange that occurs in substantiality is the same as that which took place before in the matter at hand. This necessary course is substance. Accidentality is also actuality in its immediacy. Substance first takes the form of being accidentally there.

(§151) The substance is the totality of the accidents. The One is explicated so as to become immediate actuality. The substance is thus *absolute power*, the reduction of actuality to mere immediate actuality. The substance is the power to reduce actuality, and with that it is negative. Here violence finds a home, in that actualities are posited over against one another. Power explicates the form of substance, the form of the conversion [of opposed actualities into one another] within necessity. Necessity itself is empty of any content. Its content is merely this exchange [of prior actualities for further ones], this mediation [of actual beings one with the other], a mediation that raises itself up beyond itself [into the sheer power that prevails over all actualities]. Necessity is only this manifestation of power. Hence it is said that necessity is *blind*, i.e., it is devoid of any determinate content that would make up the absolute end.

In the Spinozistic system, the absolute is determined as the absolute substance, as the One from which the world falls away. This state of having fallen out [of the one substance] makes up the world in its externality, in its immediacy. Everything actual internally breaks ups, and so is only temporary. The breaking of everything actual is the power of substance over whatever is actual. It is the explication of substance. There is only one substance, which is purely affirmative, which remains equal to itself in the exchange of actualities [in their rise and breaking up.] All figurations [in the actual world] are determinations, negations, vanishing [entities]. Thought is swept clean of all ends. Here is the greatness of Spinoza. The oneness of his substance is the fire in which the soul cleanses itself of all particularity. That is liberation, but it is only formal freedom. In that Spinoza proceeds to the human spirit, he makes emancipation from bondage into his vocation. Bondage lies in human affects [or passions], since by such affects we posit ends. Human freedom [from bondage to the passions] lies in the love of God. Such freedom is the direction taken by spirit toward the one single substance. Everything particular consumes itself. The affects make up human bondage [*servitus humana*] insofar as they are what is determining.

Yet from this determination of substance [as object] the transition must be made to the subject in which the human being attains to freedom. What is revolting in Spinoza is the determination of his substance by which human beings are considered only as accidents, as beings in which there lies no absolute end upon and for itself. What is incoherent in the Spinozistic system shows up in this its content. Divine revelation takes the form of divine [self-]manifestation. This manifestation is the world itself. The two forms [or attributes of substance] are for Spinoza extension (physical) and thinking (spiritual). That there are two such forms, extension and thinking, is accepted empirically. They are what they are, and are simply come upon. Where do these two forms come from? For Spinoza what is determinate is not conceptually grasped. But we fail to grasp conceptually how thinking and extension should come out of the one substance.

Everything [coming out of Spinoza's substance] merely goes *back* into it. But what is particular fails to be explicated as the self-movement of the substance itself. Spinoza did not proceed from his substance on to the correlation of causality [as deduced from the substance]. The causal correlation lies in something [of the nature of a process] which further differentiates the self-referential substance from its [eternal] attributes. Substance posits itself merely as undifferentiated, but [in causality] it is nonetheless different from what is thus posited, the substance is different from its differentiation [in causality]. Causality is thus a [self-]differentiation as posited within Spinoza's substance. So the substance comes to be the cause as the original matter at hand, as reflection within itself, as infinite negativity within itself. The substance in its determinateness is now one-sided merely as cause. In the totality of its form, substance then raises up its one-sidedness [as cause] beyond itself, and posits itself in the form of something further that is merely posited, of something relative. It thus posits itself as effect [*Wirkung*], and what is now actual, merely posited [as effect], comes from an original cause that [within its effect] is at once different from itself. Cause and effect are different only through the differentiation that lies [undeduced from the substance] within the correlation of substantiality[, i.e., the correlation of substance and its accidents]. Causality consists in negating the form of originality [as mere cause] in order to posit itself as something relative, something that essentially comes to bear reference to its other as effect.

We first have the representation of a finite cause. A finite cause is present wherever the cause comes to meet up with its end in its effect. The effect is also a finite actual existent [*Wirklichkeit*]. It is immediately determined as finitely actual, as [previously] illustrated by force [*Kraft*] and its expression. But this cause [unlike a force] does not need to be *solicited* in order to act as a cause. A force was thus at first only inner. The cause is the matter at hand, the whole, something actual. We now hold in representation two actual existents: cause and effect. The finitude [of the cause] consists in the fact that the cause is separated from its effect. The cause is thus off to its own side, and is independent. The cause is thus blind and mechanical to the extent that it is an actual existent, and the same holds for the effect. This finitude of the form [of a cause] is at once a finitude of its *content*. This finitude of such content follows from the finitude of the form of causality. Yet we have already beheld the identity of form and content. The determination of form [as active] at first operates against [the form of] the effect. The content is identical with the form only as the [essential] form of what is inner as distinguished from itself in the [outwardly] explicated form.

[2. The correlation of causality]

(§153) The difference is now posited between two actual existents that in point of content are both finite. Yet if we consider the self-concept of each, the cause is cause only insofar as it is at once the effect. The cause consists in raising up its one-sidedness beyond itself [into its effect]. The cause is immediately actual, which is a one-sided determination. The cause lies in raising its immediacy up beyond itself and in positing itself as the effect. The effect itself belongs to the self-concept of the cause. Only a single such concept is present. The cause, like the effect, is only one of the two determinations of form—which make up but one being. The cause's being posited belongs to the very concept of the cause. According to their concept, cause and effect thus do not fall outside each other. It is only in its effect that the cause becomes cause. The cause [in being the cause of its effect] is self-caused [*causa sui*]. Spinoza says that God is *causa sui*. Only in its effect is the cause just such a cause. It is within the effect that the cause posits itself as cause.

The identity of cause and effect in concept is the same identity that we find between them in representation. If a stone strikes a man dead, the stone and his death first appear to be two separate actual beings. But the stone merely in its being for itself is no cause. Only in its effect does it become a cause. The stone is a cause insofar as it sets itself in motion, while the effect is the fact that through the stone and its mass a [further] movement is posited, a jolt [in the dying man] which contradicts the original self-movement [of the stone]. Both before and after the impact, the [quantity] of movement remains the same. A law of mechanics is at work: the movement that is in both cause and effect has [quantitatively] one and the same determination.

The rain dampens the ground. The rain itself, as water, causes the ground to be wet. What we have here, in both cause and affect, is one water, one and the same thing. This is the identity of the two in point of content. We so represent matters to ourselves that the cause comes before the effect, but in fact the cause has its being only within the effect. Time is not the distinguishing factor between cause and effect. Water falls to the ground. This falling is the negating of the immediacy, of the independence of water [from the damp ground]. This rain is thereby *the* cause which this effect has. Cause and effect are inseparable.

But the oneness of cause and effect is also marked by their externality. Here infinite progress enters the picture. The above inseparability of cause and effect is one determination, while their diversity is the other. We now have a contradiction. The infinite succession of causes and effects merely expresses this contradiction, with its alternation of the two determinations. Given finite causes and effects, the same contradiction holds throughout—whatever we determine as cause we must also determine as effect. The cause is an effect. The cause has again a cause, so it is itself at once an effect. We thus separate them, so that the cause has an effect, but on the other hand is an effect. We thus have a separation of causes and effects backward or forward on into infinity. This infinite progression is only an expression of the contradiction.

(§154) If we leave the self-concept of the [infinite] cause off to the side and take up what now is to be posited, what we have is the course run by cause and effect as each cancels itself in favor of the other. Cause and effect differ from each other: the effect is another actual existent [*Wirklichkeit*]. At first the effect is what is posited by the cause, but what is posited turns out to be itself an actual existent in its own right. It is an actual existent because it attains [self-]reflection within itself. Inasmuch as this is so, being posited by the cause is at once raised up beyond itself, so the positing of the effect is really a matter of positing it in advance, i.e., of presupposing it [*Voraussetzen*]. The cause in its positing is in advance of the actual effect as the original existent from which the effect springs. If we separate an effect from its cause, we must at once determine the effect to also be a cause in its own right. The effect is something posited in advance, and with that the effect is also another actual being, another substance to which that effect happens. This further substantial cause is passive insofar as the effect of the first cause happens to it, acts upon it. But this new cause is [self-]reflected within itself. It at once functions as that from which a further effect springs, which is the negating of its being posited, of its being an effect. Yet it happens to the first cause that it becomes an effect, since only by virtue of being an effect is it a [further] cause. The effect, insofar as it is posited, negates its cause as a cause[, i.e., as positing]. In other words, the effect posits its own cause as its own effect. This is what reaction consists in, reciprocal interaction [*Wechselwirkung*].

[3. The correlation of reciprocal interaction]

We have now fully explicated the correlation of finite causes and effects. The cause is itself substance. Being an effect lies upon that same substance, and so the effect is also a cause. This differentiation of cause and effect [in their oneness] is necessity in its developed form. Our own reflection on necessity [within the science of logic] is that both sides, both cause and effect, are the same [§155]. Each is cause and each posits its own effect within the other. They are both immediate as cause, and in both cases the other of what is immediate contains the effect. They are upon themselves one and the same.

(§156) The oneness of cause and effect has being for us, but not merely for us. Rather, reciprocal interaction [*Wechselwirkung*] itself consists in raising up the difference that underlies the interaction between them beyond itself into identity. For us, their difference has already disappeared. Each of the posited determinations is raised up beyond itself into the reciprocal interaction of cause and effect. The cause within its own effect bears reference to what is a further cause.

But the other cause is itself a substance, which subsists for itself. In that the effect is posited within another substance, the second cause persists for itself. This other cause negates having an effect merely posited upon itself, it negates merely receiving an effect from another cause. The second cause reacts against the first cause, and thus cancels its own initial determination merely as an effect of the first. It posits the first cause as something negated as such, i.e., it posits it not as a cause but as the effect of the second substance. It cancels the first cause as cause. But the first substance is still cause, and so it negates having the effect of the second substance lying upon itself. It thus reacts, and cancels the effect upon it of the second cause [in favor of acting as a further cause]. What is thus posited within reciprocal interaction is that cause and effect are undifferentiated, so that neither substance differs from the other. Reciprocal action thus shows that cause and effect negate not only the difference between them, but also their difference as actual beings [*Wirklichkeiten*], and their difference as substances as well. In the reciprocal interaction between cause and effect, the *necessity* of the causal correlation is now stripped bare, and the nature of necessity becomes fully manifest [§157]. Given anything that is, it is by the mediation of its other. But this mediation raises itself up beyond itself, and the result is simply what necessity itself is. And with that the exposition of the development of cause and effect is complete. They, cause and effect, at first appear as actual beings, but the reference they bear to each other directly negates their independence as any such beings.

(§158) What is necessary [*Notwendigkeit*][27] remains inner. Some-

___

27. I.e., what is subjected to necessity.

thing else, something hidden, comes forward as something alien to whatever is subjected to necessity. The bond, the connection between the two, is hidden. But all mediation has now disappeared. The result is that necessity at first is freedom merely upon itself, but is then raised up into freedom [not only upon itself but] for itself. What comes to be shown is that the independence of the two is merely the show of distinct independent actual beings. What is brought forward here is the same as what was first present [as we considered the matter at hand]. Necessity is the mediation, not of diverse substantial actual beings, but of the matter at hand with itself. But that is exactly what freedom is.

Either I obey the law as something alien to me, as something that is not mine; or, as I recognize within the law a determination of my own reason, in referring to the law I refer only to myself, I remain with myself [in my reference to the law]. That is freedom. It is the self-concept [*Begriff*] that is free. Freedom in general, when taken abstractly, is the abstraction of being and remaining by oneself, at home with oneself, even within the other. More exactly, the different beings are each totalities, but these totalities are only a showing forth within one substance. The self-concept is independent. It is the repelling of a thing from itself, but what is repelled is identical with what does the repelling, it is a movement of reciprocal action by which the first thing remains at home with itself in the other. That is the simple determination of the self-concept, in which opposed beings are one, so that their substantiality is one and the same.

(§159) The self-concept is the truth of both being and essence. In the logic of the essence there is only show. True, the distinctions within the self-concept have their being, but they have only a posited and finally negated being. We have now witnessed this show [of the essence of immediate being] in its development. Everything within the logic of the essence has shown itself in the end as a totality, as substance, as the original matter, and yet has done so only as an original matter that repels itself from itself in the form of different actual existents. The simple determinations of reflection are compressed into being only one, but into being such as one whole. That is freedom, that is the self-concept.

The self-concept now appears as a result, but it is the truth, which is why it is really first rather than last. At first the self-concept lies [hidden] upon itself in its immediate form as being. With that comes what is external to the self-concept, i.e., being, immediacy. Now we have the sheer developmental emergence [of the self-concept]. Its determinations already fall within one [substance], and in their development they show that they belong only to the one [substance]. In the logic of *being* we first had being, then something, then something else. Each of these categories had immediate being for itself. In the logic of *essence* we have had a showing forth of each category in another, we have beheld immediacy with mediation linked to it, but have only witnessed a showing.

Every category of essence is, but is such that another category appears upon it. The cause is only cause insofar as its mediation by its effect belongs to it. Now, in the logic of the self-concept, the two sides are still posited as beings, as [distinct] substances, but in such a manner that they are in fact but one substance. To be sure, they each have being only within the other, and they are the one only insofar as their oneness merely lies [hidden] upon each. But they themselves then negate each other's [merely posited] independence. The differences are posited to be throughout the same, and these differences have meaning only within their oneness with the other. The self-concept is the result [of the logics of being and essence]. The form makes up the differentiation. Being is the self-concept merely in its immediacy.

Being, mere self-identity, is a poor abstraction. That being belongs to the self-concept is what is least of all within that self-concept. The self-concept now shows forth upon itself [as immediate being], but in such a manner that it comes to be certain of itself [in its other]. The other of the self-concept has its independence, its foundation, only insofar as it has the self-concept as its ground. The transition from necessity to freedom is the hardest transition of all. The opposition between necessity and freedom appears absolute. Nature contains within itself necessity. But [through the science of logic] we come to grasp nature and necessity conceptually. We accord to ourselves the freedom to so grasp it. In nature things are ever and ever other actual existents, and they destroy one another when they collide. But when we grasp nature conceptually, we know that everything attains to the determination to which it is destined within its opposite, and within its opposite it comes together only with itself. The show of nature lies in the being of things outside one another. Within the sphere of all that exists we found the field of necessity. But insofar as we conceptually grasp nature, we are free even in our act of bearing reference to nature. Within spirit, the self-concept comes to enjoy being for itself. Within nature, spirit merely lies [posited] upon nature without yet attaining being for itself. Nature as such has, to be sure, a bond with us, but it is a bond that is not yet conceptually grasped by us. In spirit the self-concept exists within its own proper form as the self-concept, emancipated from the independence of its differences over against one another.

Subjugation to necessity is the hardest subjugation of all. Within it what rules is the relation of violence [Gewalt], of passing outside oneself, of self-negation. But to think necessity is to dissolve its hardness, and this is emancipation. The abstract emancipation of Indian hermits or the heroes of antiquity is no longer in question here. True emancipation is to be and remain by oneself, at home with oneself, in all that is different from oneself. Emancipation is the I, the pure self-concept itself. A concept of course can be a concept of something or other, of something external. But at that point the self-concept is caught up in the forms of externality, and is not yet for itself in simple self-reference. Spirit is free in that it is at home with itself in being at home with the I, and there we have the fullest form of freedom.

The self-concept merely on the level of sensation is love. In love I am totally free [in my reference to the other as reference to myself], and yet I am at once immediately [for the other who loves me] a rigid singular being [who is loved in all my singular interests]. I am also capable of withdrawing from this rigid being into the abstraction of my self [from all my diverse interests, as the one who loves me does]. I am also capable of surrendering all my singular interests [connecting me to others and to the world]. But I then again become [for the other who loves me], completely and absolutely, a rigid central point [from which all my singular interests radiate]. But in loving I myself leave this rigidity of mine behind, and expand my interest to include my relationship to the beloved, who is now for me just as much a rigid central point of diverse personal interests as I am for him or her. The sensitivity [of love] is here, in its determinateness, the unity of both individuals in their rigidity, who are thus still both distinct independent beings [for each other]. Each rediscovers his or her own [surrendered] rigid personality in the full rigidly centered personality of the beloved. This makes for the feeling of the identity of the two. To be sure, there is a contradiction here, since each has given up its rigid personality and diverse interests in his or her love for the other. Such is the contradiction that is here present on the level of sensation.

Love is completely speculative. Commonsense is speculative in the same way, but in reflection upon itself it forgets its true speculative character. In law I assert myself, my personality with all its singular interests. Law is a field in which the difference of persons is held fast in their respective rigidities. Within love, within the form of the self-concept, this whole field as found in law has disappeared. Blessedness is the actuality of the feeling of being in complete harmony, the feeling of satisfaction and of this peace. The self-concept thus attains to a being that is free at once upon itself and for itself [in its being for the other].

A "concept" often means nothing more than this or that determination of thought, some representation or other. If I say "man," that is no self-concept. Just as little is "blue" a self-concept. These are not "self-concepts" in the true sense of the term. A self-concept is strictly only what is, within itself, concrete, within itself something differentiated, but so that the oneness of what is differentiated also has being. The self-concept is abstract, but is also within itself absolutely concrete. The self-concept does not merely have its being in the form of simplicity, but rather in the form of being determinate within a differentiation that is at once posited as identical with itself. What is one-sided releases the contradiction that it has engendered. The result is the self-concept, the contradiction's state of being released, a state which, however, still retains that contradiction [as the moment of difference within the self-concept].

We human beings have hold of self-concepts. But only within spirit does the self-concept exist as such, only within spirit is it cast into relief for itself. For only spirit is free, existing as free within itself. But self-concepts taken generally are something else; they are not merely this freedom of existence which we come to enjoy. Everything, not merely self-concepts lodged within our human consciousness, is a self-concept.[28] With the category of the self-concept we do not remain stuck in our own human subjectivity. The substance of all things, their ground—all this goes back to this truth of the self-concept. We can say "God is the self-concept." The [concrete] essence of anything is itself its self-concept. The self-concept is absolute freedom. What is absolute is at home with itself in its difference from itself.

28. For example, a tree is upon itself a self-concept which holds itself within a single whole through its trunk, roots, branches, and leaves (cf. §161). But it is not self-consciously or for itself a self-concept. A thinking human being is self-consciously a self-concept. And, when the human being thinks the tree as a self-concept, the human being exercises self-consciousness on behalf of the otherwise un-self-conscious self-concept of the tree.

THE SELF-CONCEPT

3

The Self-Concept

(§160) The self-concept is free by virtue of its substantive power of having being for itself. It is what is concrete, not by growing together from what is by nature externally two, but by being one by its own very nature. It is from the very beginning only one. What is concrete is a totality. It has the form of simplicity, but it is not simple being for itself. Every moment in the self-concept is at once the whole, the entire concept. We have the whole at the level of its greatest purity as a whole, in its absolute infinity, only in God. In everything else, in every other self-concept, something else, something different from that self-concept, is also present. The highest truth is God. This truth bears the august determination of the Trinity. Every one of these three moments is itself the whole. God is Father, is Son, and is Spirit. We count them as three, but they are only one. Here is the self-concept in its absoluteness, as absolute not only upon itself but also for itself. Each of the three moments is the totality for itself, and not merely upon itself.

This divine totality is the one which on the sensory level is love, and which in the form of delectation is blessedness, i.e., spirit in its the most concrete form. This is how the self-concept must be taken. Spirit has hold of the self-concept as such. We find ourselves, here within the self-concept as such, on the ground of spirituality, of freedom, of the highest universality within which everything else is but a moment. This universal is not any original matter lying at hand, but is rather the universal substance within which everything is merely momentary. Yet every moment is upon itself the whole. This totality for itself, this absolute one, we call "God." Such being for itself as a whole is missing in Spinoza's substance, which is merely upon itself the whole, which is neither freedom itself nor freedom amid differences in any way permitting the differences to be each the whole.

(§161) Here [in the logic of the self-concept] we no longer have *transitions* into something else [as in the logic of being]. Nor do we any longer have any *showing forth within an other* [as in the logic of the essence]. We no longer have any necessity, any inner conditioning and outer showing forth, but rather only a *development* within which everything has within it the nature of the one as its truth. Within a whole grown tree nothing ever comes forth that does not already lie, within the seed, upon the seed itself. In the seed, δυνάει [potentially], is the trunk within which the whole tree is contained. The nature of the roots, the branches, the determinate bark of this tree, and so on—all that is contained, so to speak, spirit-like within the whole tree. There in the seed even the tree is already in the form of the self-concept. Everything else is only its further development. Everything is already [in its general or universal character] determined beforehand. Whatever comes out of the development bears upon itself the imprint of the whole. Everything that develops in a plant has the whole nature of the plant imprinted upon it, just as every part of any living organism has lying upon it the nature of the whole living organism. This, then, is development.

Subdivisions [of the Logic of the Self-Concept]

(§162) 1. The self-concept as such shines forth within itself so that the determinations of its [internal] differences make up its whole. The differences are posited as still remaining and contained within the oneness of the whole, but merely as shining forth within the self-concept itself. This is the subjective or *formal* concept. 2. Within itself the self-concept passes judgment on itself. When we formulate our end we project before us our entire plan, but the plan is still something inner, it is still held as something subjective, not yet freely released [into the external world]. What comes further, then, is for the self-concept to release itself into objectivity, to give itself the form of immediacy, to posit the being it has *within* itself in its being at once *outside* itself, so that the moment of difference also now receives its due. This being outside itself of the self-concept is, then, the *object,* which has being but which nonetheless contains the totality of the self-concept. 3. What is immediate [as object] is not in the true form of the self-concept. The object itself raises this immediacy up beyond itself and brings the self-concept to be for itself within the *idea,* which is the reality of the subjective self-concept together with its objectivity. The idea is a reality that is posited only through the self-concept. It has been called the "subject-object." It is commonly thought that *logic* is purely formal, but it also contains content. We have seen how form catapults itself into content. The idea is all-determining within itself and is the substantial truth of everything. Yet the difficulty, to be sure, is to get to know the oneness the self-concept within whatever is concrete.

III.A. The Subjective Self-Concept

First comes the self-concept in general, the subjective concept, the self-concept still held within the oneness of the subject. Whatever is objective lies upon the self-concept only insofar as the self-concept has forgotten itself. We will then see that subject and object each catapults itself into the other. In the subjective self-concept we have the self-concept *as such*. In *judgment,* then, we have the self-concept determining itself such that its determinations[, e.g., subject and predicate,] are posited as different from each other and yet also as one. The third form assumed by the oneness of the self-concept and difference is the *syllogism.* Here the oneness of the differences is posited [in such a manner that] the self-concept[, unlike the form it takes in judgment,] reaches closure with itself.

III.A.1. The Self-Concept as Such

Let us now see more precisely what lies within the self-concept. What we have are determinations of the self-concept that are no longer as abstract as determinations of reflection [in the logic of the essence]. Rather, every moment of the whole self-concept comes to be known as the whole itself. The relation of the moments to one another will first come to be considered in the logic of judgments. The self-concept is three in one, the oneness of three, and among these three it is the one itself, the oneness of the other two. The self-concept, proceeding forth out of necessity, is equality with itself, free equality. Within difference is posited self-identity. The self-concept within its reference to itself is [1.] *universality.* Universality [within the logic of the self-concept] is the same as being [in the logic of being] and identity [in the logic of the essence]. But the determination of universality is not as abstract as that of being or identity. Being is totally abstract, and the same is true of identity. But universality is posited as identity only as falling under the determination of being oneness with itself [within its other]. 2. [Further, the subjective self-concept in its reference to itself] is *particularity,* and 3. is *singularity* [§163].

When we say "the universal," we represent it as including everything particular within itself. The universal runs through everything. It does not have the particular outside it, but rather contains it within itself. What we know of the universal is that it is absolutely prolific, encompassing everything within itself. Universality now posits itself *for us* much as identity and being have each posited or determined themselves for us. *Particularity* likewise contains universality within itself. For the species includes the genus within itself. But the species also contains within itself *singularity,* individuality. Each also contains the other two moments, every moment is posited as inseparable from the other two.

Whatever is singular can be expressed more exactly as *subject.* As something that simply is, the subject falls within the form of immediacy. As a more abstract category [than singularity] we found being for itself, the one [within the logic of being]. Singularity, as subject, is the concrete unity of universality and particularity. This infinity of the singular subject is reflection within itself as the negation of what is different, so that the latter is posited as a purely ideal moment within the singular subject. The subject is the negative unity of things differentiated. It is determinate not only upon itself but also for itself. The subject is subject insofar as it has the two moments of universality and particularity, and that makes up the whole concept. The subject [when taken abstractly] is being for itself, having determined itself as the simplicity of being.

Everything is contained in the self-concept. One can thus analyze its moments [out of the self-concept itself]. Universality is being. Reflected being is identity, i.e., being as the moment of showing forth within difference, its other, in the logic of essence. The subject is something that is, and it is further being for itself, the one. All these categories lie within the self-concept. The subject, as being for self, is the negation of mere universality and particularity. The subject is something universal and at once determinate. These are the simple moments of the self-concept. The horse is first an animal, and that is its universality. It then has its determinateness, which is particularity—the species horse. But third it is *this* horse, the singular subject. Its particularity steps forth as the species of the genus. To grasp something conceptually is to recognize upon it this procession from the universal to the particular and from the particular to the [singular] subject. Its subjectivity emerges as a quite trivial determination within the definition of the thing. The subject is simple self-reference, something universal [referring at once to itself] as something particular. It is something complete. The self-concept is absolutely concrete [§164]. The moments of the self-concept cannot be held outside one another. We speak of the *clarity* of the concept. But this comes to mean nothing more than a representation, such as the representation of blue. The self-concept of what is blue is something else again. Further, if one speaks of *distinctness,* one should indicate the criteria of distinctness. That we are able to take note of [or refer to] something is purely subjective. Having an *adequate* concept of the thing is higher [than merely identifying it or referring to it under an abstract determination]. To lay hold of the thing in the adequacy of its self-concept is to lay hold of what we will shortly determine as the idea, in which differences have a being such that all are equal to one another, in which the different ways of being determinate [*Bestimmtheiten*] are each the same self-concept. That will be the self-concept in its realization.

We now come to speak of the distinction between concepts as *subordinated* and as *coordinated*. In the self-concept as subordinated or coordinated we have a universal determination. The true representation of something, such as animal, is the universal. The particular, such as the mammal, consists in concepts subordinated under the universal. In the case of coordinate concepts, the particulars lie next to one another on the same level, i.e., the different species of the same universal. Thus mammals and birds are coordinate. Then still to come are contrary and contradictory concepts. These are enumerated empirically. They are abstract thought determinations. Contrary concepts are diverse, while a contradictory concept is internally set in opposition to itself. Beyond that, we can tick off yea-saying affirmative concepts and nay-saying negative concepts[, e.g., not being a mammal].

(§165) If we wish to explicate the self-concept further, this is what it comes to: singularity first posits its moments as diverse. The singular subject's negative reference as mere being for itself to itself at that point becomes exclusive. The subject posited in its immediacy is exclusive. Yet being for itself here is in fact this very subject posited concretely. Strictly speaking, if we posit being for itself merely for what it is, it is abstractly simple. The moments that belong to being for itself remain, but they lie outside the abstract self-concept of mere being for self. In other words, abstract being for itself distinguishes itself from what is other than itself, and so it excludes the self-concepts that are in fact held within it. Within mere being for self, the subject is thus immediate, it is the identity of the self-concept with itself in its simple oneness. The abstract determination of being belongs to the subject [as the subject of predication], and with that it acquires the determination of something that simply is.[1] This is a matter of distinguishing the subject within the whole concept, and it is from such distinguishing that the particularity of the self-concept arises.

We have first posited the self-concept in general, in its universality. Now it is posited in its particularity, which brings us to *judgment*. The self-concept is subject, with that comes something particular as well. What is originally given [at the present stage of development] is the subject rather than cause and effect as before. For the self-concept remains one with itself, and what it excludes from itself [as subject] is at once also posited as belonging to itself [as predicate]. And with that we have judgment. "The rose is red." "Red" is distinguished from "rose," but their oneness is at once posited. The rose is what is here distinguished from itself. "Judg-

---

1. A singular subject by itself becomes a subject of predication in judgment. Cassius by himself develops into the Cassius who is judged to be mortal.

ment" [*Urteil*] is a fine word. It will be said that we have a swarm of predicates in our head, and that we attribute them to a subject as if they were to be superadded to it from the outside. That would be a matter of colligation. But judgment is a matter of original division, not of composition—it is a matter of the [self-]division of the self-concept. The self-concept [as subject] is exclusion, but what is excluded is the entire concept [as projected outside the subject in the predicate].

III.A.2. Judgment

(§166) [In judgment] the self-concept comes to be posited in its particularity. "The human being is rational." The human being is here the subject, and being rational is the predicate. The predicate has greater generality than the human. But the distinction between the human being and being rational is no sooner made than it is raised up beyond itself into the identity of the two. Judgment is not a bringing together of [external] determinations. Rather, the self-concept is one, but posits itself under different determinations.

The judgment [*Urteil*] in its abstract form is expressed in the proposition [*Satz*] "The singular is the universal, the subject is the predicate." Further formal determinations of judgment are: "The singular is particular" and "The particular is universal." [Introducing determinate content into the abstract form, we have] "The rose is red." "The rose" expresses the form of singularity, while "red" expresses that of universality. Another example is "God is absolute spirit." "[Being identical with] absolute spirit" is the predicate of God.

It is said that the content of [the terms of] any judgment does not concern the [logical] form of the judgment. But anyone who says this [as we shall see] evinces the greatest absence of mind. The understanding will at once assert [as a possible further form of judgment]: "The singular is *not* the universal." Yet every judgment [at least implicitly] asserts that the singular is not the universal. That this is so the simplest of all experience.

(§167) We usually understand "judgment" only in the subjective sense, [i.e., as judged by a thinking subject,] just as we usually also understand the "self-concept" in general in the same subjective sense. But the judgment is now the matter at hand, the matter itself in its determinateness, the particularization of this matter with its differences posited. The creation of the world we also designate as a "judgment." To create the world is to effect the most original division [between God as subject and the creation of the world as predicated of God]. To be God [as creator] is to posit difference. In creation we lay hold of thought determinations [predicated of God].

Judgment is to be taken in a completely universal manner [without being restricted to subjective judgment by a consciously thinking subject]. Everything is a judgment. Everything is a subject that has within itself some inner nature, which is its universality. Everything is a oneness of what is singular and universal. Every animal as animal is [both universal and] at once singular. The human being as such is universal, but the human being is at once singular as *this* human being. The species preserves itself, while the individual dies off. Singularity occurs on the side of immediacy, and it is what vanishes. Body and soul are separable. We can take the body as immediately singular, while the soul is what is universal in its being for itself. The two are thus separable, and yet are also identical. The vitality of a human being lies precisely in this identity. So there is a oneness between them, but also a difference between the two that every finite being brings with it [as its mortality] in the very hour of its birth. With that the human being is condemned to be fleeting, since the human being is caught up within an identity in which body and soul in their [contingent] identity are at once [contingently] different [§168].

We represent judgment to ourselves as if, within judgment, we attribute a predicate to an object. For example: "This painting is beautiful." Yet it is not *I* who make the painting beautiful. Rather, it is itself beautiful. The correctness of a judgment either belongs or does not belong to it as a subjective judgment. Yet, leaving subjective judgments to the side, if an action is bad, the judgment that it is bad is the action's own substantive being. Gold is metal, but *I* need not [subjectively] say this of gold in order for it to be metal.

Proceeding from the Latin term *propositio* for judgment, as also with *judicium*, judgment is the form of universality. Every purely historical statement is only a proposition [*ein Satz*—i.e., without showing any *judgment*]. "Something happens to something"—that is a proposition, but not a judgment. Of a subject something accidental may be said, something quite external to that subject. We may say, however awkwardly, that a human being is *now* transitory. But time has no place in true judgment, and temporally determined occurrences are likewise doings that remain external to the subject—they are not its [internal] predicates.

(§169) Judgment in its first abstract form lays outside of each other the most widely separated determinations, something singular and something universal. The singular subject is immediate, it is what is concrete. "The rose (which is concrete) is red (which is a universal, related [at once to other singular subjects])." The two determinations are linguistically connected by the copula "is." The predicate is connected with the subject by "is." In being referred to the subject, the predicate ceases to be a merely abstract universal, but now becomes a determinate universal within that subject. The predicate is identical with the subject, and is thus also itself determinate. Insofar as the universal within the subject is determinate, the universal comes to be particular. Being determinate thus falls to both subject and predicate, and in that respect they are posited as identical with each other.

This identity [of subject and predicate] must now be distinguished from their difference. Their difference is one of *form* [as subject and predicate]. Their identity is thus different from that form by which they are distinguished. In contrast to the form of the judgment, the identity of the two makes up the *content* of the judgment. Being determinate first falls on the side of the predicate. "Red" is a determinate predicate, but it is [implicitly] the entire concept, the entire [singular] oneness of what is particular [as red] and what is universal. As such a oneness, what is red is the whole concept. Suppose I say "God is most real" or "God is absolute spirit." The predicate gives out the content, and the content, what is most real, is God. For "God" [as the subject of predication] is at first only a word, but what God is, is expressed by the predicate. Thus the habit of attributing logical determinations to God is superfluous. For the content, which God himself is, lies within the predicate, and the predicate we already have [prior to judgments of attribution].

(§170) We have two sorts of terms: [concrete] subject terms and [concrete] predicate terms. If we hold to what is abstract, we do not need such concrete names. We could as well say "the singular" and "the universal." But, in the progression of judgment, the *subject* does not remain on the level of abstraction as merely singular, and the *predicate* does not remain merely universal. "Subject" and "predicate" are names for what is singular and universal, no matter how determinate what is singular and what is universal may also be. If we say "The rose is red," one term is in the form of universality and the other is in the form of particularity, but the subject bears reference to what lies on both sides of the copula, not merely to what is on its own side. The subject refers to the common content of both sides.

The subject is generally the whole, ὑποκείμενον, the [substratum or] foundation, and thus the predicate is not fully independent of it. The rose as what is actual is the bearer of redness, as the thing and its properties where the thing possesses the properties. Thus we say that the predicate *inheres* within the subject. The predicate is a determinate content within the subject taken as a totality. But the subject as a totality has within it a greater number of determinations than merely those expressed in the cited predicates. Thus the subject is richer, more encompassing than any such predicate. That is one side of the matter.

The other side of the matter is that the predicate is universal in point of form. It has the determination of being universal. The universal now passes as what is substantive, as subsisting for itself. It is [posited as] the identity of the entire concept with itself while remaining indifferent to any one singular instance. "Red" is more encompassing than "the rose," it goes far beyond the rose as subject, since it is a predicate that also belongs to many other things besides the rose. The universal now *subsumes* the subject, whereas before the predicate *inhered* within the subject. Inherence of the abstract universal within the concrete singular subject and subsumption of the singular instance under the self-subsistent universal concept are the two sides of [subject-predicate] judgment, the two ways of viewing it. Finitude falls within this diversity [of the universal's subsumed instances]. But absolute spirit is the absolute identity of subject [as totally concrete, not as abstract or subsumed] and the universal predicate [as equally concrete, not as abstract or inherent within a larger whole].

(§171) At first both sides, subject and predicate, appear to fall outside each other. They are simply different. Each is taken within this difference as something immediate. The rose is independent of being red, and so at times is not red. The existence of the singular subject is entirely indifferent to being red, to this universal. Yet by their concept, subject and predicate are identical. The copula expresses this identity, it is the dry "is," empty of all content, which upon itself constitutes the identity of the two. Identity [of the subject and the predicate] lying implicitly merely upon itself must be expressly posited, and the empty "is" then comes to be filled with content. That is the further determination of judgment. When the "is" comes to be filled with content, we will, as we shall see, have the syllogism.

The self-concept lies at the foundation of all content. Whether something is true to itself depends on its self-concept. The subject and predicate in their distinction from each other lie upon the face of judgment. The further determination of the self-concept falls [beyond the subject] on the side of the predicate, which is the universal determination of the subject. So the self-concept first assumes the form of universality in the predicate. The different determinations assumed by the predicate lay out the succession of judgments. 1. The first determination of the predicate is the totally sensory universal, i.e., the universal in its immediacy. 2. Second comes the universal of reflection, of allness. 3. In the third place is the universal as genus. 4. And finally, we have the universal as the self-concept. We thus have [four] different classes of judgment: 1. qualitative judgments, 2. reflective judgments, 3. necessary judgments, and 4. conceptual judgments.

When I say of a flower that it is red and they say that it is a plant, being a plant is a different sort of universal from being red. If I say "This plant is a perennial or annual plant," that is an important point about the plant, but it does not yet get at its genus, at the simple nature of the thing itself. That plants form a genus is expressed by their substantive nature. Whether a plant corresponds [in its external existence] to what it ought be is something further. When I say "good" or "bad," I compare what the object ought to be with what it is. The judgment is necessarily nothing but the positing of the self-concept in its determinateness.

[III.A.2.α. Qualitative judgment]

The first judgment, then, is the immediate qualitative judgment. The subject in its universality is immediate, and qualitative, and with that it is something sensory. That is the first, *positive* judgment. What is singular falls under a universal, and universality generally becomes determinate by being imprinted on something singular. But with that the universal itself becomes something particular. With respect to qualitative judgment, subjective *correctness* enters—for example, as to whether the rose is in fact red or white. There is no *truth* here. Were I to say "Now is daytime," that could be *correct* but at another time not correct at all [§172]. Such correctness or incorrectness is not what is true. The entire content here, being immediate, is empirically sensory.

We distinguish [within the realm of qualitative judgment] *positive* and *negative* judgments, and then *infinite* judgment. If we start with the positive [qualitative] judgment "The singular is something particular," we have immediate singularity and immediate particularity. If I now say "The singular is something universal," that, too, may be quite correct. But if I say "The singular is *not* something general or universal, but rather is something particular," that as well may be correct. Thus we also arrive at a *negative* qualitative *judgment.* In this case the [qualitative] positive judgment is as much negative as it is positive.

(§173) The infinite qualitative judgment is an ancient type of judgment that comes to us from Aristotle. He calls it an *"indeterminate* judgment." If I say "All singular individual . . ." this singular individual falls within reflective judgment [§174]. Take "All men are mortal" or "The rose is red"—no further determination yet exists here beyond mortality and redness. But with the negation "The singular is not a particular," e.g., "The rose is not red," the meaning is that the rose has positively some particular color or other, but that its color is not red. Thus I have only negated one determinate color, but I have left in place the universality which here is called "color." In negating "red" I have only negated a determinate color. "The rose is not red." There we have negation, but we still have an implicit reference by the subject to some other particular predicate.

Reference is still present. Reference merely as such starts off as abstract reference, which is [reference to mere] universality. I have a hold in my reference on something purely abstract: "The singular is something merely universal." But I must now negate that judgment. "The singular is something merely particular," which again ends as a positive judgment. "The singular is *not* merely particular" is then once more a negative judgment. Universality is already negated. What remains [after negating mere universality and mere particularity] is only the singular thing's empty reference to itself as identical with itself. "The singular is singular" is a judgment of empty identity. But such a judgment as a judgment is as nonsensical as the infinite judgment, which is the judgment of the bad infinite.

More concrete than the positive infinite judgment[, e.g., "Spirit is something"] is the negative infinite judgment, the absence of all reference of the subject to any [determinate] predicate at all. Reference to the predicate here remains neither in the form of reference to the subject's universal nor particular character, but only in the form of reference to the predicate that is required by any negative infinite judgment. What remains is only the subject's reference to its predicate by which the predicate corresponds to the subject neither according to the predicate's particularity nor according to its universal character. An example of such a nonsensical [negative infinite] judgment, which nonetheless may be quite correct, is "Spirit is not an elephant." What is said here fails to make reference to spirit, the subject, whether in the particular or universal character of what spirit is. For spirit does not belong to the genus to which elephants belong, since it is no animal at all. [We are in effect saying here that] spirit is only spirit, in its perfect singularity. As this mere singular individual, spirit would be something completely empty, absolutely this and only this singular being. Insofar as we hold fast to this result, namely, the result that "The singular is the singular," we have the subject as singular, and it is designated simply as something singular. But the singular as singular is still a judgment: it harbors the self-concept within itself, and hence bears reference to [singularity as its] universal character.

III.A.2.β. Reflective judgment

Despite the fact that some singular thing is merely something singular, it stands connected with something universal, with an external world. Everything that exists is relative. As something existent, such a singular thing stands within a relation. "Useful," "dangerous" are such universal predicates. The reflection on what is singular falls within its [hypothetical] interconnection [with something else]. What is singular is useful, heavy, dangerous [in the reflected light of similar singular things].[2]

Consider first the *singular* [reflective] *judgment* [§175] according to which the singular as singular is something universal. What is singular does not flee the self-concept. But the singular is thus raised above its

---

2. Reflective judgments of "allness" are commonly called dispositional judgments today. A wolf is dangerous because it is placed in the universal class of all wolves, past members of which have actually caused harm, so that we posit a dangerousness upon *this* wolf before any immediately perceived harm. We posit a disposition toward causing harm.

own singularity. Singularity as [such exclusive] singularity is not a true determination of anything. We cannot posit ourselves as [exclusively] singular. What is singular is thus immediately [posited as] something in particular [in the reflected light of what is not singular but universal].

What is singular, having become determinate as something in particular, is found in judgments of "some" [members of a class, the second type of reflective judgment]. "Some animals are tame." "Some celestial objects move around the sun." Here the negative is also expressed: "Some animals are not tame." With that the determinateness of animals exhibiting tameness is raised up beyond itself.

The third [type of reflective judgment] is [the judgment of] *allness* [i.e., of all members of a class]. To be merely particular [*Partikularität*] is to be completely indeterminate, but in such a manner as to bear the imprint of singularity. Given singular things, what is universal is then posited as being identical with [an all-inclusive class of] such beings. This universality is allness, the universality of all singular things [in a universal class]. Singularity lies at the foundation of such universality, and the all, the universal in this sense, falls within the sphere of comparison [of members of the class as all similar], within an external composition [of singular things by comparative thinking]. What is universal is posited here as invested with [repeated] singular beings, as identical with them all. The "all" makes up a closed circle, which again is something singular at a higher level, bearing reference to itself alone, excluding every other singular matter. "All metals are electrical conductors." All metals are at once singularly separated off [as a universal class from other matters], and what is other than electrical conductors is excluded by all metals. Universality, in the sense of such allness, includes within itself all singular things [in the class]. But it is also posited as determinate not only upon itself but equally for itself [through its being relative to or for other matters], as itself identical with something singular. Universality, taken in this way as concrete within itself[, e.g., as that which is singularly metal,] is substantial universality.

III.A.2.γ. Necessary judgment

The concrete universal at which we have now arrived, the universal as itself singular, is the *genus* that is clearly distinct from the sort of allness in which universality is merely a matter of a composition [of singular things]. Being red, being green, and so on is universality as taken up in its various outer abstract forms. By contrast, with the genus we have the concrete universal. The universal as a determinate genus is exclusive [in relation to other determinate generic universals]. This mutual exclusion gives the various species within a single genus their specific differences. Each species within a genus is determinate as exclusive of other species. This relation of exclusion enters into the classification of species. The genus in its determinateness grounds the differences between the species. The genus is necessarily the source of our differentiation of its species in their juxtaposition. Here we have arrived at the *categorical* [necessary] *judgment* [of the genus as divided into its species]. Without laying out the species in this way, our account of the genus will remain indeterminate.

The [necessary *categorical*] *judgment* "The elephant is an animal" posits the subject in its generic substance. Just as we saw a transition occur [in the logic of the essence] from substance to causality, so now the same transition occurs [as a transition from the categorical] to the hypothetical judgment. The genus is upon itself a substantial unity, but a substantial unity particularizing itself [into the species], and so it sunders itself into two. The genus itself is its different species as they hang together. The genus holds the species together. This yields the *hypothetical judgment:* if one species is given, the other species is also given. If something is blue, something else must be yellow. This particular hypothetical judgment does not immediately appear in the external representation [of something as merely blue or yellow], but yellow and blue are nonetheless interconnected through the nature of color. What is bright shows forth in what is dark, and dark shows forth in what is bright. If the one is, the other is. The one is the being of the other, though the other is distinct from it. Thus the one is its own non-being [in its other—§177].

What comes in the third place[, beyond categorical and hypothetical judgments,] is the unification of the two. The connection, the bond between them, now comes to be posited. And with that we have the *disjunctive judgment* [§177]. In the disjunctive judgment we have universality, e.g., color. Color is either blue or yellow or red or green. It is thus articulated into its species.[3] Color is every bit as much each and all of them. It is as much the one color as the other. Universality in its particularization is either/or as well as both/and. The universal is first the genus, and is then at once the circle embracing its species. Here in disjunctive judgment the subject is genus and the predicate its particularizations. The predicate, as the entire circle, is the same as the subject. The predicate is thus identical with the subject, which is the concrete universal. The generic universal bears reference to the species, which are thereby determinate. Universality is posited with its particular determinateness. The content [of the predicate] is now posited as corresponding to the entire concept.

---

3. Note that yellow and blue are cited as species. Since they are each simple qualities, they are not "species" in Aristotle's sense. Neither yellow nor blue is a genus differentiated by a specific difference. Each in fact appears to be what in the twentieth century came to be called a determinate of color understood as a determinable.

III.A.2.δ. Conceptual judgment

We now come to *judgments of the self-concept*. Here the predicates become "good," "true," "correct." Good is something substantial that belongs to the will as its object. It expresses the species' reference to what is universal and substantial. The good lays down a general rule. Something comes to be subjected to the rule, and it either conforms to it or does not. What is substantial is the foundation, and what is true is true because it conforms to it. Whatever is false is untrue. A thing's determination [as false] is known on the very face of it. It has an untrue existence. Thus a bad action or bad state is not a true action or state. There is still a degree of agreement [with the self-concept] present, but the thing has within itself an existence consisting in merely ramshackle scraps of what it would be in its true existence.

Only such judging [by the rule of the self-concept] is truly judgment. If I say the painting has this color, or is of this master, no one will ascribe to me a great power of judgment. Only when I say the painting is beautiful, and know how to point out how it is beautiful, do I truly show judgment [or discernment]. The predicate [in judgment of the self-concept] expresses the conformity of the subject of predication to its self-concept. Conceptual judgments first take the form of *assertoric judgments,* in which the ground supporting the judgment is not given in the judgment. As human beings we have the right to put forth assertions in opposition to one another. In this way, assertoric judgment at once reduces to subjective particularity, to *the problematic judgment* [§179].

The third conceptual judgment is the *apodictic judgment* [§179]. Some particular objective thing is posited in the subject of the judgment. The predicate then expresses the conformity of the thing's nature to the determination [for which it is destined by its self-concept]. "House" is a genus, but each house has its own particular manner of existence. Thus a house, constituted in such and such a way, may be a bad house. Within both the subject and predicate the same foundational determination [or end] is posited. The subject is "this house." Being constituted in such and such a way is its particularity. All three moments of the self-concept[—singularity, universality, particularity—]are posited within the subject itself, and at once within the predicate as well. So judgment is only a comparison of the destined determination, of the thing's purpose, with the way it is constituted in its existence. The apodictic judgment [unlike the assertoric judgment] contains the ground and demonstration of the predicate. Everything is of a particular constitution and occurs with a singular actuality. The finitude of things arises from the fact that a particular thing can fail to conform to the self-concept as well as succeed in so conforming [§178].

Transition to the syllogism [§180]. We have here reached the identity of subject and predicate, with the same determinations in both, so the immediate constitution of the subject grounds the judgment of its conformity to its concept in the predicate. This mediation [of the judgment with itself through the ground for asserting it], insofar as the mediation now comes to be explicitly posited, is the *syllogism*. The syllogism is the posited oneness of both the subject and the predicate. They differ only in form. We have here the oneness of both in their difference from each other—the oneness of subject and predicate. With that the copula "is" is filled with content, insofar as it is a posited oneness, the posited oneness of both extremes, of singularity and universality. Yet both are at once different in form from each other. There is nothing dryer in formal logic than the syllogism, and the entire doctrine of syllogisms remains without application and has by now gone out of fashion. Yet we ought not push the syllogism so entirely off to the side, but rather must be alert to where the defect in it lies. The working up of the syllogism is the work of thinking by the understanding and it contains essential thought determinations. These determinations must be recognized as belonging to the very nature of the syllogism. The old ballast of the syllogism remains, since ordinary logic manuals have no idea how to get any further.

III.A.3. The Syllogisms

The syllogism shows itself in the end to be rational. One may thus speak of the "rational syllogism" [in contrast to the syllogism of the understanding].[4] Rationality and purely formal syllogisms appear to be unconnected with each other. The syllogism in general, however, is the self-concept itself in its self-explication. "Everything is a syllogism," it is said in the note to §181 [of the 1830 *Encyclopaedia*]. The syllogism of the understanding is so represented that a subject, through its external property [in the syllogism's particular middle term], comes to reach closure with itself in a third [external, universal] determination. The

---

4. The contingency of a line of inference in syllogisms of the understanding means that the *author* of such a syllogism is an external *authority* who determines the direction of the syllogism. In a rational syllogism the course of the deduction will be autonomous and self-determining merely by considering the assumptions and premises from which it begins. The deduction is immanently self-propelling, as has always been the case with the dialectic invented by Zeno, which today is called indirect proof or the reduction of existing premises and assumptions to the absurd through discovery of the contradiction in them. It is a tautology—certainly no great discovery—to say that formal logic is formal or empty of content. Dialectical logic unites the content of initial assumptions with the formally valid deduction of their consequences. It tests the content of the assumptions from which we start by exploring the consequences that formally follow from it for possible contradiction. See Clark Butler, "Hegel and Indirect Proof," *The Monist*, vol. 75, no. 3 (1991), pp. 422–437.

result of the syllogism of the understanding contrasts with the true self-concept as explicated in the rational syllogism. In the latter the subject reaches closure through self-mediation[, not by the mediation of something external to it].

The *universal* first enters as simply being there, and second comes to be particularized, i.e., to acquire a relationship to the external world. Then, in the third place, the universal finally becomes the subject. The universal nature of something substantial particularizes itself. It thus becomes the negative oneness of both universal and particular [negating each in its one-sidedness], and so it becomes subject. Everything must be apprehended as just such a [rational] syllogism. God himself is such an eternal syllogism. He is for himself, and thus negates all that is differentiated from himself, taking it not to be so differentiated. He is identical with himself in what is different from himself.

Conversely, we may begin in the [rational] syllogism from what is *singular* [instead of, as in the preceding paragraph, from what is universal]. The singular subject is propelled by an inner drive, it wants something, and posits itself as becoming something other than itself. It realizes itself in the other, negates what is different from itself in its difference, and so becomes identical with itself [in its other]. The subject's own drive thus finds satisfaction. Reaching closure with itself within the other, the subject is at once actual.

The other, what first is different, we may name the Son, who remains [eternally] included within the idea of God. But the other lying beyond the Son, posited in the freedom of being ostensibly there, is the world. But God loves his Son, and is in identity with him, and so God is Spirit. Within the world as spiritual, within human beings, God attains consciousness of distinguishing himself from himself, and becomes identical with himself [in his other]. And so God is [now more concretely] Spirit.

God first becomes Spirit syllogistically, by [divine] reason. The syllogism thus attains theologically high meaning. Our own human action is always one of reaching closure with ourselves through the mediation provided by our means of nourishment, by air, etc. By the mediation of these processes, we give ourselves actuality and are actual.

(§182) *The syllogism of the understanding.* In the syllogisms of the understanding reason finds itself in a fallen state in which both sides, both subject and predicate, pass as subsisting outside each other. Here the concrete self-concept is reduced to the simple determinateness of being something particular. The moments of the self-concept in such syllogisms of the understanding remain external to one another.

We will now pass in review the different species of syllogisms along with the development of the syllogism in general, laying out their various determinations, and concluding with the posited identity of the moments that first appear to be diverse in reference to one another. This development of the syllogism will come to a conclusion in the logic of the objective concept with its complexity condensed as simplicity, with that negation of all mediation which is the immediate object in its contrast to the subject.

We must first hold principally to the *qualitative syllogism* [§183], and to indicate what is defective in it. In German we say "syllogistic conclusion [*Schluss*]," in Greek we say συλλοίζεσθαι, meaning reasoning through judgments coming together in a conclusion, what in Latin we call "ratiocinatio," *ratiocinium*. To the qualitative syllogism belong the three determinations [of the self-concept]: singularity, particularity, and universality. The middle term is what is particular, harboring the singular and universal terms within it. It is in Latin that these three determinations are designated as "terms," the two external ones being the extreme terms, *termini extremi*, and the middle term being the *termininus medius* [§184].

Of the two extreme terms one is called the major term, to which the form of universality belongs; the other is called the minor term, to which the form of singularity belongs. The three terms also entertain three referential relations to one another. The minor term immediately refers to the middle term, to what is particular. If we take "Cassius is a human," the reference is immediate: the judgment is propositional in an immediately given judgment. The second reference goes from the middle term to the other extreme beyond the middle term, to the major term ["All humans are mortal"]. The middle term, humans, thus bears this double reference to both Cassius and mortals. These two judgmental references, one containing the minor particular term and the other containing the major universal term, are designated as two propositions, respectively the propositional minor and major premises. From these two references a third mediated proposition comes to be drawn as a conclusion ["Cassius is mortal"]. The minor term posited in its oneness with the major term is the mediated[, i.e., demonstrated] proposition. It is the syllogistic conclusion.

III.A.3.α. The qualitative syllogism

The first syllogism conforms to what has just been stated: first the singular [S] is particular [P], then the particular [P] is the universal [U], and so the singular [S] is universal [U]. The propositional premise containing the major universal term is "The particular P is the universal U." The premise with the minor particular term is "The singular S is the particular P." Therefore, the singular S is the universal U.

We reach a conclusion regarding the subject, something singular, through a particular quality, taken together with some more general or universal form of being determinate. What is particular, here in the conclusion, pertains to what is singular: it *inheres* in it. But the particular in the major premise also inheres in a further determination, which is universal. Therefore, this other more universal determination also inheres in the subject. The particular is included in the universal, and the singular is contained in the particular. Therefore, the universal also *subsumes* the singular.

What is defective here is that we have a subject such that, the more concrete it is, the more determinations it has within itself. One can tick off a whole swarm of a thing's qualities, as is fully allowed within the syllogism of the understanding. The quality that happens to be selected makes up the middle term of a syllogism of the understanding. But the middle term contains still further determinations. It is more abstract than the subject. This sheet of paper is green. But this particular, the green, itself contains still further determinations. For example, green is pleasant to the sight, and I so include together with the subject this second determination of the particular. In fact, any subject within a syllogism of the understanding swarms with diverse qualities. It also has a swarm of middle terms, and what I choose from among these qualities is quite contingent. This choice is already quite generally a contingent one.

I then proceed, from whatever quality I select as the middle term, to see what determinations that quality contains within it. Every particularity of the subject is once again a middle point from which, when the particular term is taken from another perspective as relatively universal, ever so many lines of alternative further particularization extend outward. The particular line of inference with which I conclude regarding the subject is thus quite contingent. These qualities of the middle term can even be set in opposition to one another. Indeed, by syllogisms of the understanding one can demonstrate everything and anything! It only is a matter of my selecting some further determination. I simply choose some other quality in order to arrive at the most opposite conclusion.

For example, an action of stealing [S] falls under appropriation [P], which is legal. The thief defends himself by holding appropriation[, e.g., of life necessities] to be his duty [U], and so his action is completely justified. But if we select some other middle term, [e.g., deprivation of another's rights,] it follows that that the man deserves a hanging. The middle term contains within the man numerous possible ways of being determined.

Beyond that, there is a whole swarm of determinations that [not only oppose but] contradict one another. For example, a chief predicate of the world is that it includes evil. It is said that this predicate evil—as the middle term—is against the will of God. Hence the world is not of God. But it can also be said in contradiction that the world falls under another middle term, that of being good and thus not evil. And so it goes.

Or, to cite a second example, consider conflicts within criminal law. The state determines punishments for violations. Such punishments are threats. But there are thus diverse sides to crime, and according to these different sides the punishment determines itself differently. Rehabilitation of the criminal is one essential aim of punishment, and so the punishment is then not a threat but is rehabilitative.

Now consider, in the third place, the following antinomy. A human being has free will. He determines himself freely. But he is also wholly determined by others things, and so he has no free will. Or, to give a fourth example, a body that is not supported from below falls toward its center of gravity by centripetal force. The planets are not supported below, and the sun is their center of gravity. Yet the planets do not fall toward the sun. One thus adopts an opposing centrifugal force as a further particular predicate of bodies.

(§185) What comes in the second place [beyond the singular subject] is contingency with respect to the form of the reference. Drawing the conclusion syllogistically occurs by the mediation of two extreme determinations that come to be exhibited within a third middle term as within their unity. Each extreme term bears reference to the middle term. The singular S is the particular P, and the particular P is the universal U. The first two references are immediate. Within this syllogism they are the presuppositions, and it is concluded from them that the singular S also refers to the universal U.

Two immediate propositions occur here, and it is concluded that what is laid out as mediated by those two propositions is alone correctly inferred. Yet by the principle of the syllogism the two premises of any syllogism must each also be mediated, since immediacy [non-demonstrability] is not to be allowed to pass muster. For each of the two premises two further premises are thus again demanded, and for each of these once again two more premises are required, and so on into infinity. Yet the mediation [demonstration] is so constituted that it rests upon immediacy [undemonstrated first premises]. This is the defect quite generally of syllogisms of the understanding.

The three syllogistic terms are each held fast in their respective abstract determinations, the first being universality, the second being particularity, and the third being singularity. The progression is such that, of each of these three, it is posited that it holds within itself the two other determinations. With that the one-sidedness of the understanding [abstracting and separating each term in negation of the other two] is raised up beyond itself. The inclusion of the other terms in each term grounds the derivation in the doctrine of the syllogism's *figures*. This inclusion is the source of the figures, which we may now briefly note.

(§186) Given that I myself have constructed the syllogism to be the syllogism that it is, we see where the contingent character of this syllogism (the first figure S–P–U syllogism) lies. The true result is that two extreme determinations, the singular minor and universal major terms, are only *contingently* bound up with each other. The conclusion of a syllogism depends on the middle term, which, as we have seen, can always at will be determined differently. The two extreme minor and major terms are with each other in the conclusion only in [different] singular ways. Insofar as we express the bond or connection between particular and universal within the form of the syllogism, it is what is singular [defined as the oneness of these particular and universal extremes] that makes that connection as the middle term. The universal U is the singular S, and the singular S is the particular P [in the second figure].[5] Here S [rather than P, as in the first figure,] is the singular middle term that binds. That is the meaning of the result of connecting the particular and universal terms. The singular is the universal [and the particular]. The singular term binds together the two extremes of universal and particular, and to that extent the singular is itself the middle term. The singular [in the second figure, U–S–P,] is contained as the middle term, with the particular and the universal off to the two sides.

Three positions can be occupied by the middle term within the syllogism: the three positions of singularity, particularity, and universality are all possible. Yet [by the syllogism's internal self-development] the universal comes to step into the middle place occupied [in the second figure] by singularity, and [the singular steps] into the place of particularity [yielding the third figure, P–U–S]. If we now first take contingency in the form of an immediately singular subject, if we second take up each of the two predicative moments of particularity ["The horse has four legs"] and universality ["The horse is white"], and if we third form a conjunctive proposition according to this form, the concluding proposition shows itself to be equally contingent: "The horse is white and has four legs." But if we then want to go on and say "Whatever is white has four legs," that is of course a false conclusion. Only the [empirically contingent] horse here binds together being white and having four legs.

5. The bracketed addition comes from the German editors. The conclusion is "U is P," the universal is particular. By today's logic manuals, this syllogism is not a second figure syllogism, since the premises contain the middle term in both the subject and predicate places. It should also be noted that current expositions do not classify syllogisms according to whether their terms are singular, particular, or universal. That is a matter of content that does not enter into purely formal logic. Current convention makes a figure depend on whether its middle term assumes the predicate or subject place in the premises, not (as with Hegel) on whether the term is universal, particular, or singular in content. For Hegel, the particular is the middle term in the first figure; the singular term is the middle term in the second figure; and the universal term is the middle term in the third figure. Since there are only three moments of the self-concept, there are only three figures, not the four of usual formal logic. There may be nothing wrong with Hegel's classification of figures, but to prevent confusion it must be noted.

But then[, given the contingency of "The horse is white and has four legs,"] comes the [equally possible] negative conclusion: "The horse has four legs and is not in particular white." Whence the syllogistic conclusion "Some things that have four legs are not white," or conversely "Some things that are white are not horses." The syllogisms of the understanding, as we know, are susceptible to being enumerated: Barbara, Celarent, Darii, Ferio, and so on.

The third figure [S–U–P] occurs when universality becomes the middle term. We may, quite dryly, take up this universal middle term as implying different singular determinations in the preceding [conjunctive] subject, and we may then help ourselves to some common immediate particular predicative quality of each. Thus we have a syllogism with the premise "The horse is white and the snow is white." Here the universal middle term [generalized from the singular subjects, the horse and snow,] is in particular "white." In the conclusion the horse and snow [through the mediating universal class including them] come together within the white. Here the conclusion that emerges would be that the horse is snow [§187]!

(§188) Every one of the three moments of the self-concept is itself a middle term, and every one of them also takes the position of each of the two extremes. If we hold fast to this fact, the result is that the determinateness of each moment [as middle term or one of the extremes] over against the others raises itself up beyond itself. What we then arrive at is the *mathematical syllogism:* if a first thing and a second thing are identical with a third, the first and second are identical with each other. This mathematical syllogism occurs without any distinct determinateness of the three moments [since it can be indifferently expressed as the second and third thing being identical to each other by their identity with the first, and so on]. Consider, for example, three lines, each just like the other two. All differentiation of the moments of the self-concept [as the middle term] is gone. With which line I begin depends on a purely external determination. I already know, of such lines, that they are all identical to one another.

(§189) The negative result to which we have now arrived is that every moment of the self-concept[, each negatively displacing the two others,] has assumed the place of the middle term. Each moment of the self-concept has assumed the mediating function of the whole. The mediation of any two moments by the third is now complete. Within the first qualitative syllogism, "S is P" and "P is U" hold immediately [or empirically], not mediately [or demonstrably]. In the second figure [P–S–U], the singular S does the mediating, and the conclusion reads "P is U." This proposition was one of the premises in the first qualitative syllogism, but now it is posited as mediated or demonstrated. The other premise, "S is P" is posited as mediated by U according to the third figure. Every premise finds its proof in the two other figures. These figures presuppose each other reciprocally, and form a single circle of mediation. Particularity is posited in its development. The singular along with the universal makes up the concrete particular. We no longer have abstract particularity as the middle term. Rather, particularity now occurs within a developed form [as the particularity of some singular thing within a universal genus].

III.A.3.β. The reflective syllogism

The first form in the *syllogism of reflection* [§190] is the syllogism of *allness*. The major premise reads "All singular individuals . . ." If I say "Bodies without support beneath them fall toward their center of gravity," the major premise abstractly intends bodies in general. But if I instead say "All *singular* bodies," all bodies in general are no longer meant abstractly. Rather, bodies only in their singularity are meant. The planets and heavenly bodies are also conceptually included as such bodies. But one singular one-sided determination of a singular thing excludes the singular determination of another singular thing. If I say "Green is pleasant to sight," green is apprehended abstractly. But if I say "Every [singular thing that is] green is pleasant," green is no longer abstract, but is apprehended concretely.

"All humans are mortal, Cassius is human, therefore Cassius is mortal." But in order to assert the first proposition of this reflective syllogism I must already know of Cassius that he is mortal, I must already know the conclusion of the reflective syllogism! The conclusion of this syllogism rests on a prior *inductive syllogism*. All singular humans, human beings taken extensively, are here the middle term [establishing "All humans are mortal"]. What all humans are is only determined by all the singulars within the class of men. *Induction* contains the same determination[, e.g., humanity] in the conclusion, but does not contain all humans in general in the premises. It contains only this or that many singular human beings. In induction it must first be established that certain singular things—platinum, gold, silver, etc.—are metal. Secondly, platinum, gold, silver, etc., are established to be electrical conductors in an empirically immediate way. Therefore, inductively, *all* metals are electrical conducts. That is the conclusion of the inductive syllogism, based on experience. But this syllogism is once again defective, since to prove the conclusion I must show the conclusion to be true in *all* singular cases, not just in some. The induction can never be made completely.

At this point we are driven to take flight to *analogical* reasoning. The middle term here is also singular, but it is singular in the sense of [the] universality [of all singular members of a class]. [1.] At least up to now, we have historically found no human who in the end has not died. But this represents only a limited class of men, though one from which we [analogically] draw a conclusion about the rest of us in the present. [2.] The earth as a celestial body has inhabitants, and the moon is a [kind of] earth or celestial body. Here, based on the earth and the moon, the universal character of being a celestial body is taken as inductively inferred. Therefore, [by the moon's analogy to earth as a celestial body] the moon has the characteristic of having inhabitants in common with the earth. Yet maybe the earth has inhabitants according to the particular quality it has upon itself as the earth, and not according to its universal qualities common to all celestial bodies. These syllogisms of reflection [taken as including inductive and analogical syllogisms] allude to one another.

III.A.3.γ. The necessary syllogism

[1. *The categorical syllogism.*] The first necessary syllogism is based on the oneness of what is universal and what is singular[, e.g., of all metals and that which is metal]. Copper is metal. Metal is an electrical conductor, so copper is an electrical conductor. But if my meaning is "Metal [as a singular genus] is an electrical conductor" [on analogy with "The human being is rational"], the assertion is meant to hold according to the very nature of metal. This copper body is metal, that is its genus. And what is true of the genus is necessarily, categorically, true of this body. That is the categorical syllogism [§191].

2. *The hypothetical syllogism.* The universal [in an antecedent clause] is given in its immediacy [without being demonstrated]. Secondly, the particular P [falling under that universal] is necessarily given by the universal, and with that we have the connection, with a [singular] being of its own, between antecedent and consequent clauses. This immediate being of the hypothetical connection by itself is the middle term, and it is at once the mediation [of the conclusion with itself as one premise through the other premise categorically asserting the antecedent clause]. The universal U has an immediately given being. But [in the hypothetical middle term] the universal determination U is no longer immediate but is mediated by the consequent clause, and with that we have the particular P [as the consequent clause detached in the conclusion—§191].

3. *The disjunctive syllogism* lies in the disarticulation of the universal into its particularizations. Color is red, blue, green, and so forth. Here at once enters the mutual exclusion of singular colors. One and the same universal color is posited in the circle of its particularizations, in such a manner that each one of these particularizations is posited as at once singular, and so as exclusive of the rest. The universal color is posited as the totality of its particularizations, but is equally posited as but one singularity in its own right, posited as singular in a manner excluding the other particular colors.

If we hold to the form of the *disjunctive syllogism,* we have within it one and the same thing explicated within the differences as contained in the whole [§191]. The singular color is what it is thanks both to its particularization and to its universality. The whole is so posited that the different colors, which are each extinguished as each singularly being for itself on its own account, are posited as ideal [*ideel*]. The different ways of being determinate are negated [in their mutual independence]. The subject reaches closure with itself, not through what is other than it as such, but through the other as raised up beyond itself into the subject itself. With this closure reached by the subject with itself [in its other], the self-concept is realized [§192].

The self-concept comes to be a totality withdrawn within itself, whose differences are each within themselves likewise such totalities. Such a totality is the *object* [§193]. The distinct moments of the self-concept are covered over, becoming indistinguishable within the simplicity of the self-concept reduced to an object. Within the syllogism up to now, these moments were posited differences that were present at hand. The moments are now present as only raised up beyond themselves, and with that the self-concept turns back into simple oneness with itself. The meaning of the [necessary disjunctive] syllogism is that every moment of the self-concept is in its turn posited as the whole concept. With that what now is present is a oneness with being merely in itself, with its differences [erased], raised up beyond themselves—hence a oneness with the determination of immediacy. And that is the *object*.

The transition from the subjective self-concept to the self-concept as object is now accomplished. The self-concept is the unfolding of its differences, and now is the negating of them. Every moment is at once mediated and mediating. Through the negation of the differences, the totality is posited in its simplicity. The self-concept is so posited that this oneness without posited differences has now arisen. But it has not only arisen for us. Rather, its undifferentiated oneness results out of the self-development of the determinations already in place. The self-concept posited [as a whole without posited differences] is the object.

III.B. The Object

The object is something existent, something actual. But it is the totality. It is identical with itself, and is such a totality as contains [unposited] differences condensed within itself, and indeed so that each of these differences is also a totality. Every differentiation is also the entire self-concept. Every moment within the object is itself the totality, and yet all the moments, all these totalities, make up only one totality. In the Leibnizian system [as distinct from the science of logic] the monad is the atom, and yet every monad is itself the whole. Differentiation within the monad comes to be more or less developed, but no monad has connection with the others. Any differences are ideal.

Within the object we distinguish between mechanism, chemism, and teleology. The object is a totality such that the differences within it are each also a totality. [1.] The referential relation is at first an external one [of one atomic unit to others within mechanism]. [2.] In chemism the reference [to another unit] is posited as immanent [within the first]. 3. In teleological reference the self-concept steps forward in being for itself [before the objective external world or object], and then posits itself within the object.

III.B.a. Mechanism

The difference between units is at first, within mechanism, an indifferent one, where every differentiated being is independent, and is itself a totality. There the object is an external unity of units, an aggregate. Insofar as the different objects within the mechanical whole do come to be set by me in reference to one another, they still remain external to one another. A stone, a tree, is such an object. If I cast each apart into pieces, every piece is itself a new object. And if I bring them together again, they still remain external to one another. This external unification of the external pieces into which we fall is the category of external composition. It is said that a human being is composed of body and soul, and then that the body is further composed of blood, nerves. It is imagined mechanistically that each unit exists for itself, and can so exist. This is *formal mechanism* [§195].

The mechanics of push and pull are also brought forward in physiology. We say that we know something by heart, which is a good way of saying that we know it "mechanically." Sense, understood as the understanding, is a unifying activity connecting words. But it connects them purely mechanically, so that *spirit* itself makes itself into a *thing*, into something external. Yet spirit as such, not reduced to such a thing, alone underlies the whole, sustains all, and is the disrupting power capable of breaking up what is established. Within spirit, dependence, i.e., non-independence, is posited as the negation of atomistic mechanical units now held within the one.

The positing of a first object as negative toward other objects within a total external mechanical object is not external to that first object. Rather, its negation of other objects generally belongs to that object's own being upon itself, to its immediate being. Moreover, the first object's negation of the second is its own negation of itself. The negation of other objects first appears quite generally in the form of *centrality*, which is still mechanism, but is mechanism as differentiated from the above mechanical aggregate of purely indifferent ones. The center is the unity within which many ones are posited as dependent. In the case of a physical body, the many show themselves to be dependent by falling toward the center [of gravity]. But the bodies still form a mechanism, since in their manyness they inconsistently still remain outside one another [§196].

The subject, the feeling subject, the thinking being has also found its own particular center. Desire is also a seeking, a drive, and by desire a human being shows that even as an atom he, in self-contradiction, is not independent. A human not only has personality, but is also an animal, a living being driven toward centers outside itself, a being which seeks out an [an embodied] middle point in other animals. Among human beings, the center of attraction is relatively more independent than among animals. A human being, as an object, has its center only in another centrally placed body. This implies the dependence of all bodies that tend to that [more independent] bodily center.[6] Here we have the opposition between what is independent and what is dependent, between the center and objects belonging only to the periphery.

The objective syllogism of *absolute mechanism* [as contrasted to the already-examined subjective syllogism of formal logic] takes form here [§197]. We may call it the syllogism of the [universal] center and [particular] periphery. It is the syllogism of objects absolutely separated from one another as in all mechanism, but of objects that nonetheless, in contradiction to that separation, bear reference to one another. The universal center refers throughout to what is not the center[—to the periphery, the particular term]. The third, middle term here is the unity of the two previous terms, centrality and lack of centrality, and that makes for a *syllogism*. But in fact there is a triad of syllogisms, as has resulted from our inquiry into the nature of the syllogism.

Within the [first] syllogism as completely laid out in its different determinations, the immediate determinations of center and periphery raise themselves up beyond themselves into what is concretely singular. Every member within the objective totality runs through all three positions [of universality, particularity, and concrete singularity]. Each object within the total object takes its turn 1. as concretely singular, 2. as immediately [or abstractly] singular [as universal], and 3. non-independent [as particular]. Even within their concrete singularity, the peripheral objects, the particular planets, are dependent, all referring through the mediation of their unity to their other extreme, to their universal center in the sun. The common reference [which the particular peripheral planets at one extreme and their universal central sun at the other extreme bear to each other] is now the concrete middle term of the syllogism, something other than either of the two

6. A possible interpretation is that Hegel is referring here to the great man of history as a center of human attraction.

extreme terms. This concretely singular middle term is as much center as periphery, as much independence as dependence.

Thus the sun is imprinted upon the particular dependent planets as their universal center. The planets are independent centers in their own right, but at once are dependent since they rotate around the sun, since they have their common universal center of gravity outside themselves. The planets seek out the sun in the heavens, they have their center in the sun, but are themselves common universal centers for their footmen [, i.e., moons] rotating about them. (Comets are also non-independent, a kind of excrescence, and yet placed in the train and service of the planets, and indirectly in the service of the sun like those footmen.) The moons, satellites of the planets, have their center in the planets, which in turn have their center in the sun. And so indirectly these footmen are themselves bound up with the sun. The sun is to this degree the abstract universal center for all particular peripheral objects including the planets, while the planets also function as the more perfect concretely singular centers. Here we place planets, which were first non-independent objects, under the determination of concrete singularity, but they fall just as much under universality [as the center of attraction for their moons] as under such singularity. The sun functions as the extreme of common universality for concretely singular planets in their particular dependence on the sun. But the sun can at once function as the extreme of concrete singularity. And in that case the independent singular central sun and dependent particular periphery together make up the universal all. And that is one syllogism, in the heavens above as everywhere.

A magnet is also a syllogism. First the north and south poles are the extreme terms related in the conclusion, while the middle term connecting them is the magnet itself. The conclusion is that the north pole is what it is only by the mediation of the south pole[, i.e., through the magnet which concretely points both to north and south]. [1.] The [particular] middle term, within which the two extreme poles collapse into one, is called the *point of indifference.* So this particular point [of demagnetization] becomes the middle term between the collapsing poles, and we have here one form of the syllogism. [2.] Concrete *singularity* [or the oneness of universality and particularity] must in turn also assume the middle position, as when dependence becomes the concretely singular middle term precisely to the extent that centrality [universality] itself occurs in and through dependence [particularity]. 3. Third, the absolute center as the abstract [universal] center also becomes the middle term. The absolute [as the abstract center of the system of philosophy] will rightly be called "the idea" in the science of logic. At the level of mechanism the abstract [universal] center comes to bear reference to what is other than it precisely through its non-independence, i.e., its dependence. That is the third syllogism, in which the *universal* is the middle term. This universal abstract middle term in physics is seen in *weight,* where weight is the abstract mutual reference of physical objects by which one [singular] physical object refers to other [particular] objects by weight, by the universal attraction of all bodies. Those are the three syllogisms.

If we also view civil society and even the state as a mechanism, they contain persons who are [first singularly] concrete, but who thus have needs and drives, both spiritual and physical, by which they bear reference to [particular] objects [around them that can satisfy their needs]. The third or middle term connecting individual persons is here the universal term, civil society in general. My self, my person taken as my need is the [particular] side of myself, my dependence on others. I bear reference within my need to things external to me belonging to others, which form the bond between us in human society. Through my particular needs I am bound to that great complex which is civil society. And, still further, I am bound to the law, to the state and government [which regulate civil society]. Civil society and the state are here what is universal. Due to their particular needs men have been compelled to form states. The formation of the state is itself one great and true syllogism, and here again is the objective syllogism in one of its forms.

Singularity is also the middle term, the subject as such, personality with reference to the law. The activity of the subject is essentially the middle term, connecting [particular] needs with the universal in general, making them conform to the requirements of justice. The mediation of my particular needs and their just satisfaction mean that my needs are made to accord to the universal, to the state, to the law. That the law is also the middle term occurs through this subjective activity of mine. I activate the universal law. Here the subject is present as the activity that mediates the two sides of law and needs, so that needs may be brought under the universal law. The law is the abstract universal [of the state] so long as it is not mediated by the inner conviction of the individual [identifying with the state].

Within the third mechanical syllogism, the state, government, and justice are the foundation, the [concretely singular] middle term. This substantial middle term penetrates everything: needs, convictions, all particularities. We thus have these three syllogisms. Every objective whole is a unity of all three such syllogisms, and knowledge of this unity is what is implied by the objective [*objectiv*] knowledge of objects [*Gegenständen*]. [Going beyond the syllogism of the mechanical object to that of the whole system of philosophy,] the science of logic proceeds through nature to what is spiritual. What is logical also does duty as the [relatively abstract universal] mediating term, as the foundation. Spirit likewise is the [concretely singular] middle term that binds what is logical with nature. We again have a triad of syllogisms.

We may go from what is logical to spirit through nature [as particular], and that, too, is one form of the syllogism [§198].

What follows is the transition from mechanism to chemism [§199]. Chemism is nothing but these references which, as we have already seen, the moments of the self-concept [in their objectivity] bear to one another. These references are now posited in their existence as objective. The planets wander in their orbits as isolated bodies. This is the form of immediate independence present within whatever is mechanical. But dependence among the planets is upon itself likewise present. Their reference to one another is the negation of their independence. It is by their mutual dependence that they bear such references. This is how the object is to be posited [in its dependence]. The immediate independence of the object has its being as something negated, and this is how it is to be posited. The object is a being such that, within its behavior toward the other, it also bears reference to itself.

III.B.b. Chemism

(§200) We have now reached *chemism* in general.[7] An acid is a body or object. Taken merely as acidic, it is something differentiated off from potash the base, each object having its determinate character over against the other. The celestial bodies [within mechanism] are also differentiated from one another, but their scarcely detectable self-differentiation remains purely inner. The true form assumed by objects is their self-differentiation over against one another. One the one hand, an acid cannot exist merely for itself as acidic. The acid is, on the one hand, independent. Yet, on the other hand, it harbors an inner drive [*Trieb*] to posit itself in identity with what is other than itself. The acid is itself the totality of its identity with what is other than it, and the base is the very same totality. But with that we have a contradiction. The totality is present only within the acid and base taken together. But since they exist outside each other, each is one-sided and yet is upon itself the totality. This is the contradiction, and at once the drive to overcome contradiction. To overcome the contradiction, the base is

7. Chemism, like mechanism, is a logical category. Although examples from chemistry and physics fall under these categories, chemism and mechanism are not exhausted by examples from physical science. Thus we may speak of the chemistry between two people. For Hegel, this may be understood as literal, not merely metaphorical. Chemism is the negation of atomism, monadology, objects as merely independent. It depends on an internal selective reference or targeting of partial objects by one another. Whereas chemistry endeavors not to psychologize the bonding between atoms and molecules, chemism goes beyond chemistry by doing so. When Hegel says that objects have a selective drive toward oneness with one another, it is hard not to interpret chemism in psychological terms stemming from Schelling's panpsychist philosophy of nature.

unconditionally driven toward something acidic, and the acid toward its base. The contradiction of their independence and mutual dependence from each other finds its resolution in the chemical process itself. The product of that process is neither acid nor base but their neutralization [§201]. The acid and base each brings upon itself the same neutralization, and the chemical process is the bringing forth of that totality. The totality is the oneness of both acid and base, and is neutral, neither acid nor base. In their neutralization neither is accentuated more than the other.

The three syllogisms [with respectively universal, particular, and concretely singular middle terms] are also present in this chemical process. The concept is the foundation within both acid and base, but merely lies upon the surface of each.[8] An acid cannot be without its base, and the acid is thus upon itself also the base. The same is true of the base with respect to the acid. The substantial ground then reaches closure with itself, within the neutralization of acid and base. The totality is this closure of both within one. So acid and base can bond because of their inner drive toward each other. Their activity is this pure form which is, in and through each, their difference from each other. It is what achieves the closure of the two sides. Yet the inner totality is particularized within its species, within opposites. The universal, to be neutralized, reaches closure through its particularity with singularity as immediate [un-self-mediated] subjective being.

(§202) This immediacy of this subjective being is what is one-sided within chemism. According to chemism, the self-concept reaches closure with existence, and yet both extremes, both acid and base, are presupposed as independent of each other. In the neutralization of acid and base, the chemical process itself is extinguished, so that what is neutral is a quiescent immediate object. The bespiriting principle no longer exists within the neutral object, but must come upon that object from an external source[, i.e., from us]. What is neutral must be posited from the outside in its differentiation respectively as acid and base. Neutrality does not sunder itself directly into the extremes of acid and base. The chemical process rather presupposes that a beginning is made with independent differentiated objects. And these differentiated objects again presuppose that they have been externally separated out from their neutral state, and have come to be placed under tension in order to be differentiated.

The reduction of what is differentiated to what is neutral is one process, while the reverse process is the placing of what is neutral under

---

8. The acid and base form a single concept for us, but not for either acid or base. An alternative reading is that we act on behalf of the acid by forming the self-concept of the acid as including the base. The totality of acid and base by itself does not activate itself as a self-concept, so that the concept simply lies upon that totality for us.

the tension of opposed acidic and base objects. Each process presents itself as a particular one, independent of the other, and with its being for itself to the exclusion of the other. Yet each has the other process for its presupposition in the background and is not in fact independent. This presupposition sets itself apart into products. The differentiated [products] are presuppositions, and with them the beginning is apparently made. Yet that these products are not what we really begin with is shown by the process itself. These products as existing separately fall to the ground. The chemical process is a totality that separates itself into different parts—it is judgment. The separated beings emerging from judgment do not truly subsist for themselves to the exclusion of each other, so that it is posited that they are not independently present beings. Their immediacy is again independence, but as immediacy it is at once something untrue that sunders itself out of the totality.

Such is the self-concept as it quiescently lies upon the surface of the chemical process, lying there for us to grasp. This self-concept lying on the chemical process is a concrete universal that particularizes itself within itself, that passes over into reference to itself as singular, i.e., over into an exclusive negative unity with itself. It comes to differ from itself, excluding itself from itself [as an acid excludes its base]. The exposition of the concrete universal is laid out for us to grasp within the chemical process itself. Indeed, this concrete universal is what the chemical process upon itself is. What now comes to be posited is that the two diverse courses—now separating acid and base from each other and now neutralizing them, two courses which in the chemical process first appeared to be external to each other—are now negated as mutually external courses. The self-concept in being posited, in the posited ideality of its previously independent courses or moments, is the self-concept in being for itself. Here in its [abstract] being for itself, in its being for itself as its own end, the self-concept breaks *free* of whatever is external to it, it is upon itself the free self-concept.

III.B.c. Teleology

The self-concept, no longer lying quiescently upon a chemical process, is posited in its [abstract] being for itself over against what remains external to it. But the result is once again that the self-concept is [subjectively] one-sided, and is posited as negative toward the object that is external to it. The subjective self-concept thus bears reference to what is objectively external to itself as well as to its unrealized being for itself, and with that double reference it becomes [the pursuit of] its *end* [§203]. Given this subjective self-concept, with this its being for itself [fixated as something absolute], it becomes self-contradictory that anything at all should be external to it. For what is external to it to be sure lies already within the self-concept, but it lies within it only ideally—so that the self-concept still remains to be posited out there within what is external to it. Abstract being for oneself as being for one's end then raises up its one-sidedness beyond itself into oneness with what is objectively real, but the objective realm to which the self-concept now bears reference is still posited only ideally [*ideel*] within it. The self-concept still harbors merely upon itself what it would be concretely for itself in the realization of its end. It is not yet its own accomplished activity of having posited objectivity within itself as an ideal moment of itself. Within the teleological goal-directed self-concept, the external object remains to be posited [by external action] as non-independent, as dependent on the self-concept itself, with a being that conforms to the self-concept. And positing the object with a being that conforms to the self-concept yields the *idea*, the truth itself.

The self-concept in its external realization is within itself the infinite self-concept. But the infinite self-concept first comes to enjoy being *for itself* as infinite only through its being infinite *for us* in our science of logic[, i.e., as we bestow being for itself on it, on its behalf]. Its own activity is not initially that of negating its immediate external object. The finite self-concept contains the contradiction of being held back within its subjectivity, without having the determination of being in its immediacy lying yet upon it. Accordingly, the subjective self-concept is placed under tension. This is the tension of self-contradiction, where the subjective self-concept is the activation and then the resolution of its own self-contradiction. Teleology is the self-concept as the [practically] rational self-concept. It exhibits practical rationality itself. For within teleology what reigns is totality, a totality that is reason itself stripping the self-concept of its subjective one-sidedness as it objectifies itself outwardly.

In modern philosophy a prejudice has arisen against the teleological relation[, i.e., against final causation in nature]. God is wisdom, goodness. He was previously presumed to have prepared the content of the whole world for the realization of these ends. In a way the teleological content of the world may not appear to be worth mentioning. For the adaptation of means to ends can be seen everywhere. For when it comes to references to such adaptation of means to ends, we think first of our own finite activity, where the material we act upon is externally present to us. Our human action, unlike God's providence, is only a finite adaptation of the world to an end, where the objective world remains external to us. *Internal teleology* [§204], contrary to the external teleology of human action, we come to know only in beholding a living organism. All needs, all drives within the organism refer to ends, to the organism's own being for itself. In the product of a mechanical or chemical action or reaction, on the other hand, what comes out in the end differs from what was there at the start. But in the realization of a purpose within living beings, the beginning is at once the end. For example, if I as a living being build a house, I start with a plan. But the house must in the end turn out to be exactly as called for by the plan. And so it is among living beings generally, including the animals.

From the seed of a pear comes only a pear tree. Already within the seed all the determinations of the pear tree are contained. This is what, within nature, inner adaptation to an end consists in. Aristotle recognized, within nature generally, the self-concept of a living being, and of its internal teleology. He called it *entelechy*. What comes out in the end is what was there from the beginning. The product, the end is what motivates the beginning. The house as my end is what moves me to build it. In teleological activity the content [of the self-concept] is maintained within my activity. My activity is that of bringing something forth in which the content reaches closure with itself [in the realization of my end]. But the self-concept is still subjective, just as the pear tree is still subjective within the seed. Beyond this bare subject or seed of the tree, the object requires favorable external conditions. This requirement is what restricts the teleological relation of living organisms to the external object to being only finite teleology [§205].

If the subjective end reaches self-closure with the object, it becomes the entire soul of what is objective. Through a middle term, the [singular] subjective end or being for itself reaches closure with initially alien objectivity[, i.e., with the universal]. This middle term is activity upon the object, adapting it to an end, and such activity is at once a utilization of *means* [§206]. And that makes up one whole syllogism.

The subject is singular. Ideality is then expressed within the subjective activity that holds its means at its disposal. This activity is the middle term that brings forth the other extreme, the object [as the realization of the end]. We thus have the three terms of the syllogism, [namely subjective activity, objective means or tools, and objective material,] but each term is also the whole syllogism within itself. The *subjective end* [taken as the middle term] is itself a syllogism [§207, §208]. In German one says "I have subjectively decided [*entschlossen*] to do something," but one also says "Doing something is concluded upon" [*beschlossen*]. "To decide" [*entschliessen*] literally means to "to open up" [*aufmachen*] what is subjective to the objective world, while "to conclude with doing something" [*beschliessen*] means "to settle fixedly on a decision, making it fast." But we rightly say both "I myself decide to do something objective" and "I open up the simple abyss of the [subjective] I to the world." Deciding outwardly expresses the content of my decision. Within my decision a content steps forth. But it steps forth only subjectively as conclusively intended within me. I conclude with some decision which is to be the content of my will, I posit it as identical with myself, as a particular decision to the exclusion of alternative equally particular decisions.

This syllogism we call either a decision released into the world or a conclusion [of deliberation—*ein Beschluss*]. The house that I only intend to build, which I have in representation, is within me a negation [of what is objective]. This is the defect in the end being pursued, stemming from the fact that it is so far merely subjective, that the content of my decision is only subjective. Here is the contradiction. For the self-concept [my being for myself in being for my end] is upon itself objective, not merely subjective. The self-concept holds within itself the self-certainty of *reason* [§209]. According to this self-certainty, the self-concept must necessarily *realize itself* [§210]. The end is the self-concept with the infinite certainty that it is irresistible power, and that the alien object over against it is null and void. Yet that object is essentially a judgment [dividing itself off from the subjective self-concept]. What is objective thus gives itself the form of being immediate[, not mediated by the self-concept]. The [subjective] end is the contradiction of having unity [with what is objective] only as something ideal [*ideel*], not yet as something developed before it within the form of immediacy. The raising of this contradiction up beyond itself into the realized end is *activity*. That gives the second premise, an immediate overpowering of the object by the subject.

The self-concept in its being for itself, in its being for its own end, thus by activity gives itself immediate objective reality. The self-concept has the self-certainty of being itself the totality—what is objective is no longer independent of it. This overpowering of the object is the utilization of the available means. Mastering the object remains in its one-sided immediacy until the mediated process of utilizing the means also intervenes. The particular object which the end takes unto itself is the object understood as the *means* to the end. Among human beings, these means are first of all our own hands, which are the tools of the senses. Living beings have these means contained immediately upon their hands, and yet they must develop the habit of using these means. By their utilization I must proceed to overpower whatever is immediate in the object. I have here, within the means, the middle term of a syllogism. My [singular] activity thus arms itself with the necessary means with which to realize my [universal, general] end. The middle term thus brings with it a break between my activity and the means. The means are something external that is taken up by my activity in light of my end.

In the third place, the possibility now exists for activity on behalf of the end, as it is resumed again in the light of one achieved objectification, to objectify itself still further. Activity is again directed over against the object, but is so directed to another object mediated by its function as a means to the end. With these objective tools at hand, my activity proceeds to direct itself against another object beyond these tools, against the *material* [§211] on which, with the tools at my disposal, I continue to act. Objects [as means] now come to stand over against other objects [as material]. Here we find the ruse of reason, the ruse of the end pursued by deploying objects against one another. Reason brings on the means. The third place [or middle term] is now occupied by the realized end. The external material is transformed by activity according to the requirements of the end, and that is once more a syllogism. This syllogism is the true fundamental form of the whole teleological relationship. The teleological relationship is at first the finite adaptation of the material to an end. The material remains something external to the goal-directed activity. The object serving as the means or the tool is also something external to it. The content in this finite adaptation to the end is a limited one. The achieved end is no sooner achieved than it becomes an object which falls back into finitude, but which can progressively also again be made into the means and material for still other ends. To be sure, the achieved end represents a satisfaction which the world spirit prides itself upon attaining, but what is achieved is always a mere means for the further endless progress of spirit.

(§ 212) But what now follows is the transition to the end internal to the means and material, to the idea, to the end that has within itself both the means and material adequate to itself as the end. The finitude of an end lies in the fact that the means and material are at once still independent of the end. The activity on behalf of the end is the explicit positing of what at first lies quiescently upon the material, of the nullity of the difference [between end, material, and means]. The end is the self-concept which negates the subjectivity of activity on behalf of it, and which is certain of that activity as a mere ideal moment. Within realism or empiricism [in contrast to idealism] objects are independent—I, the subject, am off to the one side, and the object is off to the other. But not a single human being really believes realism stated as such. Even the animals consume grass with the gut feeling that in the grass they chew there is nothing fixed or independent standing over against them. The animals themselves thus posit this independence of the grass as something null and void.

Human beings [in knowledge] penetrate the far reaches of the heavens and stars with their self-concept, and thereby make independent celestial beings over into dependent ideal beings within themselves. The self-concept from the very beginning has been a matter of the end reaching closure with itself, and it has reached closure with itself only when the moments of itself lack independence, only when they are mere moments of the self-concept. The end itself bears, imprinted upon itself, the very means, as also the material, by which it posits itself objectively. The end thus becomes the infinite end. What is true as such has now become our object. The self-concept in its own mere being for itself is one-sided being, the being of only the [subjective] self-concept. That subjective self-concept now raises this its own one-sidedness up beyond itself into its own self-realization. What holds truth is this self-realization of the self-concept, and this we call the *idea*.

III.C. The Idea

The term "idea" has often meant "representation" [as in, e.g., Locke]. Kant called attention to the distinction between this former usage and the meaning he assigns to the term. The "idea" [in the present lectures] means the infinite, the limitless, but only in the sense of being concretely infinite. Finitude finds total fulfillment within the idea, the infinite self-concept. The concrete infinite is subjective, but it is also objective, since it is real. We now lay hold, within the idea, of the oneness of the subjective and the objective. This oneness is the truth. What holds truth is no mere subjective representation of mine. What holds truth, what is true to itself, is rather the concrete self-concept, the self-concept as not only *upon itself* [potentially] infinite but equally *for itself* infinite.[9] What is true, the concrete self-concept, at once contains within itself the infinite realm of all that is objective. For this objective realm is absolutely adequate to the concrete self-concept and to it alone. The content of the concrete self-concept is this very process [of constituting the oneness of the subjective and objective self-concepts with each other]. Objectivity, taken as ideal [*ideel*], is the form assumed by the self-concept. This infinity of the self-concept is what makes for truth. Essentially the idea is *subject* [§213]. *Substance*, if it is to become true, must be apprehended as subject. What has been differentiated as subject and substance is, for substance, the oneness with itself of the subject as its other. But substance and subject are not neutralized within their oneness like acid and base. Rather, what comes in the third place [beyond the abstract substance and abstract subject] is the concrete self-concept as the subject [overreaching the substance or object].

What is *ideal* [*das Ideale*] is to be distinguished from the idea. The idea taken in its sensory immediacy is ideal. Ideal Greek sculptural figures embody the idea. The beautiful embodies the idea. Yet within a beautiful work of sculpture there is always something extraneous to the idea merely as such. What is extraneous is, to be sure, one side of the work, but

9. In Aristotelian terms this statement may be taken to mean that what is *upon itself* or potentially infinite is infinite *for itself* by first actualizing its potential within itself and then reflecting upon its own successful actualization of its potential. Our grasp of the infinity of the heavens in science is the infinite's grasp of itself in and through its human members. Scientific knowledge becomes the full realization of our end in teleological activity, so that nothing is left to the side as unassimilated by knowledge, i.e., as a field of alien objectivity challenging further teleological striving.

it is a finite side of it. Even so, when a work of art is taken as ideal, externalities of color and space come to be spiritualized, and such figuration
upon the work thus comes to express something spiritual. The form of
the artwork imbues it with soul. Far from being abstract, the form is self-
revealing spirit. Every single characteristic, every spatial figuration, every
point is pregnant with meaning, laying bare not itself but its soul, its
meaning as unseparated from the art object as sensory. But what is true
is the idea without any such extraneous aspects. The idea, as the oneness
of the inner and outer, is alone actual. Contrary to ideal classical sculpture, the outer of the idea is the totality of all that is objective. What is
subjective has its content in that totality, and that totality is actuality.[10]

(§214) Reason, truly expressed, is the idea. The self-concept reaching
closure with itself, the idea, is the oneness of what is subjective and objective. The idea is found wherever [1.] the end as intended, [2.] the
means utilized, [3.] material at hand, and [4.] the end as carried out
into reality all coincide. All these limited categories are consumed in
the unity of the idea. The understanding has an easy time of saying that
the subjective and the objective each has its being for itself. Quite correct. Yet it is quite perverse to simply talk of their identity, since all difference is then left aside. The idea is an identity to which the moment of
difference also belongs. The idea is the [concrete] self-concept laying
hold of itself within freedom, within blessedness, within what is other
than the [subjective] self-concept.

(§215) The idea is essentially the process of absolute negativity [or
double negation, negation of the negation], and it is thus at once dialectical. [1.] The idea is at first the universal, which is immediate. As immediate, it is *nature* or, putting it more determinately, it is *life*. First or
immediately, the idea is nature. But this immediacy is the judgment belonging to the idea, it is the idea divided off from itself within its externality. When the idea is displaced outside itself it is nature. The highest
stage of nature, of the idea in *being outside itself,* is life. [2.] The [subjec-
tive] self-concept in its being for itself then posits itself over against
what is objective, over against the world stretched out before it. Thus the
idea is, in the second place, finite knowing [*Erkennen*].[11] The subjective
self-concept [in its mere being for itself] truly knows [*weiss*] that this re-

10. What is actual may be understood as the actualization of the concrete self-
concept with a being for itself through reflection on the actualization of its potential as that potential already lay upon itself (*an sich*).

11. *Erkennen* appears to mean cognition of the forms of the idea in the external
world without conscious recognition of them there, so that it is a finite cognition
which is for itself limited by the world it knows. In context, *Erkennen* thus appears
to mean re-cognizing (*wiedererkennen*) for Hegel. *Erkennen* contrasts with *Wissen*
in Hegel's text. Where *Erkennen* originates for Hegel in a Kantian context, *Wissen*
means true rather than false or finite knowledge.

cognizing falls short of the truth, and that the world remains external to it. For itself, the [subjective] self-concept, merely as such, is [a finite] knowing [of the world]. The self-concept as finite knowing proceeds from the certainty of reason, reason's certainty that it has being. [3.] What comes in the third place is *absolute* knowing [*absolutes Erkennen*],[12] true absolute knowledge [*Wissen*], spirit as such.

III.C.a. Life
[III.C.a.1. The soul]

(§216) The self-concept realizes itself within the body as the soul. The soul within such [corporeal] externality is immediately within itself. The oneness of the soul is the fundamental determination here. The soul is what is speculative, and exists as such. Taken externally, the body is something material. As a body it is in space, and is one among beings which are all outside one another. The soul, by contrast, has no belief in bodies external to one another. It is simple, and is identical with itself. It is a sensitive soul, residing within the body. It becomes determinate insofar as its body is determinate. For the determinateness of the body is the simple determinateness of the soul. The soul remains within its universality.

Space also remains everywhere equal to itself, as also does time. And so the soul retains its universality, an all-penetrating oneness with itself. The self-concept [as a soul] holds fast here to its ideality. The simplicity [of each sensitive soul] appears wherever we reach out and touch with our fingers. We are thus sensitive souls that feel, sensitive beings, souls one and all. Mutually external bodies make no difference to a sensitive soul. Within [the activity of] sensitive intuition we behave [toward bodies] in an external manner, but this sort of sensory intuition holds no truth. What holds truth is rather ideality within the soul. Being sensitive is only [the activity of] the soul that is sensitive from a single standpoint. Sensory externality holds no truth for the subject.

The wonders of animal magnetism [hypnotism] have their root within the [universal] oneness of the soul. A healthy rational soul restricts itself to its own body. Yet if, as happens when one is under a magnetic spell, the rational soul is weak, it steps outside itself. It itself comes to be sensitive within [the sensitivity] of another [soul], and represents to itself what the other represents to itself. The rational soul's [state of] being closed-off from all else, its singularity, is weakened, and even whether or not different sensitive beings are spatially more remote from one another makes no difference. Such is the ideality of one soul.

---

12. *Das absolutes Erkennen* is the subject's conscious recognition of itself in the whole objective world. It is infinite knowledge, the same as *absolutes Wissen* or absolute knowledge.

The soul stands within the real interconnection of sensitivity and does not restrict itself to its own body. As for the individual's state within sleepwalking, it is similar to the state of the child within the womb. Particularity is sunken deep within universality.

[III.C.a.2. The bodily organism]

What comes, in the second place [within life], is the particularization in which differences are now posited outside one another in space. A living *organism* has parts, while the *soul* is without any parts that would be independent of one another. The organism has independent organic members. The bodily organism [*Körper*][, by *having* independent members,] does not consist in precisely such and such isolable parts. Rather, the body [*Leib*] contains no distinctions beyond those of the self-concept. Its distinctions are those of the self-concept. Getting to know how this is so is the difficult point. Each moment [of the self-concept—universality, particularity, and singularity—]makes itself into a complete *syllogism,* and is the totality [§217]. These moments are present within the living body. The insect divides into head, breast, belly, etc., and so does a human being.

The head is the seat of universality [sensibility],[13] the breast and heart [are the seat of particularity, irritability], and the belly and stomach are the seat of singularity, of reproduction. To grasp the body conceptually is thus to grasp it in the image of the self-concept. The subject as such is singular. Universality is present as sensitivity[, as being open to all]. What is singular exists as a sensitive being. The [singular] subject negates the difference between universality and particularity [as that difference occurs in their separation].

Life is the dialectic of objectivity, where beings lie outside one another. In the solar system, living subjectivity is not yet present. Each living subject is an individual closed off [from what is outside it], no part of which can maintain an external subsistence of its own. The process of things outside one another is a continuous one. In universal sensitivity the process is simple, while it is developed when the subject is differentiated into organs and members belonging to the ongoing process. Every part has a life of its own, every one begetting itself anew. Every part consumes within itself the other parts that are themselves organic. Every member is a means, all members set ends for themselves, all are consumed by the others, and all beget themselves ever anew. Even the bones are included in this life process. The members are ends unto themselves, and yet are fluid, sacrificing themselves to the organism as whole. A living being is [always] beginning anew, but is essentially an end [*Zweck*]. It forever begets itself, and continually makes itself into the result. Death enters

---

13. "Sensibility" is added in brackets by the German editors.

should life no longer be begotten. Life is the tranquil activity of self-pres- ervation [*Erhalten*], but as the begetting of itself it both preserves itself and receives itself [*erhält sich*] as begotten.

The particularization of the members is negated within the [abstract] universality of life. To be alive is to be a subject, a living being. Here, within life, is the sphere of finitude where body and soul are separable. Whatever is finite is born to die. A living being has the simple vocation of positing itself as something different. Quite generally, that is what the living body is. It posits itself as different from itself in its object, its means, its inorganic nature whose differentiation from itself must be negated. The individual thus feeds off itself and wastes away in the con- sumption of its own organs, consuming its means [of self-preservation], for those means are its very own organs.

What comes, *in the first instance*, is the [life] process of the individual within itself [§218]. The individual, feeding on itself, wastes away in consumption, as in the related tubercular disease. This process of wast- ing away lies at the basis of what is known as the hunger cure. Less nourishment is given than meets a human being's need, so that the or- ganism feeds on itself, consumes itself, and thus reconstitutes itself within itself. Every organ, every nerve is consumed and begotten anew. This begetting is the very activity of self-preservation.

What comes *in the second instance* [as a life process, after self-regenera- tion through consumption,] is that the subject relates itself to its exter- nal inorganic nature, to an inorganic nature with a free existence of its own [§219]. Life is the idea in its immediacy. This immediacy must at once be determined as something posited. The universal life of nature [outside the living being] is something created. The living individual [returning to health after self-consumption] finds its inorganic nature outside of itself. The living subject relates itself to something alien. But this subject enjoys infinite certainty of self, and negates the independ- ence of whatever is alien. To relate itself to something else is to negate its own self-feeling, and this negation occurs within the living subject itself. Life is within itself a contradiction. It is the feeling of deficiency, of need, where the deficiency is particularized in each species. Every animal has its own particular inorganic nature [or environment]. A whole world can surround an individual without holding any interest for him. An animal has no need of anything that, at least upon itself, is not already contained within it. Nothing purely foreign to it can ever enter it. Here we have absolute self-determination. Every deficiency in the organism bears reference to a specific content [in the organism's external inorganic nature]. Such is drive, need, self-feeling, the infinite certainty of self, the certainty of its oneness with itself, and hence the negation of the contradiction of life. The resolution of that contradiction is satisfaction. To reach satisfaction is to preserve self-feeling.

[III.C.a.3. The species][14]

The third process of the immediate idea as nature is that of the species [§220]. The first life process was one of reaching closure with oneself through [regenerating] oneself from within. The second life process consisted in reaching closure with oneself through something abstractly other than oneself[, i.e., through one's external inorganic nature]. The third relation is the unity of the prior two processes, a relation to another living being of one's own species, so that the other has an original [species] identity with oneself. It is the relation that consists in reference to something concretely other than oneself which is nonetheless of one's own species. This *sexual relation* is the life process of the species. The subject [participating in this relation] attains its satisfaction, and in its satisfaction is a singular [individual]. But its grasp has already overreached what is alien and has posited what is inorganic as identical with itself. This is the life process of the species. Kinds within the species are particularizations of the [individual] subject.[15] The species process brings together these different particularizations in one. The process brings the species to [the point of] being for itself in the newly begotten individual, in the new subject.[16] The one side of the matter, then, is that a living individual is begotten. The beginning and the end proceed here to the fore out of each other.[17] As an individual[18] one reaches closure together with oneself, and yet there are not one but two individuals. Because life is still the idea in its immediacy, the first individual reaches closure with itself together with another individual, who is the one begotten and mediated by the first. The one-sidedness of immediacy is laid hold of, and the species is now posited [beyond the mere individual—§222].

The other side of the matter is that the individual goes under, the individual in its mere immediate singularity dies. Natural death lies in the fact that the subject lives its [particular] life into universality. The body ossifies itself as natural, not abstract, universality. In the old age of a human being, everything has become habit. The opposition of his or her subjectivity [to an other] is no longer present, but has completely yielded to habit. Singular individuality yields itself up. Habit is rightly said to be second nature. Beyond the life of habit, the interest

14. The German word in this section is *Gattung*. *Gattung* may mean species as well as genus. I have chosen "species" because it makes sense to speak of the sexual process within a species, but not within the genus.

15. The easiest interpretation of these "kinds" is that they are the two sexes.

16. Following the interpretation in the previous note, this "new subject" would be the newborn infant.

17. The "beginning" and "end" may be interpreted as parent and child.

18. This "individual" may be read as the parent, keeping in mind that parent, infant, child, etc. are to be taken merely as examples of logical thought determinations on the level of pure thought.

of a living being is aroused solely where opposition is present. My activity consists in overcoming what is alien to me, in positing it as identical with me. A human being who has experience with life comes to be used to whatever happens. Whatever happens never presents anything new. The individual knows how things are, and so is indifferent toward them. Old age holds to the universal. Such is the dulling [of interest in the world] and, at once, the transition of the individual into what is universal. The species preserves itself, but only by way of an individual [infant] who is likewise merely transitory. The species again immediately falls into singularity, and that is the alternation [of newborns] between the two genders.

While the single individual disappears, the species begets itself within the self-concept. The single individual disappears. This individual is not the true existence of the species. Rather, such an individual is rather always in the course of disappearing. The species has itself for its object. The demise of the individual living being, who goes under within his or her immediacy, is at once the rise of spirit. The process [of this rise], which goes on to infinity, lies in the contradiction of the species as it arises out of and yet falls back into the form of immediate singularity. Yet the line followed by this progression is that of a circle, a return upon itself. The species reaches closure with itself as a species through negation of the moment of individuality, which is the rise of spirit. The self-concept is realized, and its realization, within which the [concrete] universal has its being, is itself the universal. It is the universal that has being *for* the universal. Both sides are themselves the same concept.

III.C.b. Recognizance [*Erkennen*][19]

The self-concept exists freely with being for itself. Within this form the self-concept is itself. What, within a human being, we call the "soul" is the simple subject, the process of positing one's body as identical with oneself while falling into individuality. The self-concept, the idea, now has itself for its object. Such, in general, consists in knowing oneself in the other. Spirit is at home with itself as true knowing [*Wissen*], consciousness, thinking. Those are the forms assumed by this realization of the self-concept within its object. I know myself to be this simple being, bearing reference to something there that has its being as transparently as my very own being. The universal is here at home with itself. Hence, the I is I only as this return within itself. Only in spirit does the self-concept have existence as the self-concept—only in spirit is the self-concept in its own element.

---

19. *Erkennen*, translated as "recognizance," here implicitly connotes re-cognizing [*wiedererkennen*], the identification of familiar markers in what is experienced to be alien territory. Hence, it is finite knowledge.

Here we have the idea of spirit itself, but at first [only] as finite spirit. Subjectivity has reached universality, pure oneness within itself. The idea as referring simply to itself is the subjective idea, but the idea is also the activity of distinguishing, judgment [or division—*Urteil*], repelling itself in its totality from itself [§223]. This is the moment of otherness, of difference. The movement is that of positing both [subjective and objective] ideas within one. The idea as subjective, as enclosed within its simple oneness, is merely its activity of intuiting what lies already within itself. This is the abstract idea within the form of one-sidedness. It is the idea unmuddied and unconscious, since to consciousness belongs the differentiation of an object.

The subjective idea is not yet the activity of distinguishing understood as an opposition falling within it, but rather only distinguishes the object as its other. The universe, the world generally, is the subjective idea outside itself. So the idea as the world lies out there presupposed by the subjective idea, as something immediately present, a world that is immediate. Yet the idea as the subjective idea has, within the world, a being for itself. Within the subjective idea, then, the externality of reality is already negated. The universe is at first a negation over against the subjective idea. Yet the negation is already upon itself lifted. The idea is upon itself subjective. Subjectivity is for the idea itself a lack—it is the need, the drive to raise its subjectivity up beyond itself, and at once to lift up beyond itself the one-sidedness of what is objective, the idea in its externality. Subjectivity is the certainty that such externality is pure show. Subjectivity is reason—it has the certainty of being, upon itself, reason itself [§224].

Reason enters the world with absolute faith in itself, with the drive to lift its self-certainty to the level of truth. Certainty is subjective, while the truth is the idea as objective. This is the drive behind [Kantian] finite knowing [*Erkennen*] [§225]. It has two sides. It is impulse, finitude—where finitude lies in the fact that the total process falls apart into the double process in which subjectivity and objectivity are distinguished. The process is one of raising the one-sidedness of each side, of subjectivity and objectivity, up beyond itself. In one direction the impulse is directed toward what is objective [taken] as what ought to be, while in the other direction it is directed toward what is subjective. (The opposition [between the two impulses] is to be lifted up beyond itself.)

The other is what is, what is immediate, what has validity. On the one hand, being as external is the standard of validity, and what is subjective has to bring itself into conformity with being. On the other hand, conversely, what lies in the subject is valid, is what ought to be, so that objectivity has its one-sided validity removed. These are the two sides of finite knowing. They respectively go by the name of *theoretical* and *practical* activity.

Rationality is the possibility inherent in finite knowing, it is the idea within its simplicity. The idea ought to be given fulfillment, but in such a way that the very ideality of the idea nonetheless remains. But where is the content of the idea to come from? If the content is to be taken from the world, it is the latter that will pass as valid in its being. The subject is then deficient and ought to be filled with being. This is finite *knowing* [*Erkennen*] in the strict [theoretical] sense, [implying] curiosity and inquisitiveness. Inquisitiveness consists in filling the I, taken as simple, with content. My certainty of self remains unperturbed. The true knower [*Wissende*] makes him- or herself into a universe, into an infinite manifold of content. The idea remains within the ideality [of thought contents], and the I is still this simple being even if a fullness of content exists in this well of the world. A fullness of content, buried out in the world, is there to be mined. I must be the master of it, I must have true knowledge [*wissen*] of it. This is *theoretical* reason. Reason is certain of its ability to know the world. Reason proceeds from this conviction, the conviction that the world is there to be apprehended by it. Certainty is filled with the content of the world—I come to know the matter as it truly is.

The other [impulse] is known as *practical* reason, which shows the reverse relationship. The individual's own determinations now hold validity for that individual as the true determinations. I believe in myself over against whatever is external. What is practical are ends, self-determinations that are valid for themselves. The absolutely valid end is in general the *good*. What now holds validity is what is subjective over against the external world. The practical direction consists in going out to fulfill the subject's aims and to carry out the good. The impulse to the good alters the world in order to make it conform to what is subjective.

III.C.b.1. Recognizance as such

[The analytical method]

The starting point of all [theoretical] knowing as such is the presupposition that nothing is to be alien to us. Rather, every content is to belong to us, and is not be an independent content of its own. But all material comes to be assimilated to us. This is our basic relationship [with the world], and to this extent our knowledge of it is finite, in that a [still unassimilated] content is always posited as fixed somewhere beyond us [§236]. Finite knowing, however, is at once active, and its first activity is the *analytical* method [§237].

The world is infinite both within its external expanse and within the singularization of its every content. But now the world is touched by the simplicity of the I. What is outside me can enter into me only insofar as I bestow upon it the form of simplicity that we call "universality" or "abstraction." To the extent that I take up the material of the world, I am

I, and I then become active over against its externality. My action is one of simplifying whatever is external. This doing of mine has only the form of self-identity, the [abstract self-]identity [of A with A] as seized upon by the understanding. What is given to me as concrete must be dissolved in its concreteness, and it is this that is known as "analyzing," the dissolution of whatever is manifold, which is an unconscious [activity of mine].

But to analyze is not just to abstract [universal determinations]. It is also to separate, but to separate in the sense of isolating something that, prior to its abstraction from other items, was already there as a single item bearing reference to itself.

Color lies upon the surface of a body. In analyzing a body, I consider its color for itself. I pick out, one from another, determinations previously bound up with one another, and posit each determination for itself. Universality has two modes: either a universal is entirely formal[, i.e., abstract], or it is apprehended as determinate within itself[, i.e., concrete, synthetic]. I intuit the object, I make an image of it for myself, and in so doing I have already abstracted it from its [original] space and time [location], and have already negated its singularity. Moreover, even if the image is still fresh, the singular traits of the object grow fainter. This is the generalizing [activity] of the I. Each determination is still [in fact] bound up with all the others. Each determination as particular bears reference to others, and yet I lift it out [by abstraction] in isolation from them. More exactly, I do not lift out the more particular determinations. Rather, these I simply leave to the side, and abstract the universal from all this, which yields its various genera and species. This abstracting is what makes up what is called the analytical method.

[The synthetic method]

Next [within re-cognizing as such] comes the *synthetic* method [§228]. The analytical method has a universal, the universal genus, as its point of arrival. This universal, the result of analysis [as abstraction], is now rather the point of departure for the synthetic method. This is the method that goes after the particular, which analysis has left aside. The end presupposed by the method [of finite knowing, *Erkennen*] is to truly know [*wissen*] the universe to be the idea. The first direction taken by finite knowing was to give the form of universality to what is external. That is what we have called analysis [as abstraction]. In whatever is empirically concrete, one particular will be alongside another. What comes first is to give this form of universality in general to the object.

Finite knowing [as contrasted to *Wissen*] is finite, and its finitude lies in the fact that it still holds the moments of the self-concept outside one another. But the self-concept itself is the driving force. It leads the way. What the object is upon itself comes consciously to be real-

ized [within the self-concept]. The manner in which the object is realized is finite, since determinations united within the idea still fall outside one another within finite knowing. The first action, we said, is
analytical [or abstractive], yielding merely the single form of universality. Each universal is essentially one among the determinations of
form within the self-concept, and the finitude of knowing lies in the
fact that these determinations of form [which are in fact unseparated]
are invoked in isolation from one another.

The analytical method uncovers genera and species. Only the given
content is taken up. But mathematical analysis is a special case. It is said
that, when we proceed analytically, we start with what is known and
move toward what is unknown. We always start with what is known.
A [known] equation contains unknown magnitudes. Certain relations
between such magnitudes are known: x is given with a certain arithmetic ratio assigned to it. Thus x is completely determinate—as determinate
as it is will ever be. But x is still to be discovered [as a numerical con-
stant]. This is simply done by freeing x of all connections of equality
with a ratio[, e.g., of y to some number]. The entire content of x is given,
but [in the course of solving the equation for x] it comes to be posited
within a different form. The variable x takes for itself the form of self-
reference according to the underlying determination of the equation.
The start is always made from what is known[, i.e., a ratio]. We can also
start from the unknown [and proceed to the numerical constant as the
solution], and as long as it remains unknown the operation we perform
is directed to making the unknown known.

The form of universality has a content, it is determinate. We have
proceeded [in analysis] from singularity to universality. This operation
effects a transformation. What is singular is no longer as it was in its
original immediacy, but now is in the form universality. What is singular in its original immediacy is incomplete, since it does not correspond
to its concept. The self-concept only demands what is its right, the right
to have the content of what is singular fall within the determinations of
the self-concept itself. The self-concept proceeds from universality back
toward *singularity*—and precisely this is the *synthetic method*. It proceeds
from universality to particularity, to explication within the self-concept. This method is called synthetic insofar as the universal comes to
be developed within its [particular] determinations. But when these
determinations are developed, something new comes to be added—a
synthesis. The whole is itself synthetic.

The right-angle triangle is explicated by laying out its determinations, setting them outside one another. When I come to re-cognize
the triangle as the unity of its determinations, I know it completely.
That to which I come [by the synthetic method] is not immediately
given. This is also the case with the analytical method, in which the

universal I find was not yet given. [Scientific] laws are not immediately given, and to this extent there is also something synthetic in them. The synthesis goes from universality toward singularity.

[Definition]

What comes first [as we move from universality toward singularity] is the genus. The self-concept requires *definition* [§229] of its species, and the determinations [contained in a definition] themselves come forth as [analytically] required. The self-concept is the universal presented in an understandable manner. What is understandable is that the genus of an object be given along with the other determination, which is the species' *differentia specifica*. Particularity [as the specific difference] is delivered by analysis, it comes from what is given. Fashion nowadays has strayed from the logic of definitions, much as it has also strayed from that of syllogisms. But in definition we strive to lead determinations back to their simple components. Gold is metal, and that is the genus. The specific difference is its weight. It is nineteen times heavier than water. But gold has still many other determinations. The definition of it would be that it is metal of a specific weight. If all its other determinations could be led back to the one determination of specific weight, that would be the one definition. The entire wealth of determinations reduced to one determination, that is what is demanded of definition, and this demand conforms to the requirements of the self-concept.

In abstract objects like those of geometry, which have their being only in abstract space, such definitions [in which everything is derived and nothing is accidental] can be given. A determination is sometimes called an "earmark" [i.e., a criterion]. But the term is poorly chosen, suggesting that the determination lies only in the fact I am able to remark it, which would mean that it is not essential to the thing itself. The synthetic method begins [as we have seen] with what has been yielded by the analytical method. The equation of the ellipse is the result of geometry. From this equation particular determinations are derived, and with that the universal is delivered by analysis.

[Classification]

What comes second [after definition] is *classification. Division* [§230], the specific difference within the genus, particularization, essentially has its more exact meaning over against another particular. Classification is a completion of the definition. The triangle comes to be classified into right-angle, acute, and obtuse triangles. But the question is: how does one get from the universal to its particularization? In finite re-cognizing the procedure is understood, so to speak, as an external one. The particularizations are simply found, they are come upon as externally given. Law is classified and divided into civil law, criminal law, church law, and so on. The word "church" comes to be added externally to the determination "law." A ground for classification will here be demanded. This ground is the universality of the particularization. The equality or non-equality of the sides is the ground for classifying triangles, but the classification is interpreted externally. The principle of classification is found. But true classification through the self-concept would have to proceed from that self-concept in its determinateness, from the fact that out of that determination itself the different species could be developed.

Color is a genus. It is a perturbation of light and dark. That is what defines the genus. Now as for the various particular colors—they are yielded through the relation of light and dark. If darkness is the basis and what is light is drawn over into it, we have blue. Or, conversely, if light is laid down as the basis and is then perturbed, we have yellow. Thus the differences between colors follow from the determination of the genus. If the color yellow is intensified to the level of individuality, we have red. But if the intense individuality of red is peacefully neutralized, we have green. Here we see reason itself at work within the process of classification.[20]

[Proof]

The right-angle triangle is perfectly determinate within the Pythagorean theorem—an example of one great and true *theorem* [§231]. The mediation of a conclusion is its *proof* [§231]. The mediation of this Pythagorean conclusion includes a third statement containing the equality of triangles—or whatever the determination may be in which this equality of triangles is contained. To prove the Pythagorean theorem we must draw lines. It is never said why just these lines should be drawn, the task is simply externally laid down of drawing them in such and such a manner. A swarm of possible figures arises, only a few of which are selected as usable for the proof. The procedure is entirely external, an external construction. Only after this construction do we see into the ground for the conclusion.[21]

The mediation of a conclusion is its proof. A proof exhibits the necessity of the conclusion. But the full necessity of a conclusion contradicts the presupposition [of unproven immediate premises] made by finite recognizing, by finite knowledge. This presupposition thus now yields to the subjective idea wanting to fill whatever immediately is with its own subjective content. May this subjective content, this object, have being! May I give being to the subjective truth by taking the material of being up

20. This paragraph illustrates the disjunction of determinations within the genus by drawing on Goethe's theory of color.
21. The arbitrary postulation of figures by the proof's author makes the proof the result of subjective volition. The following paragraph introduces objectively realized volition into proof, which thus becomes truly necessary and hence free.

within myself! May the subject set what has being in correspondence with itself, so that the subject may be this very being! The full necessity of proof contradicts the presupposition that what is simply is, the contradiction that reason is allowed to set itself in conformity with what is. What passes as true in proof is merely what has been yielded by mediation. But a presupposition was whatever immediately is, while the necessity of what is immediate becomes immediacy mediated by the striving of the subject. Therein lies the transition to *will* [§232].[22]

III.C.b.2. The will

The idea as subject has reached the threshold of the truth. The truth lies, not within the given object, but rather within what is both upon itself [potentially] and for itself[, in reflection on its actualized potential,] self-determining. In volition, finite theoretical knowledge has pulled back from its prejudice[, namely the prejudice that reason and intelligibility can be found theoretically as already present in the world]. In willing, the idea as subject first knows reason to lie within itself, not yet outside itself in the world. The idea as subject knows itself as the positing of the determinations internal to it for which it is destined. These internal determinations of the willing subject, not

22. If proof starts with unproven, unmediated premises to which we must merely submit, the proof fails to make the conclusion truly necessary, where "true necessity" means freedom. "The moon is a blue cheese, and all blue cheeses are dairy products, so the moon is a dairy product" is inferentially necessary. But because it is not sound, the proof confronts alien necessity in the hard facts. Freedom, true necessity, occurs when the premises are supplemented by corresponding assumptions postulated by the *will:* "May all men be mortal, may Cassius be a man, and lo and behold all men are mortal and Cassius is a man. Hence, Cassius is mortal." Only a sound argument enjoys the true necessity of freedom. "May all men be mortal" expresses the consent or will of the argument's author that all men be mortal. We then distinguish realized and unrealized acts of will. A master of ceremonies who says "May the curtain rise" normally makes his or her will effective, but it is also possible to will what is already the case. "May I leap over the moon" expresses an unsuccessful volition. When our proofs begin with willed assumptions that are also factual, they do not begin with unmediated statements to which we involuntarily submit. The assumptions will correspond to the facts, which thus cease to embody alien necessity. The assumptions are mediated by our will. But if our will is unsuccessful, the mediation of assumptions by the will still finds unmediated necessity in the facts. Only when our assumptions are correct, only when our will is successful and knows itself to succeed, are the facts fully mediated and necessitated. And only then is our conclusion fully proven with a necessity that sets us free. Our conclusion lifts the hard necessity of the premises into the freedom of the will's self-objectification in the world. This coincidence of what we will and what we know to be the case will constitute the transition to the "absolute idea" in the next and final section of the lectures.

what is objectively given, now pass muster as the truth. What is objective, far from being true by itself, first attains to truth by being determined by acts of will. The idea as subject, volition as self-determining for itself, in which *necessity* [as encountered in the logic of essence] assumes the form of freedom as the self-determining subjective concept, brings forth the thought determination of *the good* as lying there before itself [§233]. The good is to be realized, and so it is not walled off merely in itself, but is the *end* that willing holds in view.

The will, with its end in view, attains certainty as to the nullity of the object as presupposed independently of itself. Inasmuch as the good still remains a finite good, the will for its part still remains a merely subjective will. Its own activity likewise remains finite [§234]. The will is a finite will by harboring the contradiction of the good, realizing itself within the objective world and not being realized within it. The will as both realizing itself and yet not fully realizing itself makes for the infinite and endless progress of the will. The good is the will insofar as it goes beyond being walled off in itself by at once being for itself [in reflection on its own self-actualization]. The will is always the will of a single subject, of a particular singular being. This singular will is the will upon which the good is potentially to be realized objectively.

For Kant, such infinite progress carries with it the postulate of the immortality of the soul. If the striving, willing subject were ever to become perfectly good, no willing would exist any longer. There would no longer be any activity, any struggle, any opposition of a willing that runs up against the sensory obstacle. Yet this doing of the will, this activity, is itself the refutation of its presupposition that such an obstacle exists. The contradiction of the will lies only in the fact that the two sides, the will on the one hand and the good that is willed on the other, are presupposed to be independent of each other, each being merely for itself on its own account. Yet the activity of willing on behalf of the good is the refutation of this presupposition that the good and the will are independent of each other. The activity of the will is always that of raising subjectivity beyond itself into the realization of the good. This doing of the will is unconscious—it has being for us but not for itself. But the very doing of it, the very raising of subjectivity up beyond itself into realization of the good, contradicts the initial presupposition of the independence of the good and the will. Reason is first merely walled off in itself, separated from nature. But, in the form of externalized reason, reason assumes the being of nature itself, of the world itself and of all that goes with it. The essence of both, of both reason merely in itself and reason in the world, is the connection between them.

Theoretical reason presupposes that whatever has being is as such true. But what theoretical reason merely presupposes here comes to be actualized only through practical reason. Yet practical reason is as one-sided as theoretical reason, and as the one-sidedness of both is lifted, the good is actualized not only potentially upon itself but equally for itself [in reflection on its actualized potential]. The [absolute] idea is thus realized, but such that it still lapses into positing itself anew as an end in view whose actualization is to be brought forth again and again, forever. The idea is this game of differentiating oneself from oneself, and thus falling into finitude by virtue of this differentiation. The idea is the activity of forever carrying out finitude into execution. Here we arrive at the *speculative idea* [§235], the abstract logical truth in general. The difficulty is to gain re-cognition of it. When matters get serious, when we come to speak of God, we must [from the practical standpoint] have *faith* that the world is powerless to prevail over him, but that he eternally realizes himself within the world and is realized by the world. The difference between God and the world exists only for the consciousness which makes such a distinction. It must also be conceptually grasped that the good is not merely abstract or untrue. Rather, the world contains within itself the absolute idea, the unity of the idea as subjective and as objective. But the objective world itself at once contains the very subject that differentiates itself from the world as object.

III.C.c. The Absolute Idea

The *absolute idea* is the subjective absolute idea for which the objective world is that same idea [§236]. Through the subjective idea the objective world comes to be known. Such knowledge of the world by the subject is the absolute philosophical idea. The absolute idea, as the oneness of the same idea both as subject and as object, is the idea as the concrete self-concept, subjectively conceiving itself in its object. To this concrete self-concept the absolute idea now has being at once as object and not merely as subject. Here we have absolute truth [conceived as fully as the science of logic can conceive it], i.e., as God above.

Aristotle says that, for God, theory, theoretical contemplation, is what is most excellent. As surely as God is, just as surely is he blessed and most excellent. Yet for Aristotle God is eternally blessed, while we human beings are blessed only now and again. Here, at the end of the science of logic, we return to the standpoint in which we found ourselves at the beginning of this science. For us, as practitioners of this science, the self-concepts have thus far been treated as external objects for our own subjective contemplation. But it is now the absolute idea as subject which, in and through our human scientific thinking, thinks the logical content. The two sides of the absolute idea, both subject and object as self-identical under these two determinations, now come to be the object of our contemplation—they become the absolute idea with a being for itself in and through us. We reach here the self-concept raised to the level of the absolute idea.

We surmise that it is here with the absolute idea that matters first in earnest truly begin, that here alone do we find ourselves lodged within the very heart of truth. Yet what we have is the absolute beginning [in its potential] as much as the absolute end [in its actualization]. More precisely, we have in the absolute idea, not something with a being for something other than itself, but with a being for itself. Within its very own being the absolute idea enjoys the simple being of being at home with itself. In having being for itself, the absolute idea is its own object, and thus is also at once differentiated from itself. The absolute idea is the judgment by which it self-divisively distinguishes itself from itself, and this judgment is the eternal *creation* of the world posited as differentiated from itself.

Posited as self-differentiating, the absolute idea will now fall [externally] outside its simple oneness with itself, and inaugurate the process of raising this differentiated being of the created world [nature] up beyond itself back into oneness with itself [as spirit]. The absolute idea upon itself falls into being other than itself. It therefore exhibits the absolute drive to raise its being other than itself up beyond such external being. The absolute idea is unto itself its own object [*Gegenstand*], it is the object for which the subjective idea has being as being for itself. The process of the objective idea [*objective Idee*] consists in negating its being for what is other than itself, in its restoration of its identity with itself. This negation of its otherness and restoration of its identity with itself make up the full content of the absolute idea. The absolute idea is object unto itself, and is the process of negating its external objectivity [*Gegenständlichkeit*]. But the absolute idea fallen [internally] outside itself, along with its drive to lift its being other than itself up beyond otherness, is what we have already beheld even prior to the creation of the world throughout the science of logic. All along we have beheld no more than the absolute idea distinguishing itself from itself.

The content of the absolute idea lies in all that has now preceded it in the science of logic. The absolute idea repels itself from itself, and its process at once restores itself to itself in what is other than itself. This is the system of logic. In that the absolute idea is for itself in being for its own object, the object is its manifestation, its differentiation of itself from itself, the sphere of external beings holding forth with a being for one another. Lying within this sphere of external beings with being for one another is differentiation in general, where to differentiate is to bestow determination. The posited determinate forms deposited along this process are themselves the content as retained within the absolute idea. The absolute idea, when taken as objective, is *being* [within the objective logic]. But this being is at once different from its other standing over against it, which is its *essence* [also within the objective logic].

So the absolute idea as object unto itself is being, while its essence is being's difference from itself, differentiation. The logic of essence is that of difference, the activity of differentiating being taken as the absolute object from itself. The spheres of being and essence are [upon themselves, potentially] the absolute idea [in which the subjective logic of the self-concept culminates]. The logic of being lifts itself up beyond itself, and so passes into the logic of its essence. Yet the essence of being remains, within itself, different from being taken as immediate. These spheres of being and essence have laid out the absolute idea in its content. Within the third sphere, the logic of the self-concept, the essence of being lifts its show of being other than being up beyond itself and determines itself as the self-concept. *Necessity* [in the logic of the essence] now becomes true freedom in the logic of the self-concept, the self-concept as posited. The self-concept developing upon itself into its totality is the absolute idea, the absolute idea as objective unto itself. Here in this objectification we have the full content of the absolute idea. Mere being, we now come to truly know [*wissen*], arises from the primordial internal judgment or self-sundering of the absolute idea. Mere being is posited within the absolute idea. Potentially it is upon itself that very idea, but it at once sets itself forth over against the idea.

(§237) The above objective content is the system of all that is logical. What remains for the absolute idea is only to supply the form for that content. Whatever was content [in the objective logic of being and essence] is now destined to be but a formal moment deposited within the absolute idea. The *Platonic absolute idea* or form has the defect, which Aristotle exposed, of being devoid of self-movement. For Plato the absolute idea fails to encompass what Aristotle highlights as energy, entelechy, dialectic, in contrast to mere motion [*Dynamis*]. These determinations of energy, entelechy, and dialectic are posited by Aristotle as forms within the absolute idea itself. Aristotle tells us that thinking, for God, is the *thinking of that which is thought*. Thinking here has itself [νοητόν] for its object, and so is set free of anything other than itself. Such thought thinking itself is unmoved, but what is unmoved, as something that persists immovably in being, has only itself for its object. Yet what is unmoved is, for Aristotle, also the mover. This one, being for itself with solely itself as its object, implies that no unintelligible darkness survives in the object. Perfect clarity immovably reigns within it, with nothing to muddy it.[23] Its content is to be apprehended merely as the determining of form, as the activity of the absolute idea, not merely as any one form among its formal determinations, but as the determining of form in its infinite activity.

---

23. This is to say, in Aristotelian language, that the absolute idea, as thought thinking itself, has no unactualized potentiality in need of further illumination.

This unmoved form is the universal activity of the absolute idea. The self-activation of the absolute idea occurs within all of its moments, in the logic of being as within that of essence. Each of these two circles is within itself a circle of circles, each such circle contains the whole larger circle imprinted upon itself. Within each moment the very same activity occurs, and the universal form of this activity we call the [dialectical] *method*.[24] We already re-cognize this method, since it has been implicitly active in each of the circles we have already traversed in the science of logic. We call the universal form of this activity "the method" to distinguish it from its variable particular content. Yet the form exhibited by the method has a content of its own. What we call "method" is distinguished from the variable particular content so that the [continuing] form of the method has its own content. The method is not the form as it comes to be explicated upon any particular empirically given material. The method is rather the universal inner life of every self-concept, it is the dialectical process of development as subjectively re-enacted.

(§238) *Being* is the immediate *beginning* of the science of logic. This being is immediate. We have already seen being's one-sidedness when taken as immediate. The absolute idea has being for itself, is an object unto itself. What is objective within the absolute idea starts with what merely has being. The absolute idea primordially divides itself, and is self-determining as absolute negativity[, negation of the negation]. In other words, [as a concrete] universal it is not anything abstract, but is absolute concrete self-reference [under different determinations]. Negation of the negation is the living nub of the absolute idea. The inescapable conclusion, the conclusion that everything is the infinite activity of negation of the negation, has arisen upon the given determinations. Immediate being as posited being is determinate. As immediate, it is mediated by what is not immediate. Immediate being is upon itself, potentially, the self-concept. Mere being is the still indeterminate self-concept. It is the universal, but is the universal understood as abstract. What comes in the second place, beyond being, is the original internal self-division of the absolute idea in judgment [§239]. If we start out

24. The dialectical method in which the subjective logic of the self-concept culminates is thus the subjective re-enactment at the end of the history of philosophy of the objective logics of being and the essence of being in the prior history of philosophy. If the dialectic is the original self-moving, self-constructive development of history, including the past history of philosophy, the dialectic in the sense of the dialectical method at the end of the history should be understood as our subjective re-enactment or reconstruction, as speculative logicians, of the self-constructive dialectic of objective history. The objective success of practical striving is crowned only by subjective knowledge of that very success. Victory in the objective play of such striving in history is consummated by the enjoyment of a subjective replay.

with mere being, we must take judgment merely as it comes to be imprinted upon being itself, we must not take it at the start as proceeding from the absolute idea. Being bears this judgment within itself. We begin with the immediate being which being first gives itself out to be, since being is merely upon itself [or potentially, for the science of logic,] what is living. Being reduces itself to being only a determination of form, one moment within the whole. Being is not thereby refuted, but rather remains as one determination, as an essential ingredient, within the further progression. Yet being does lose its initial status of being ultimate. The moment of reflection comes in the second place in relation to being, and is the sphere of essence in general.

(§240) In the logic of being, the progression is a transition from something to something else, which is a matter of *alteration*. In the logic of the essence of being [§241], the progression is a showing forth of this essence within what is set over against it, and what shows forth within what is set over against this essence also in turn shows forth as what is set over against itself. What is set over against the other is in each case the showing forth of the one within the other. Within the logic of the self-concept, the progression is posited as judgment, where the self-concept is internally self-divided into a singular subject and universal predicate. The singular subject A continues into B, the other which is predicated of it, and so they are posited as unseparated: A *is* B—which is the continuation of A into B. The development within this sphere of the self-concept, within the logic of judgment, is a reverse movement from the self-concept back into the first sphere of being [walled off in itself as the subject of predication], a prevailing current which is quite the opposite of the self-development of being into the self-concept, a doubling back on itself of the forward movement.

It is not enough to say that we pass dialectically *from* one thing to the next, for the second thing is also the first. The other is the one-sidedness of both raised up beyond itself. Infinite progress enters with the transition from the second to the third, which are distinguished even while bearing reference to each other. Their mutual reference is what they share in common. Contradiction takes the form of [ordinal] infinite progress to ever new members of the series, where the repetition of ever new members is impotent to bring any two members together [§242]. Indeed, such infinite progress is a quite thoughtless mode in which to proceed. What is at issue is bringing the [successive] thought determinations together. Bringing them together is the third moment, the self-concept in its concrete self-determination. The unity within which the distinguished moments have their being as lifted up beyond themselves, i.e., as preserved, is the realized self-concept, this unity as posited. The unity of these moments is this very positing of unity. It is what we have already witnessed: the unifying activity consisting in negating the differences [in their separation from one another by negation of the negation].

That activity of negating differences precisely as different from one another is being for itself. The transition of one into the other lies imprinted upon the first, it is its very being upon itself. But the first being's being for itself lies in the fact that the determinations are the activity of each in negating the other as other. The object [for which the subject has being as for itself] is the collapse of the object into the subject. In positing what being is potentially upon itself, we are always jumping ahead of ourselves. We posit what being is upon itself, after which, as we have seen, the self-concept also comes to be posited through what it upon itself potentially is. What we then have is the self-concept not only as it initially is upon itself, but also for itself. The method is the soul— the living self-activation—of the material itself [§243]. But, considering the method precisely as method [from the standpoint of the absolute idea in which the objective success of practical striving is completed by subjective contemplation of that very success], it is essential for us to truly know that nothing can withstand the self-concept.[25] The self-concept is absolutely all-penetrating. It prevails over and annihilates whatever would be other than it. Within whatever is at first externally off-putting, the self-concept still comes to itself.

(§244) The absolute idea is this internal self-judgment. From this idea's self-differentiation come the spheres of being and essence. But what is even more concrete than the absolute idea, however, is for this idea to pursue its self-judgment [or self-division] beyond itself into *nature*.[26] The [self-]reflection of the absolute idea within nature is then *spirit*. The absolute idea considered in its immediate oneness with itself

25. Hegel has previously said that we have only faith (*Glauben*) that the advance of the self-concept's all-penetrating negation of the negation is irresistible. But that claim was made from the practical standpoint of volition before the end of history. From the end-of-history standpoint of the absolute idea, which is the standpoint from which the objective historical achievement of attaining the object of will (universal freedom) is crowned by subjective knowledge that it has indeed been attained, the dialectical method of re-enacting the achievement allows knowledge, not just faith, that every negation of otherness, and every negation by the other of what is first given, yields to negation of the negation. But this insight leaves open the question of whether history has now ended only in general but not yet in particular.

26. We have seen Hegel side with Aristotle's purportedly non-Platonic view of the absolute idea as the rest of purely actual activity, devoid of anything lying upon it as a potential for further self-development. Hegel now diverges from Aristotle in taking the absolute idea, Aristotle's thought thinking itself, to bear upon itself a potential for self-alienation in nature as "created," and self-recuperation in spirit, in the infinite Incarnation of the Word (Christ) in the world.

is the act of its self-intuition in pure thought, in its simplicity, the absolute idea in its immediacy. Here in nature we have the absolute idea in its fallen state. The absolute idea as given in the form of [sensory] intuition is *nature*. But within nature the absolute idea comes forth only under a one-sided determination. In fact, the absolute idea is not simply given immediately [in the sensory world], but is the infinite activity of positing itself. The absolute idea is the Word [Logos, Christ] that releases itself freely from itself into nature.[27] The absolute idea does not simply pass within nature over into life, but has resolved to freely release itself from itself as nature. Nature is then what is immediate, it is being—except that this content of the consummated absolute idea has being displaced outside itself. But nature itself, as we have already seen to be anticipated in the purely logical category of life, is its own rise up beyond itself into spirit. Nature thus bears upon itself the mark of its own self-nullification, and passes over into infinite spirit as the truth of nature. Yet it does not do so without first passing over into finite spirit, which only then will lift itself into *infinite spirit*.

27. One of Hegel's formulations in paragraph §85 of his introduction, as noted, suggests theism: the logic is an exposition of the eternal essence of God prior to creation. But the meaning of this statement is explicitly shown, in this final paragraph of the lectures, to contrast with the orthodox claim that God created the world *by* the Word, *by* Christ, hence *by* what Hegel calls the absolute self-thinking logical idea. Hegel's less orthodox language here implies that the absolute idea, Christ himself, is the creator, and not merely the instrument of creation. His reference in this final paragraph to the absolute idea as *fallen* in its passage into creation also poses a challenge to an orthodox classical theistic interpretation of creation. God needs us to actualize his self-knowledge: he attains to knowledge of himself only in and through our knowledge of him. We read in Hegel's last essay on theology, published just a year before the present lectures, that "God is not merely eternal being (substance) but also self-knowledge.... [A]s being in the other [in nature and in spirit], God is self-knowledge outside itself—God's consciousness in the world, in individual beings as the creatures of God.... If God is actual only in and with His creatures—and this is what Scripture teaches—God's knowledge is also in them—since He is only insofar as He knows Himself." See G. W. F. Hegel, "Review of K. F. Göschel's *Aphorisms*," trans. Clark Butler, in *Miscellaneous Writings of G. W. F. Hegel*, ed. Jon Stewart (Evanston, Ill.: Northwestern University Press, 2000), pp. 413–414.